Roots of Resilience:
Lessons from Appalachia for a Stronger Therapeutic Practice

By
Dr. Martin Cortez Wesley

Title: Roots of Resilience: Lessons from Appalachia for a Stronger Therapeutic Practice / Martin Cortez Wesley

ISBN 979-8-9929358-0-6 (Hardcover)
ISBN 979-8-9929358-1-3 (Paperback)
ISBN 979-8-9929358-2-0 (eBook)

WESPRESS
BOOKS
EST. 1979
SAPIENTIA PER LIBRIS

Client and student names and identifying characteristics have been changed to protect the privacy of the individuals involved. Family member's names have not been changed unless noted.

Acknowledgments

This book would not have been possible without the love, support, and inspiration of those who have shaped my life and my work. To my wife, Dawn, my partner in life, love, and purpose. Your unwavering support, wisdom, and belief in me have been my foundation. You have walked this journey with me, step by step, and I am forever grateful for the life we have built together. To my children, Destiny, Brittany, and Milo, each of you has enriched my life in ways beyond measure. Your strength, resilience, and unique perspectives inspire me daily. To my grandchildren, Landon, Logan, and Melody, you are the future, and through you, I see the continuation of the values and lessons that have been passed down through our family. Your laughter, curiosity, and love bring me endless joy. To my mother, Norma, your love, sacrifice, and wisdom have been my guiding light. The lessons you instilled in me continue to shape who I am and how I approach life and work. To the clients and students, I have had the privilege of working with, you have taught me as much as I have ever hoped to teach. Your courage, vulnerability, and growth are at the heart of this book, and I am honored to have been a small part of your journeys. To my ancestors, whose stories, struggles, and triumphs continue to guide me, this book is an extension of the lessons you left behind. Your resilience has laid the foundation upon which I stand. To the people of Kentucky and greater Appalachia, this land and its people have shaped me in ways both profound and personal. The spirit of this region, with its rich history of strength, perseverance, and community, runs through these pages.

This book is a tribute to all of you. Thank you for the roots that ground me and the resilience that sustains me.

With gratitude,

About the Author

Dr. Martin Cortez Wesley was born in Lexington, Kentucky, in 1963 and has deep roots in the state, with his father's family coming from Casey County, near Bethelridge, and his mother's family from Edmonson County, near Sweeden and Bee Springs. Growing up, Dr. Wesley lived in Kentucky, Tennessee, Arizona, and later Virginia, experiences that helped shape his diverse perspectives on life and human resilience.

From humble beginnings working a paper route and as a cook at McDonald's, Dr. Wesley's life has been one of dedication and hard work. He and his wife, Dawn Wesley, have raised three children, Destiny, Brittany, and Milo, while also caring for other children as house parents. Together, they founded "Sowin' Love Shelters" and "Sowin' Love Family Services," providing emergency shelter care and counseling services to children and families in need.

Dr. Wesley's journey into the world of counseling began with a family therapy private practice and as the director of a substance abuse treatment center, helping those struggling with addiction. He later transitioned into academia, beginning his teaching career at Western Kentucky University. After earning his Ph.D. in Academic and Counseling Psychology, he became an assistant professor at Lindsey Wilson College in Columbia, Kentucky, where he played a pivotal role in expanding the school's counseling programs throughout the Appalachian region.

As the founding Dean of the School of Counseling at the University of the Cumberlands, Dr. Wesley's leadership and vision helped shape the future of counselor education in the region and the world. He repeated this achievement later in his career when he became the founding chair of the online counseling programs at National Louis University.

Today, Dr. Wesley continues to teach and inspire future counselors at National Louis University. He remains deeply connected to his family and his roots in Appalachia. He enjoys spending time with his wife, Dawn, his mom, his children, and his grandchildren, Landon, Logan, and Melody.

Dr. Wesley's dedication to his profession, his family, and his Appalachian heritage runs deep. His journey from rural Kentucky to academic leadership reflects a life committed to service, learning, and the values passed down through generations.

To connect with Dr. Wesley, you can reach him via his personal email at wesleyphd@gmail.com.

Table of Contents

The Roots That Ground Us

Resilience is a word often thrown around in today's world, yet few truly understand its depth, complexity, and what it means to live a life defined by it. For those who grew up in Kentucky or the greater Appalachia region, resilience is more than just a concept; it's a way of life. From the worn hillsides that tell stories of generations before us to the small towns where everyone knows your name, there is an unspoken strength that runs deep in the veins of Appalachian people. It is a strength born not from ease but from adversity, from hardship, and from an unwavering sense of hope and faith that, no matter what, we will make it through.

In my life as both a son from the foothills of Appalachia and as a therapist and counselor educator, I have come to realize that many of the values I was raised with, the quiet determination, the fierce loyalty to family, the reliance on community, and the ability to laugh even in the darkest times, are the very qualities that make someone not only a good therapist but a resilient human being. This book is a reflection on those lessons, the ones learned from my family from stories passed down from generations and whose wisdom continues to shape me to this day. It is also a guide for therapists who seek to build resilience, both within themselves and in the clients they serve.

In the chapters that follow, I will explore the core lessons that have shaped my therapeutic practice and teaching, all of which are deeply rooted in the values of Appalachia. Through storytelling, reflection, and practical guidance, we will journey together through the many ways that resilience manifests itself, whether in the face of loss, change, or the daily struggles that come with simply being human. I will also share how these values have helped me become a stronger therapist and, in turn, how they can help you foster resilience in your clients.

The Appalachia I know is not one of despair or poverty, as it is often portrayed by outsiders. Instead, it is a place rich with culture, tradition, and a profound sense of community. The lessons we carry with us are the ones born out of necessity, of finding joy in simplicity, of never wasting what we have, and of always knowing that no matter how dark the night, the sun will rise again. These are the lessons that make us resilient, and they are the lessons that make us healers.

So, as you turn the pages of this book, my hope is that you find not only practical advice for your therapeutic practice and life journey but also a reminder of the strength that lies within all of us. Whether you are a therapist or someone simply seeking to understand how to weather life's storms, may you come away grounded in the knowledge that resilience, like the roots of an old mountain oak, runs deep and steady, holding us up through even the fiercest winds.

This is the story of resilience, told through the lens of Appalachian values and the stories of my family and clients.

Weathering the Storms

There was a song named "Gloom, Despair, and Agony on Me," (Brillstein, 1969) that was the center of a recurring skit on an American variety show, [1]Hee Haw, which ran from 1969-1971. Within the lyrics came an old Appalachia saying: "If it weren't for bad luck, I'd have no luck at all." This was always said with a grin, a laugh that almost seems to mock the tough hand that was dealt to someone, but beneath the humor lies a hard truth. Life in the Appalachian Mountains and foothills has never been easy. The land is rugged, the winters are harsh, and work is often hard to come by. But there's a lesson hidden in that struggle, a lesson about resilience and about how, through adversity, we find our true strength.

My grandma Doreen Wesley used to say, "Hard times don't last, but tough people do." I didn't fully understand the weight of those words when I was younger, but as I've grown, both as a person and as a therapist, I have come to appreciate their significance. In therapy, as in life, the storms come. Whether it's a client facing loss, trauma, or deep personal pain, or even the therapist struggling with the weight of vicarious trauma, adversity is inevitable. But it is through facing these storms, not avoiding them, that we build resilience.

In the hills of Appalachia, the storms, both literal and metaphorical, have shaped the people who live there. A few years back, one of those literal storms struck my family in a way that left deep scars but also revealed the depth of the community's strength. My great granduncle, [i]Vincent Wesley, his wife Margaret (whom everyone called Peg), and several of their children were tragically taken in a tornado that ripped through Casey County, Kentucky.

The storm came together violently, sweeping through the valley and destroying everything in its path. It struck their home with such force that the roof and walls were torn away. The entire family, Vincent, Margaret, and their daughters Ann and Martha, were inside the cabin as it was torn apart. Vincent, attempting to protect his family, was found in the yard missing an arm and wrapped around a piece of timber. His wife and daughters, too, were scattered and found amidst the wreckage, their lives taken far too soon.

---

[1] *Hee Haw* was a country-themed variety show that aired from 1969 to 1992, blending humor, music, and rural stereotypes. While popular for its slapstick comedy and performances by country music legends, the show also reinforced both affectionate and exaggerated portrayals of Appalachian and Southern rural life. For a deeper analysis of its cultural impact, see Harkins, A. (2004). *Hillbilly: A cultural history of an American icon.* Oxford University Press.

In those days, the aftermath of such a tragedy wasn't met with modern disaster relief or emergency counseling services. The family, friends, and neighbors who survived were the ones who stepped in to lend aid. They gathered together not just to bury the dead but to rebuild the lives of the survivors. Even as their own homes and lives were shattered, they helped one another, relying on the resilience that had been passed down through generations of Kentucky life.

In the days following the storm, Vincent and his family were mourned by the entire community. The losses were devastating, but as is the way in Appalachia, the people came together to rebuild. The barn was scattered for a quarter of a mile, and most of the livestock were killed, but friends and neighbors worked to gather what could be salvaged. The tornado left a path of destruction, but it couldn't destroy the strength of the community that rose in its wake.

A sad picture of coffin of a family member that was tragically taken much too early.

Living in Kentucky, the thunderstorms often roll down the mountainside, bringing with them the threat of washed-out roads, broken power lines, and a darkness that seemed all-consuming. But we didn't panic. We didn't give up. Instead, we prepared. We gathered candles and blankets, brought the animals in, and huddled together as a family. In those moments, we relied on each other, drawing strength from the sense that, no matter how bad it got, we would face it together. And we always did.

As a therapist, I find myself drawing on these lessons when working with clients. Life's storms can feel overwhelming, and in those moments, my role is not to fix the storm but to sit with them through it. To prepare them with the tools they need to weather it and to remind them that they are not alone. Much like the storms in Appalachia, life's difficulties may seem insurmountable at times, but with resilience, preparation, and a support system, we come out the other side stronger.

In therapy, helping clients build resilience means teaching them to embrace adversity, not fear it. It means helping them recognize that, much like the roots of an old mountain tree, their strength lies in their ability to bend, not break, in the face of life's challenges. Just as my family huddled together during those mountain storms, clients need to know that they have a network of support, whether that's family, friends, or the therapeutic relationship itself.

The lesson from Appalachia is simple: resilience is not about avoiding hardship; it's about facing it head-on, knowing that you have the strength to endure. And as therapists, it's our job to help our clients see that strength within themselves, even when they can't yet see it on their own.

Just like the mountain folk I grew up with, our clients can endure, adapt, and thrive. They just need someone to help them realize it.

This introduction helps to set the tone for this book that is not only reflective but also practical, offering insights into how resilience can be cultivated in the therapeutic process.

Resilience isn't always born out of single acts of courage. Sometimes, it's the slow, steady resolve to keep moving forward, even when life hands you loss after loss. My other grandmother, ⁱⁱArzona Carroll, nicknamed Zoni, embodied this quiet strength. Born in 1912, the year Arizona became a state, her name was meant to honor the state's new beginning. But when her parents spelled it wrong on the birth certificate, she became Arzona. It's a small detail, but one that would echo the unplanned twists and turns of her life.

Zoni was only five years old when she lost her father, William Elmore. He loved coon hunting, even though he was half-blind, because it gave him a sense of freedom and pride. It also provided extra income for the family through the pelts he sold. One night, while hunting in the dark, he slipped and fell from a cliff. That single moment changed the course of her family's life forever.

A picture of the Elmore family. In the front row is Jesse Elmore, my great-great grandfather, Edy Minerva Vincent, my great-great-grandmother, William Elmore, my great-grandfather. Above are Louisa, Seth, and Priscilla. As you can tell from this picture, William was half-blind, but his sister, Priscilla, was totally blind. Not only did he die in part due to his blindness, but she was also abandoned in a car on railroad tracks, where she was killed by a dinky train in KyRock, Kentucky.

At five, Zoni didn't fully understand the weight of the loss, but she remembers missing her father, the security of his presence and the joy he brought home from each hunt. But as the years passed, what could have been a life defined by grief took an unexpected turn. Her mother eventually remarried, and Zoni's new stepfather stepped into the role of protector and provider. He wasn't her biological father, but she was grateful for him. He took care of Zoni, her mother, and her siblings with a kind and steady hand, filling a void left by her father's tragic death.

Zoni's life could have been one of sorrow, shaped by the loss of her father at such a young age. Instead, she found comfort and stability in the man who became her stepfather. She learned, at an early age, that life is full of unexpected turns, but that doesn't mean we are abandoned to navigate them alone. Sometimes, resilience means learning to accept new chapters in life, even when they don't look like what we had envisioned. It means finding gratitude in the people who step in to help us when the world feels uncertain.

Her story, like so many others from Appalachia, speaks to the strength it takes to adapt to change and loss. Zoni missed her father, but she didn't let his death define her future. Instead, she found peace in the family that remained and in the new bonds that grew with her stepfather's loving care.

In therapy, I often reflect on her story when working with clients who have faced early losses or the disruption of their family structure. It's easy to focus on what was lost, but Zoni's life reminds me that there is resilience to be found in embracing what is new, even if it isn't what we expected. Her gratitude for her stepfather is a powerful example of how love, care, and support can come in many forms, even after great tragedy.

My grandmother Zoni Carroll as a young woman

Resilience, in Zoni's case, wasn't about clinging to what could have been; it was about appreciating what was and finding strength in the life that continued to grow around her. It's a lesson that has stayed with me, both personally and professionally, as I help others navigate their own losses and changes. Life is full of unexpected turns, but sometimes, the beauty of resilience is found in the quiet acceptance of what comes next.

In the hills of Kentucky, the land itself can be both a source of life and a heavy burden. For my grandma, [iii]Doreen (Martin) Wesley, the weight of the land, and life, came crashing down one afternoon in the barn. She was the oldest of seven children, and like many young girls in those days, she was often at her father's side, helping with the endless work required to keep the family farm running.

On this particular day, their plow horse had gotten its foot lodged in the stall. It was a difficult and dangerous task to free the horse, but my grandmother's father was strong, capable, and undeterred by the danger. He was able to release the horse's foot, but in the frenzy that followed, as the horse broke free, it kicked her father square in the chest. The blow was severe, and though he lived a short time afterward, the injury ultimately claimed his life.

With her father gone, the family was left in a precarious situation. He had been the one to work the farm and provide for the family, and now that burden fell squarely on the shoulders of my grandmother, her mother, and her siblings. They weren't just grieving the loss of a father, they were also staring down the very real threat of losing their home, their land, and their means of survival. Foreclosure loomed, and the already hard life of tending the land became an overwhelming struggle to feed their family and make ends meet.

But they didn't give up.

My grandmother, though still young herself, stepped into her father's role. She, along with some of siblings such as my great uncle Kenneth Martin, worked tirelessly on their own farm and took on extra work at neighboring farms just to keep food on the table and the farm from slipping through their fingers. The work was backbreaking and the hours long, but giving up wasn't an option. There was a resilience in her that went beyond just survival; it was about protecting the life her father had built, about ensuring that her family stayed together, and about finding a way forward even in the face of overwhelming loss.

This story of my grandma, Doreen, isn't just one of hardship; it's a story of resilience. In the face of adversity that would have broken many, she dug deeper into her own strength and the support of her siblings. They weathered that storm, and though life didn't suddenly become easy, they made it through. The farm survived, and so did they.

In my work as a therapist, I often think about this story. It reminds me that resilience isn't about avoiding hardship or pretending life will always be fair. It's about facing what comes, even when it seems too much to bear, and finding the strength within us and in the people around us to keep going. My grandmother's story, like so many from the hills of Appalachia, is a reminder that hardship is not the end. It's a part of life, but it's also an opportunity to grow, to build resilience, and to find a way through.

Resilience isn't just about surviving; it's about thriving in the aftermath of adversity, and that's a lesson that continues to shape my life and my work to this day.

My Great Grandparents, Elmer Martin, and Grace Martin, and their oldest child, and my grandmother, Doreen Martin Wesley

The Family Tree: Generational Wisdom in Therapy

In Appalachia, family is more than just the people you share a home with, it's the roots that ground you, the branches that provide shelter and support, and the leaves that continue to grow with each new generation. The family tree is a living testament to the experiences, hardships, and wisdom passed down through the ages. In therapy, this concept of generational wisdom is invaluable. Understanding where we come from, the lessons passed down from our ancestors, and the patterns we inherit can provide powerful insights into our own struggles, strengths, and paths toward healing.

As a therapist, I often encourage my clients to explore their own family trees not just to uncover genealogical facts but to tap into the generational wisdom that their families offer. It's a reminder that we are not alone in our struggles, those who came before us often faced similar challenges and can offer lessons, even from beyond the grave.

Generational wisdom is the knowledge, values, and resilience passed down from one generation to the next. It's the stories your grandparents told you, the morals and values your parents instilled, and even the unspoken lessons you've picked up simply by observing how your family members lived their lives. In many ways, this wisdom is like a well from which we can draw strength in times of difficulty.

In therapy, recognizing the influence of generational wisdom can be transformative. Many people come into counseling feeling isolated in their struggles, whether it's addiction, depression, or trauma. But when they take the time to examine their family histories, they often discover that their ancestors faced similar challenges and found ways to overcome them. This realization can provide hope, showing them that resilience runs in their blood.

For instance, I've had clients who struggled with the idea of facing hardship alone, believing that their problems were unique or insurmountable. But once we began exploring their family trees, they realized that their grandparents or great-grandparents had faced similar trials, whether it was surviving the Great Depression, enduring wartime separation, or raising large families with limited resources. These stories of resilience provide a sense of continuity and hope, reminding clients that they are part of a larger narrative of survival and strength.

In therapy, one of the most effective tools I use to help clients understand their family dynamics is the genogram (McGoldrick, 2008). A genogram is a visual representation of a person's family tree, but it goes beyond the simple recording of names and dates, it includes emotional relationships, health issues, and patterns of behavior that may be passed down through generations. By using a genogram, clients can visually map out their family's history and identify both strengths and challenges that have been passed down through the years.

A genogram helps clients see connections they might otherwise miss. For example, someone might realize that addiction runs through multiple branches of their family tree or that certain patterns of conflict in relationships have repeated over several generations. By making these patterns visible, the genogram becomes a tool for understanding not only where these issues come from but also how they can be addressed and changed.

In my practice, I've seen clients have breakthrough moments simply by mapping out their family history on a genogram. They begin to see how their current struggles are linked to generational patterns, and this understanding can be incredibly empowering. It allows them to take control of their own narrative, recognizing that while they may have inherited certain challenges, they also possess the ability to break those cycles and create healthier patterns for future generations.

While generational wisdom can provide strength, it's also important to recognize that not all family patterns are positive. Many families pass down cycles of trauma, addiction, or unhealthy behaviors that can span generations. In therapy, part of the work is helping clients identify these negative patterns and break the cycle for future generations.

For example, I've worked with clients who come from families with a long history of addiction. They often feel trapped by their family's legacy, believing that they are destined to follow the same path. But through therapy and the use of genograms, we explore their family tree, looking at both the negative patterns and the moments of resilience. This process helps clients understand that while their family may have struggled with addiction, they also possess the strength and wisdom to overcome it. By learning from the past and consciously choosing a different path, they can break the cycle and create a healthier future for themselves and their children.

One of my clients, [iv]Samantha, grew up in a family where addiction was the norm. Her father, grandfather, and uncles had all struggled with alcoholism, and she believed it was only a matter of time before she would follow in their footsteps. But as we explored her family tree and created a genogram, she also discovered stories of strength, her grandmother, who had raised her children alone while her husband was away for weeks at time, or her great-grandfather, who had stopped drinking to save his marriage. These stories gave Samantha a new perspective on her family history. Instead of seeing it as a curse, she began to view it as a source of strength. She realized that if her ancestors could overcome their struggles, she could too. This shift in perspective allowed Samantha to break the cycle of addiction in her family and start a new chapter of resilience and recovery.

One of the most important aspects of exploring the family tree in therapy is learning how to honor the past without being bound by it. Our ancestors' experiences shape us, but they do not define us. We have the power to take the lessons they've passed down and apply them in ways that create positive change in our own lives.

In Appalachia, honoring the past is a core value. We take care of our elders, we tend to our family cemeteries, and we pass down stories and traditions that keep our ancestors' memories alive. But we also understand that each generation must find its own way. Just as a tree grows new branches, each of us has the opportunity to grow in ways that our ancestors may not have imagined.

In therapy, this balance between honoring the past and embracing the future is key to healing. Clients often come to me feeling burdened by the weight of their family's history, whether it's addiction, mental illness, or trauma. But through exploring their family tree and visual tools, they come to see that their ancestors weren't just victims of hardship; they were survivors, people who faced incredible challenges and found ways to persevere. By tapping into this generational wisdom, clients can find the strength to move forward, honoring their family's legacy while creating a healthier future for themselves and their children.

In Appalachia, family is everything. It's the foundation upon which we build our lives, the source of our greatest joys and deepest challenges. We honor our ancestors not just because it's tradition, but because we understand that they are part of who we are. Their wisdom, their struggles, and their triumphs live on in us. As the saying goes, "The apple doesn't fall far from the tree." But while we inherit much from our ancestors, we also have the power to shape our own destinies.

When I reflect on my own family tree, I see stories of resilience, love, and hardship. [v]My great-grand uncle, Daniel Boone, who faced unimaginable challenges as a frontiersman and soldier, passed down a legacy of courage and perseverance. My second great-uncle, Lewis Miles Carroll, who died as a prisoner of war in Andersonville, left behind a legacy of sacrifice and devotion to family and country. My uncle, Truman Carroll, who served with valor in Vietnam, exemplifies the strength and bravery that runs through my family's bloodline.

These stories remind me that I am not alone in my struggles. I am part of a larger family tree, one that is rooted in resilience, strength, and wisdom. And just as I draw strength from my ancestors, I hope to pass on that same resilience to future generations.

For my clients, the family tree, and the genogram, is a powerful tool for healing. By exploring their family histories and mapping out their relationships, they can gain a deeper understanding of their own struggles and strengths. They can learn from the past, breaking negative cycles and embracing the wisdom that has been passed down through generations.

In therapy, I encourage clients to look at their family tree not just as a record of names and dates but as a source of generational wisdom. What can they learn from the lives of their ancestors? How can they apply those lessons to their own lives? And most importantly, how can they honor the past while creating a better future for themselves and their families?

To tap into this generational wisdom, we must know our past. I remember the first book my mother read to me, *Are You, My Mother?* (Eastman, 1960). In the story, a baby bird embarks on a journey to find his mother, asking different animals and objects, "Are you my mother?" The bird encounters a kitten, a hen, a dog, and even a big steam shovel before finally finding his real mother. The little bird's journey to discover who he belongs to and where he came from resonates deeply, as it's a question many of us ask ourselves throughout our lives: *Where do I come from? Who am I?* In many ways, we are all that baby bird, searching for identity and a sense of belonging.

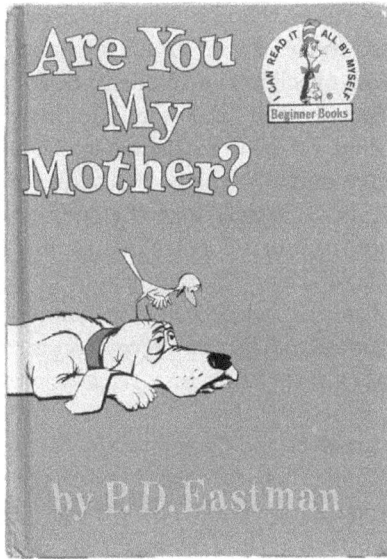

Are you my Mother? One of my first books growing up.

For people raised in small-town Kentucky or similar tight-knit communities, the importance of knowing who we are and where we come from cannot be overstated. Our identity is intertwined with our family, our land, and our ancestors. This connection to our roots gives us grounding in an increasingly disconnected world. The values, stories, and lessons passed down from our ancestors form the bedrock of who we are today. When that connection is lost, people can find themselves adrift, struggling to make sense of the world.

One of the biggest challenges I see today, especially in counseling, is the loss of identity. Many people come into therapy not knowing who they are, where they belong, or what their purpose is. Without that foundation, they feel adrift. I believe that reconnecting with our roots, whether they be family, culture, or place, can provide a sense of stability and direction.

For me, rediscovering my roots has been a deeply personal journey. I've spent years piecing together my genealogy, visiting family graveyards, and speaking with older relatives. These actions have helped me understand the values that were passed down through generations and how they shaped me. There is something powerful in knowing the stories of those who came before you, who faced hardships, and who survived. These stories provide not only a sense of identity but also a blueprint for resilience.

I remember traveling with my mother to old graveyards where our ancestors were buried. Each gravestone told a story, not just of death but of life, of family, community, and the hardships faced by those who came before us. By reconnecting with their stories, I found a deeper understanding of who I am and the values I carry forward today. Those values I have shared with my children, grandchildren and now with my clients and students desiring a career as a therapist.

For clients and counselors alike, understanding one's identity is essential for personal growth and healing. From an existential lens, knowing who you are and where you come from helps clarify the bigger questions of life: *What is my purpose? Where am I going?* Without these answers, it can be difficult to find direction.

As counselors, it's important to recognize that identity formation is not just an individual process but a cultural and generational one as well. Our clients may not have had the same experiences of close-knit communities or generational stories being passed down. It's our job to help them reconnect with who they are, whether that's through understanding their family history, discovering their cultural values, or connecting to a larger sense of purpose. Clients may need to explore their roots to find answers about themselves and their values.

For counselors-in-training, helping clients rediscover their identity is one of the most important aspects of our work. You are not there to define a person's identity but to help them uncover it. This might involve encouraging clients to reflect on their past, their family, and the values they were raised with, or it might involve helping them navigate their relationship with cultural or ancestral legacies that have been lost or neglected. The counselor's role is to facilitate this journey of discovery, not to dictate it.

For clients, it's crucial to understand that identity is not something you "find" once and then you are done. It's a process. Who we are changes over time, but the more we understand our roots, the more grounded we become. This foundation is essential when life gets difficult. Knowing where you came from, who your people are, and what values have been passed down to you provides a solid base for navigating the challenges of life. Reconnecting with family, whether through conversations with older relatives, exploring genealogy, or even visiting places tied to your family's history, can bring a sense of peace and belonging.

In many ways, this book is about answering the same question the baby bird asks: *Are you, my mother?* It's about understanding where we come from and what makes us who we are. Kentucky, larger Appalachia and my family history, for me, has always been a source of strength and resilience, passed down from generation to generation. My journey to rediscover my roots, from memories of my grandparent's family farm, to chatting with extended family members to visiting family cemeteries, has brought me not only a sense of identity but a sense of responsibility, to carry those values forward.

The lessons are simple but profound: We must understand where we've been to know where we're going. Whether you are a counselor helping someone rediscover their roots or a client searching for meaning, identity is the key. It's not something that can be given to you; it's something you must discover. But once you do, the path ahead becomes clearer.

In the end, we are all like that baby bird, seeking connection, seeking identity, and seeking to know where we belong. By embracing our roots and understanding our people, we can build stronger, more resilient lives and communities.

Working with What You Have

One of the most valuable lessons I've learned from my Appalachian roots is the power of resourcefulness, the ability to work with what you have. Growing up, I watched my grandparents and relatives practice a level of resourcefulness that was born out of necessity but also out of respect for the world around them. In a region where money was often scarce, people found ways to make do, repurpose, and reuse, ensuring that nothing went to waste. This spirit of resilience and resourcefulness is something I've carried with me throughout my life, and it's a lesson I try to pass on to my clients and students as they navigate their own challenges.

I remember watching my grandfather, [vi] [2]Cortez Wesley, straighten out old nails to use them again. It may seem like a small, insignificant act, but it spoke volumes about the mindset of the people who lived through hard times. To him, even a bent nail still had value. He would take the time to hammer it straight, saving it for future use. This kind of practical ingenuity was common in Appalachian households, where nothing was discarded without first considering whether it could be fixed, reused, or repurposed.

People found countless ways to stretch the resources they had, and these habits were passed down through generations. My [vii]grandmother Zoni would take her old dress and cut them down to size for my mom, ensuring that nothing went to waste. Hand-me-downs were common in large families, with older children passing on clothing and shoes to their younger siblings. Growing up, most kids never thought twice about it, it was simply the way things were done. Families made sure that every item, no matter how small, served its full purpose before being retired.

This resourcefulness extended to every aspect of life. Shoes, for example, were often resoled rather than thrown away. While I've never had to wear a pair of shoes until the soles wore out, my ancestors knew the value of making things last. They saved every scrap of fabric from old clothing to make quilts, often called [3]crazy

---

[2] My grandfather, Omar Cortez Wesley, was known simply as Cortez, an unusual name for rural Kentucky. His name, along with my own, carries the legacy of my family. I was named after my grandmother's maiden name, "Martin," and my grandfather's name, "Cortez," ensuring that even in my name, their influence remains with me.

[3] Crazy quilts, characterized by irregular fabric scraps sewn together in intricate patterns, are a significant part of Appalachian folk art and resourcefulness. Often made from salvaged fabric, these quilts reflect both economic necessity and artistic expression, incorporating embroidery, storytelling, and family history. For more on their cultural significance, see Turner, K. (2009). *Southern quilts: Surviving relics of a rural past.* University Press of Mississippi.

quilts, where each piece of fabric held history and meaning. These quilts were not only practical, providing warmth in the cold Appalachian winters, but they were also deeply symbolic of the resilience of the people who made them.

My mom, Norma, standing by her quilt that she made for me as a gift.

Even the water they used was collected and reused. Rain barrels were a common sight, ensuring that every drop of water was saved for the garden or the animals. And laundry? It was hung out to dry in the fresh air, not tossed into an energy-draining dryer. There was a sense of connection to the natural world, a respect for the resources at hand, and an understanding that waste was a luxury they couldn't afford.

The resourcefulness of Appalachians wasn't just about repurposing objects; it extended to every facet of life, particularly when it came to food. Chickens were raised not just for eggs but also for meat, and their feathers were used to stuff pillows and mattresses. Gardens provided the vegetables that fed the family throughout the year, and when an animal was slaughtered, every part was used. As a friend of mine once said, "When we slaughtered a hog, we used everything but the oink."

This idea of using everything, of wasting nothing, was key to survival. Every bite of food that could be preserved was canned or dried to last through the winter. While I may can some jam or jelly today, my efforts don't come close to the amount of food my ancestors needed to prepare for the months ahead. They preserved every bite they could, not just for convenience, but because it was essential for survival. The resourcefulness of our ancestors was rooted in their understanding that life was fragile, and that survival depended on their ability to make the most of what they had.

The resourcefulness of my ancestors teaches a powerful lesson for clients and students, particularly those looking to become therapists. In therapy, we often talk about resilience, the ability to bounce back from hardship. But resilience isn't just about enduring tough times; it's about making the most of what you have, recognizing the value in even the smallest things, and finding creative solutions to life's challenges.

For clients, learning to be resourceful can be a key component of healing. Many come to therapy feeling like they don't have enough, enough support, enough strength, enough resources to overcome their challenges. But just as my grandfather straightened out old nails, clients can learn to recognize the value in what they do have. They can tap into their inner strength, their existing relationships, and their past experiences, finding ways to use those "bent nails" to rebuild their lives.

For students training to become therapists, the lesson of resourcefulness is equally important. As counselors, we often find ourselves working with clients who feel overwhelmed by their circumstances, convinced that they don't have the tools they need to succeed. Our job is to help them see that they do have resources, sometimes in places they might not expect. Whether it's a supportive friend, a forgotten hobby, or an inner reserve of resilience, there is always something to work with. Part of being a good therapist is helping clients identify and use those resources to their advantage.

In therapy, we often talk about working with what we have, not focusing on what we lack. This mindset allows clients to reframe their challenges, to see opportunities instead of obstacles, and to use the resources they have to build something new. Whether it's an emotional tool, a supportive relationship, or even just a small piece of hope, every bit counts.

The lessons of resourcefulness from my Kentucky roots are just as relevant today as they were generations ago. By working with what we have, by finding value in the small things, and by respecting the resources available to us, we can build lives filled with meaning and purpose. And just like those quilts made from scraps of fabric, our lives become a patchwork of resilience, creativity, and strength.

In the end, it's not about how much we have, but how we use what we have that truly defines us. And that, perhaps, is the greatest lesson of all.

Rooted in Hope

In the rugged hills and deep hollers of Appalachia, life was often marked by hardship. Yet, despite the many challenges, economic struggles, harsh winters, and the unpredictable nature of farming, hope remained a constant force. Hope was not some lofty, unreachable ideal, but rather a practical, deeply rooted mindset that allowed people to keep moving forward. It wasn't a naive belief that everything would turn out fine, but a resilient optimism, a conviction that with hard work, perseverance, and faith, there was always a way through.

In my work as a therapist, I've found that hope is one of the most powerful tools for overcoming adversity. Hope doesn't ignore pain or difficulty; instead, it acknowledges them and looks for ways to persevere. Whether I'm working with clients facing personal struggles or counseling students learning how to help others, the importance of hope cannot be overstated. Optimism, when rooted in reality, gives people the strength to keep going when life feels unbearable.

When clients come into therapy, many of them feel hopeless. They've faced challenges that seem insurmountable, whether it's the loss of a loved one, the struggle of addiction, or a deep sense of failure. They're stuck in patterns of thinking that tell them things will never get better. They are stuck in a cycle of catastrophizing (Ellis, 1962), a [4]Cognitive Behavioral Therapy (CBT) term where people assume the worst possible outcome and feel it will be unbearable. But I've seen time and again that even in the darkest moments, a small seed of hope can grow into something powerful.

One of the first things I try to instill in clients is the belief that change is possible through cognitive restructuring (Beck, 1978), a CBT technique. We then look to Behavioral Activation (BA) (Ferster, 1973) by looking at small, achievable goals, steps that may seem insignificant at first but that build a foundation of hope. For instance, a client who has been struggling with depression may feel unable to make major life changes, but we might start with something as simple as establishing a daily routine. Over time, these small victories build momentum, and clients begin to see that progress, however slow, is possible.

Another important lesson I teach is that hope doesn't mean expecting a perfect outcome. It's about believing that even if things don't turn out exactly as we want, we can still find meaning, growth, and healing. This kind of optimism is grounded in reality and resilience. It allows clients to face challenges with strength, knowing that setbacks are a part of the journey but don't define the destination.

---

[4] I should note that Albert Ellis developed what he called Rational Emotive Behavioral Therapy (REBT), but REBT would be classified as a subset therapy of CBT.

One of the most practical ways to cultivate hope is by focusing on small, attainable goals. Often, clients come to therapy overwhelmed by the size of their problems. They don't know where to start. By breaking challenges down into smaller tasks, we create opportunities for success. Each small win provides evidence that progress is possible, and this builds hope. For example, a client struggling with addiction might focus on staying sober for one day at a time, rather than thinking about lifelong sobriety. Each day that passes builds confidence and a sense of accomplishment.

Many clients get stuck in patterns of negative thinking, where they assume the worst or believe that they're doomed to fail. A key part of therapy is helping them reframe these thoughts into something more hopeful. This doesn't mean ignoring the reality of their challenges but finding a more balanced perspective. Instead of thinking, "I'll never overcome this," clients can learn to say, "This is hard, but I'm taking steps toward improvement." This shift in thinking creates space for hope and optimism to grow.

Every client has strengths, but in moments of crisis, they often forget about them. I encourage clients to reflect on their past successes and the skills they've developed over time. Whether it's resilience, creativity, or problem-solving abilities, these strengths can be leveraged to face current challenges. By focusing on what they're capable of, clients begin to see that they have the tools they need to overcome their struggles. This realization fosters a deep sense of hope and empowerment.

Hope isn't about believing that everything will be perfect. It's about accepting that life is full of imperfections and learning to thrive despite them. Clients often come to therapy expecting to solve all of their problems or to find a solution that eliminates pain completely. Part of fostering hope is helping them understand that setbacks and difficulties are part of the process. By accepting imperfection, clients become more resilient and hopeful, knowing that challenges don't have to derail their progress.

As future therapists, counseling students need to understand the vital role that hope plays in the healing process. Cultivating hope in clients is not just about offering encouragement; it's about helping them find real, sustainable reasons to believe in their ability to change.

A strong therapeutic alliance is critical for effective counseling, and hope is a key ingredient in building that relationship. Clients need to feel that their therapist believes in their potential for growth and change. Counseling students must learn to communicate this belief through their words and actions. By fostering an environment of optimism and possibility, therapists help clients trust that the process will lead to meaningful outcomes.

One of the biggest challenges for new therapists is finding the balance between offering hope and being realistic about the difficulties a client may face. While it's important to be empathetic and understanding, therapists must also be honest about the work that lies ahead. Hope is not about sugar-coating reality; it's about helping clients see that even in the face of adversity, there is always room for growth and healing.

Therapists often serve as models of behavior for their clients, and that includes modeling optimism. By demonstrating a hopeful outlook in therapy sessions, counseling students can inspire their clients to adopt a similar mindset. This doesn't mean ignoring the challenges but rather approaching them with a mindset of problem-solving and possibility. Clients pick up on this optimism and begin to internalize it, believing that if their therapist sees hope, maybe they can, too.

One of my clients, [viii]Sally, came to me after the loss of her husband, overwhelmed with sadness and feeling like she couldn't move forward. Initially, Sally couldn't imagine a future without him, and the grief felt all-consuming. Together, we focused on small steps, reconnecting with friends, finding ways to honor her husband's memory, and gradually re-engaging in activities she once loved. Over time, hope began to return, not because the grief was gone but because she saw that life could continue in new ways. Sally learned to find joy in small moments and began to feel hopeful about the future despite her loss.

Another client, [ix]Jack, struggled with addiction and felt hopeless after multiple failed attempts at sobriety. Jack believed that because he had relapsed before, he was destined to fail again. In therapy, we focused on building his self-efficacy by celebrating each day of sobriety as a victory. We reframed his past relapses as learning experiences rather than failures, and over time, Jack began to see himself as capable of recovery. By focusing on the progress he made each day, hope grew, and with it, his commitment to a life of sobriety.

In the end, hope is more than just a feeling; it's a practice. It's something that we cultivate in the face of hardship, drawing on our inner strengths and resources to keep moving forward. For clients and therapists alike, hope is a lifeline, a reminder that no matter how difficult life becomes, there is always a way through.

In my Kentucky and Appalachian roots, hope was grounded in a deep understanding of life's challenges and the resilience required to overcome them. This practical optimism is something I bring into my work every day, helping clients and students see that even in the darkest moments, there is light to be found. By rooting ourselves in hope, we give ourselves the strength to grow, to heal, and to overcome whatever challenges life may bring.

The Strength of Connection

In Appalachia, there's a saying: "You don't just belong to your family, you belong to the whole town." This wasn't just a sentiment; it was the way life worked. Growing up in small communities meant that you were always part of something bigger than yourself. Everyone knew your name, your family, your neighbors, and even the grocery store clerk. If you went to town, folks weren't just passing you by; they were asking how your mama was doing or if you needed help with anything. There was no slipping by unnoticed, and that was part of its beauty.

As a kid, my dad knew they couldn't get away with much because if they were up to mischief, someone would surely see them and tell my grandparents. There's an old phrase: "It takes a village to raise a child," and in the mountains and small towns of Kentucky, that village was real. Everyone looked out for each other's kids, whether they were playing down by the creek or just walking to the store. You could be sure that if you got hurt or in trouble, someone would be there to help, and they'd let your parents know soon enough what happened.

This extended to all aspects of life. When someone in the community was going through hard times, people showed up. If a neighbor was struggling to bring in their crops or had a family member who was sick, folks would bring food, lend a hand, or simply be there to offer comfort. There wasn't a problem too big for the community to come together and try to solve. We called it "pulling together," and it was the kind of connection that made you feel like you weren't alone, no matter what life threw your way. My grandfather, [x]Cortez, would spend all day helping his neighbor bring in tobacco, even when he refused to grow it himself. He would work for hours cutting and cooking sugar cane to help a friend. That's just how it was.

One story that illustrates this perfectly comes from my mom, [xi]Norma. When she was only five years old, her father, Elbert, worked in Louisville, which was about one hundred miles away, making it hard for him to come home regularly. It was Christmas, and my mom, her siblings, and their mother, Zoni, were facing one of the harshest winters ever. With snow piled high and no money to spare, they were barely holding on. The family was out of food and coal, and with no sign of their father returning soon, they had to find a way to survive.

One day, Zoni took her oldest son, Wayne, to the local landfill to scavenge for something for Christmas for the younger kids. They found broken little cars with missing wheels and old dolls, missing eyes and limbs but these became small treasures that Norma and her siblings cherished despite their flaws. When the snowstorm worsened in late December, and food and coal finally ran out, their mother tried to chop down a tree to make firewood but ended up injuring herself in the process. They were far from neighbors and help seemed out of reach. With little choice, their mother set out for a distant store, leaving the children huddled together in bed to keep warm.

While their mother was gone, a knock came at the door. Four local men stood there, with sacks of coal slung over their backs. These neighbors, aware of the family's desperate situation, had come to help. They immediately set to work, building a fire, warming the house, and even giving the kids wool socks to wear while the house heated up. The men laughed, told stories, and kept the children entertained. But one man wasn't content to leave just yet. He feared that the fire might burn too hot and said he would stay until their mother returned. He stayed, watching over them and keeping them company until the family was reunited.

These were the ties that bound the community together, people showing up when you needed them most, even if you hadn't asked. This simple act of kindness was never forgotten by my mother, who stayed in touch with some of those men for the rest of their lives. These neighbors didn't see themselves as heroes, but to my mother and her family, their kindness made all the difference during a time of great need.

This story reminds me of the resilience and selflessness that still exists within Appalachian communities. It's a region where people still lend a hand when someone is in trouble, where you're never truly alone, and where a knock on the door can be the difference between despair and hope.

My Mom, Norma (Carroll) Wesley as a baby, being held up by her mother Zoni Carroll

During the devastation of Hurricane Helene, I remember hearing stories of how communities in Appalachia came together, just as they always had. Although many of these mountain towns were miles away from the coast, the heavy rains and flooding reached even them. Roads were washed out, homes were damaged, and many people were left stranded. But in true Appalachian fashion, people didn't wait for the government or outsiders to come in and help, they helped each other. Families shared what food they had, farmers used their tractors to clear debris, and churches opened their doors to shelter those whose homes were lost. One story in particular stands out: when a family's home was swept away in the floods, neighbors quickly organized a makeshift shelter in a local barn. They brought blankets, food, and tools to start rebuilding. By the end of the week, they had raised enough supplies to rebuild the family's home.

This wasn't an isolated event. Appalachians have long known that, in times of crisis, they can count on one another. I've heard similar stories from the coal mining disasters in West Virginia, where men and women would risk their own lives to pull others from the rubble. In more recent years, the opioid epidemic has torn through our communities, leaving families devastated. But just as we did after

[5]Hurricane Helene, Appalachians responded by coming together, forming support groups, helping with childcare for struggling parents, and providing rides to treatment centers for those in recovery. No matter the disaster, the response has always been the same: we take care of each other.

Going to church was part of this fabric. Church wasn't just about worship; it was about connection. You'd see your neighbors, catch up on news, and make plans to help out where needed. There was a rhythm to these connections that kept the community strong. Whether it was Sunday service or a mid-week potluck, everyone came together to support one another and stay involved in each other's lives.

The community also took an active role in the schools. Parents and grandparents were invested in what was happening in the classroom, and they didn't hesitate to show up for school events, volunteer when needed, or hold the teachers accountable. The saying went, "It's the town's job to raise smart kids, and the teacher just happens to get paid for it." That might've been said with a chuckle, but there was truth in it. Education wasn't just the responsibility of the teachers or the parents, it was the whole community's responsibility. Everyone was invested in making sure the kids were prepared for the future, and the strength of that support made all the difference.

These community ties are deeply ingrained in our Kentucky roots, and they hold important lessons for therapy and mental health. Humans are social beings by nature. We thrive when we're connected to others, and we struggle when we're isolated. The strength of community, the sense that someone is always there for you, isn't just comforting; it's essential for our well-being.

In therapy, one of the most common challenges clients face is isolation. Whether it's due to depression, anxiety, addiction, or grief, many people find themselves disconnected from others at the very moment they need connection the most. That's why, as therapists, it's crucial to guide our clients toward building and strengthening their social supports. We're not meant to go through life alone, and having a support network can make all the difference in a client's healing process.

---

[5] In September 2024, Hurricane Helene devastated the Appalachian region, particularly affecting areas in western North Carolina and eastern Tennessee. The storm brought record-setting rainfall, with some locations receiving up to 31.33 inches over a four-day period, leading to catastrophic flooding. Communities such as Asheville, NC, experienced unprecedented river levels, resulting in widespread destruction of infrastructure and homes.

Just as in Appalachia, where the community rallies around those in need, we can help our clients identify their own support systems. Whether it's family, friends, church, or even community organizations, there are people and places that can provide the connection and care they need. Sometimes, clients aren't aware of the resources available to them, or they may feel too ashamed or embarrassed to reach out. As therapists, it's our job to help them see the value of these connections and encourage them to lean on others for support.

There's another saying from the mountains: "A load shared is a load lightened." This is true in life, and it's certainly true in therapy. When clients feel overwhelmed by their problems, they often feel like they have to carry the burden alone. But therapy can help them see that there are others who can help shoulder that burden. While we can help share their load as therapists by encouraging them to open up to trusted friends or family members or by getting involved in their community, clients can begin to feel less isolated and more supported in their journey.

For counselors, this means guiding clients toward these social supports in a thoughtful and compassionate way. Some clients may have experienced betrayal or hurt in their relationships, making it difficult for them to trust others. In these cases, it's important to move slowly, helping clients rebuild their confidence in connecting with others. This might involve encouraging them to start small, reaching out to a friend for coffee or attending a community event, before diving into deeper relationships.

It's also important to help clients understand that seeking help and building connections is a sign of strength, not weakness. Many people, especially those who have been self-reliant for much of their lives, feel that asking for help is an admission of failure. But as we know from our Appalachian roots, "no man is an island." We all need each other, and there's no shame in leaning on your community when times get tough.

Counselors can help their clients build social connections by encouraging them to identify support systems by helping clients make a list of the people in their lives whom they trust and feel safe with. This might include family members, friends, coworkers, or community groups. Sometimes, simply identifying these people can help clients feel less alone.

Counselors can also help their clients rebuild trust in relationships. For clients who have been hurt by others, rebuilding trust is a gradual process. Encourage clients to take small steps toward reconnecting with those they care about, whether through a phone call, a shared meal, or attending a community event together.

Help them get involved in the community. Encourage clients to find ways to engage with their community. Whether it's through church, volunteering, or joining a social group, community involvement can provide a sense of belonging and purpose.

Setting healthy boundaries is also important. While connection is important, it's also crucial to help clients understand the importance of setting boundaries in relationships. Teach them how to build healthy, supportive relationships that are based on mutual respect and care.

Finally, explore group therapy. Group therapy can be a powerful tool for clients who struggle with isolation. By connecting with others who are facing similar challenges, clients can experience the healing power of community in a therapeutic setting.

In Appalachia, community ties are the thread that binds people together, offering strength, support, and care. In therapy, we can draw on that same principle, helping clients reconnect with the people around them and encouraging them to build strong social supports. Just as the community in the mountains pulled together during hard times, so too can our clients find healing and strength through connection.

In the end, the lesson is simple: We're not meant to go through life alone. Just as the mountains cradled our ancestors, offering them a sense of belonging and protection, so too can community be a source of healing for our clients. As therapists, we are here to help guide them toward those connections, encouraging them to lean on others, share their burdens, and find strength in the ties that bind.

Lessons from the Land

In the hills of Appalachia, nature has always played a central role in life. It's where our ancestors found their sustenance, their shelter, and their peace. The land wasn't just something to live on, it was something to live with. The mountains, rivers, forests, and fields were woven into the very fabric of who we were, offering not only the physical resources we needed to survive but also the emotional and spiritual solace we needed to thrive.

Growing up, I witnessed firsthand the powerful connection between people and the land. My grandfather, [xii]Cortez, was a farmer, and he had a relationship with his land and animals that seemed almost sacred. He spent hours working in his garden, tending to his crops, and caring for his animals, and it was clear that these tasks were more than just chores; they were part of his life's purpose. There was a peace he found in the rhythm of the seasons, in the simple act of planting seeds and watching them grow. The land gave him more than food; it gave him a sense of belonging and connection that grounded him in the world. When I reviewed his diary from the 1940s, I saw his notes of his daily routine and those events that impacted his life. On September 16th, 1941, he wrote the following in his diary: "helped tear down old house at Frank Hanson's, went to hospital… the baby was born." The following day, he wrote, "Done chores, went to Bloomington and to hospital… Doreen come home… cut weeds". His only son, my father, was born, but in the pages of his diary, his mind was on his work, providing for his family and the land on which he worked.

"One day, I undertook a tour through the country, and the diversity and beauties of nature I met with in this charming season expelled every gloomy and vexatious thought" – Daniel Boone

That connection to the land is something we're rediscovering today in the fields of psychology and wellness. Nature, it turns out, plays a powerful role in healing, both physically and mentally. Whether it's through ecotherapy, nature-based counseling, or simply spending time in green spaces, the benefits of nature for our well-being are undeniable.

There's a reason why we instinctively seek out green spaces when we need to clear our heads. Whether it's a walk in the woods, a visit to a park, or sitting by a river, nature has a calming effect on us. It provides a break from the constant stimulation of modern life, allowing us to slow down, breathe deeply, and reconnect with something larger than ourselves. Research shows that spending time in nature can significantly reduce stress levels, lowering the production of stress hormones like cortisol. A notable study (Hunter, 2019) published in *Frontiers in Psychology* found that a 20-to-30-minute nature experience led to a 21.3% per hour drop in cortisol levels, with the most efficient stress reduction occurring within that time frame. In a world where we're often overwhelmed by the demands of work, technology, and the fast pace of life, nature offers a kind of sanctuary. It helps to reset our nervous systems, bringing us back to a state of balance. The physical benefits are clear as well; being outside encourages movement, whether it's walking, hiking, gardening, or even just playing with children in the yard. This physical activity, in turn, boosts our immune system, strengthens our hearts, and reduces the risk of chronic illness.

But the benefits of nature go beyond stress relief and physical health. Nature also fosters social connection. Green spaces often serve as communal gathering places where families and friends come together to picnic, play, or simply enjoy each other's company. In a time when many of us feel increasingly isolated, these outdoor spaces remind us that we are part of a larger community.

On a deeper level, nature has the power to inspire a sense of existential awe. When we stand before a mountain range, gaze at the stars, or listen to the sound of a rushing river, we're reminded of how small we are in the grand scheme of things. This sense of awe can bring with it a feeling of peace and acceptance, helping us put our worries into perspective. It's hard to stay focused on life's smaller stresses when you're faced with the vastness and beauty of the natural world.

In recent years, the field of ecopsychology has emerged to explore the relationship between human beings and the natural world. Ecopsychology recognizes that our mental health is intimately tied to the health of the planet and that nature can be a powerful tool in the therapeutic process. Nature-based counseling (Dohlman, 2024) programs, which integrate the natural environment into the therapeutic setting, are becoming more popular as therapists and clients alike recognize the healing potential of the outdoors.

These programs might involve anything from traditional therapy sessions held in a park or forest to more structured activities like hiking therapy, gardening therapy, or wilderness retreats. The goal is to use nature as a co-therapist, allowing the natural world to facilitate healing in ways that a traditional office setting cannot. Many people find it easier to open up emotionally when they're outside, away from the confines of four walls. The natural environment provides a sense of freedom and openness that can help clients feel more grounded and connected to both them and the world around them.

My wife and fellow therapist, [xiii]Dawn Wesley, regularly engages in Walk-and-Talk Therapy, where she meets with clients in nature parks, integrating movement and the healing power of the outdoors into the therapeutic process. Unlike the structured and often confining environment of a traditional therapy office, Walk-and-Talk Therapy allows clients to experience a sense of openness, freedom, and connection to the natural world. The very act of walking through a wooded path or alongside a river can lower defenses, promote relaxation, and create a sense of calm, making it easier for clients to process difficult emotions. Many clients find that the side-by-side movement, rather than face-to-face seating, removes the pressure of direct confrontation and allows for more organic and flowing conversations.

Beyond the benefits of movement itself, nature plays a crucial role in this therapeutic approach. Research has shown that spending time outdoors reduces stress hormones, improves mood, and fosters a greater sense of well-being. The natural world provides a built-in form of grounding and mindfulness, with the sights, sounds, and smells offering a sensory experience that encourages presence and self-reflection. The rustling of leaves, the rhythm of footsteps on a dirt path, or the gentle motion of water in a stream can all serve as subtle yet powerful reminders of change, resilience, and renewal. Dawn often encourages her clients to engage in nature-based mindfulness, such as focusing on the feel of the breeze, the warmth of the sun, or the sound of birds, helping them become more attuned to the present moment.

One of Dawn's most memorable experiences using Walk-and-Talk Therapy was with a client named [xiv]Hannah struggling with profound grief and depression following the loss of a loved one. Hannah, a middle-aged woman, found herself unable to talk about her emotions in a traditional setting, feeling as though the walls of an office trapped her grief. However, as they walked through a quiet nature preserve, something shifted. The client found solace in the stillness of the trees, noticing how even the barest branches in winter held the promise of new growth in the seasons ahead. One day, while walking alongside a lake, she paused, took a deep breath, and said, "For the first time in a long time, I feel like I can breathe." That moment, so simple yet profound, underscored how both movement and nature can serve as powerful catalysts for healing. The trees, the sky, and the gentle movement of water became metaphors for resilience and forward motion, helping the client not just process her grief but begin to move beyond it.

This approach isn't new; it's something our ancestors intuitively understood. My great uncle [xv]Daniel Boone, for instance, found immense freedom and peace in the wilderness. As an explorer, he spent much of his life in nature, experiencing the sense of adventure and awe that came with traversing the untamed lands of Appalachia. "Nature was here a series of wonders and a fund of delight", he said (Boone, 1996). For Boone, the mountains weren't just a place to explore, they were a sanctuary, a space where he could connect with something larger than himself. (Boone, 1996).

Similarly, my grandfather Cortez had a deep connection to the land he farmed. He knew that nature wasn't just something to be used, it was something to be respected, something that could teach you patience, resilience, and gratitude. The simple act of caring for his garden or tending to his animals brought him joy and fulfillment, and in many ways, it grounded him during difficult times. The land gave him stability, even as life's challenges came and went.

For clients struggling with stress, anxiety, depression, or even addiction, spending time in nature can be a crucial part of the healing process. Nature offers a space for reflection, relaxation, and renewal. It encourages movement, which is vital for both physical and mental health. And it provides an opportunity to disconnect from the pressures of daily life and reconnect with something more meaningful.

For counselors, integrating nature into the therapeutic process can be a powerful tool. Whether it's encouraging clients to take walks in nature, like Dawn does in her practice, by facilitating outdoor therapy sessions, or incorporating nature-based activities like gardening or hiking into treatment plans, the possibilities are endless. Nature can serve as a mirror for clients, reflecting back the lessons they need to learn about themselves and their place in the world.

There's also a deeper lesson in the way nature operates. Nature is a constant cycle of growth, death, and renewal. There are seasons of abundance and seasons of scarcity, but life always continues. This cyclical process can be a powerful metaphor for clients who are going through difficult times. Just as the land goes through seasons, so too do we. And just as the land always renews itself, we too can find renewal, even in the darkest moments.

One of the most beautiful aspects of nature is the sense of freedom it provides. Whether you're walking through the woods, tending to a garden, or simply sitting by a creek, nature has a way of reminding you that life is bigger than your immediate worries. It invites you to let go of the noise and reconnect with what truly matters.

In Appalachia, this freedom was a part of daily life. Daniel Boone felt it as he explored the wilderness, and my grandfather Cortez felt it as he worked the land. There is something deeply human about connecting with nature, something that speaks to our need for freedom, for space, and for quiet reflection.

In our fast-paced, technology-driven world, it's easy to forget this. We spend so much time indoors, glued to our screens, that we often lose touch with the healing power of the natural world. But nature is always there, waiting for us to return to it, offering its gifts of peace, freedom, and renewal.

In the end, nature is one of the greatest healers we have. It doesn't require a prescription, it doesn't judge, and it's always available to us. All we have to do is step outside, breathe in the fresh air, and let the lessons of the land guide us toward healing and renewal.

Finding Joy and Song in Struggle

In the mountains of Appalachia, life was tough, and there was no getting around it. But if there was one thing mountain folk knew how to do, it was to laugh. Laughter wasn't just a reaction to something funny; it was a way of life, a method for pushing through the struggles and hardships that were as common as the rocky hills themselves. People in the mountains knew that while life wasn't always easy, it didn't mean you couldn't find joy along the way. As the saying goes, "You might as well laugh as cry," and my people took that to heart.

Laughter in the mountains wasn't just an escape from hardship, it was a way to survive it. The healing power of laughter has long been acknowledged in both folk wisdom and science, and today we know it goes far beyond a good chuckle. Laughing has real, tangible effects on our bodies, decreasing stress hormones like cortisol and epinephrine, boosting the immune system, and even relieving pain. For those who lived hard lives in the hills, laughter was like medicine, handed down from one generation to the next, offering hope and comfort in the face of whatever came their way.

I think about my own grandmother, [xvi]Zoni, who always had a funny story or a sharp-tongued saying ready. She was the typical Appalachian granny, just like the one from [6]*The Beverly Hillbillies*, complete with her 410 shotgun by the door and her unfiltered humor. She didn't mince words. One of her favorite sayings was "Well, shit fire and save the matches!" She'd say it with genuine surprise when something caught her off guard, which happened often since she was nearly blind. And while her language might have been a bit colorful, her laughter was infectious, and her wit was sharp.

Granny Zoni's laughter wasn't just about cracking jokes, it was a survival tool. She'd lived through her fair share of hard times, but she always found a way to laugh at life's absurdities. Whether she was telling a story from her youth or laughing at the present, she knew that humor lightened the load. And, more

---

[6] *The Beverly Hillbillies* was a sitcom that aired from 1962 to 1971, following the fictional Clampett family, a rural Appalachian clan who strike oil and move to Beverly Hills. The show played on exaggerated hillbilly stereotypes, portraying the Clampetts as kind-hearted but naive in contrast to the sophisticated yet often shallow city dwellers. While beloved for its humor and cultural satire, the series also contributed to long-standing misconceptions about Appalachian people. For more on its cultural impact, see Harkins, A. (2004). *Hillbilly: A cultural history of an American icon.* Oxford University Press.

importantly, she shared that gift with everyone around her. Her laughter was infectious, and it spread through our family like a balm for the soul.

Modern science has confirmed what Appalachians like Granny Zoni always knew: laughter is good for you. Researchers have found that laughter triggers a cascade of physical benefits in the body, helping to reverse the effects of stress. When we laugh, our brain releases endorphins, the body's natural feel-good chemicals, which promote an overall sense of well-being and can even temporarily relieve pain.

One of the most significant benefits of laughter is its ability to lower stress hormones like cortisol and epinephrine. These hormones, when left unchecked, can lead to chronic stress and a host of health problems like heart disease, anxiety, and depression. Laughter acts as a natural antidote, lowering these hormone levels and reversing the body's stress response. A systematic review and meta-analysis (Kramer CK, 2023) found that spontaneous laughter was associated with a 31.9% reduction in cortisol levels compared to usual activities, suggesting its potential as an adjunctive therapy to improve well-being. Additionally, laughter enhances oxygen intake, stimulates the heart, lungs, and muscles, and increases endorphin release, contributing to stress relief and a relaxed feeling. It's no wonder that in places like Appalachia, where life's challenges were constant, people turned to humor as a way to keep their spirits high.

"Shit fire, and save the Matches."

Laughter also boosts the immune system, helping to ward off illness. Studies show that laughing increases the production of antibodies and activates immune cells like T-cells, which help fight infection. One study found that mirthful laughter led to significant increases in natural killer cell activity and immunoglobulin levels, suggesting that laughter may bolster the body's defense mechanisms (Dalezman, 2012). Furthermore, Berk and colleagues (Federation of American Societies for Experimental Biology. , (2010, April 26).) demonstrated that laughter decreases stress hormones like cortisol and epinephrine, while increasing the activity of immune cells, including T-cells and natural killer cells. These findings suggest that laughter not only reduces stress but also enhances immune function, contributing to overall health and well-being. In a place like Appalachia, where access to modern healthcare was limited, staying healthy often meant relying on natural remedies, and laughter was one of them.

And then there's the mood-boosting effect of laughter. It's hard to stay angry, anxious, or sad when you're laughing. Laughter improves mood by releasing dopamine and serotonin, the body's natural antidepressants. Countless notes that laughter replaces cortisol in the bloodstream with beneficial brain chemicals, including dopamine and endorphins, thereby enhancing mood and promoting relaxation.

Another phrase and song you might hear in the mountains is "Keep on the sunny side." It's a reminder to focus on the positive, even when things seem dark. Appalachian folk were known for their resilience, and much of that resilience came from their ability to stay optimistic in the face of adversity. Laughter was the spark that kept that optimism alive. Even when things looked grim, they found humor in their daily lives, and it helped them keep going.

Take, for example, the ways in which people used humor to deal with the hard work of everyday life. Chores in the mountains were never-ending, hauling water, tending gardens, chopping wood, but laughter was never far behind. Whether it was cracking a joke about how "you can't get blood from a turnip" when the harvest was slim or poking fun at a broken-down wagon with, "Well, I reckon it'll be faster to walk anyway," humor kept the work from feeling too heavy. It wasn't about ignoring the hardship, but about making it bearable.

In my work as a therapist, I see time and time again how laughter can play a crucial role in healing. For clients dealing with trauma, depression, or chronic stress, incorporating humor into therapy can be transformative. While it's important to address serious issues with care and attention, humor can provide a safe space to process emotions, offering relief from the intensity of the therapeutic process.

For example, I often encourage clients to find moments of lightness in their day-to-day lives. Whether it's watching a funny movie, sharing jokes with friends, or even reflecting on the absurdity of certain situations, laughter can be a powerful coping mechanism. I've seen clients who've been stuck in deep depression begin to lift their spirits by allowing themselves to laugh again, even if it starts small. A little humor can go a long way toward easing emotional pain and opening the door to deeper healing.

Counseling students, too, need to learn the importance of humor in their work. Therapy doesn't always have to be somber and serious. In fact, bringing a little levity into sessions can help build rapport, reduce client anxiety, and foster a more open, trusting relationship. Laughter, used appropriately, can break down barriers and create a sense of connection that's essential for effective therapy.

Appalachians knew that laughter could turn even the hardest situations into something manageable. It didn't take away the struggle, but it made it bearable. Whether it was sitting around the porch after a long day's work, swapping stories with neighbors, or poking fun at the missteps of the day, they knew how to find joy in the struggle.

One of my favorite examples of this resourceful humor is the saying, "Don't get your knickers in a knot." It's a reminder not to let the small things get you down, a saying I've used many times in therapy when clients find themselves overwhelmed by everyday stresses. Much like Granny Zoni's colorful "Well, shit fire and save the matches!" when she was surprised, these sayings were ways of shrugging off life's annoyances and keeping the bigger picture in mind. "Laughter is the best medicine."

Music, like laughter, holds a special place in Appalachian culture, offering joy, healing, and connection. Mountain music, bluegrass, and southern gospel quartets remain central to the traditions that bind the community together. In the old days, you might find people gathered around with guitars, banjos, fiddles, and bass, filling the air with music that told stories of hardship, love, and faith. In some churches, you'd hear acapella harmonies sung in four-part style from shaped-note hymnals, with melodies that lifted spirits high and brought people together.

Much like laughter, music has profound effects on both physical and emotional well-being. The benefits of music range from reducing stress to boosting the immune system. It's known to lower blood pressure, decrease levels of cortisol (the stress hormone), and release endorphins, much like laughter does. A recent study published in *Frontiers in Psychology* (Arnold, 2024) examined the neurochemical effects of music and found that listening to music can lead to the release of endorphins, enhancing mood and promoting relaxation. Music therapy has been shown to improve mood, relieve anxiety, and even help with pain management. Arnold (2024) also showed that music-based interventions can influence pain perception at multiple levels, including the periphery, spinal cord, brainstem, limbic system, and cerebral cortex. What's more, music can tap into deep emotions, helping people express feelings they can't put into words. When used in a therapeutic setting, music provides an outlet for clients to process difficult emotions, find relief, and strengthen their sense of connection with themselves and others. Research indicates that music can facilitate emotional expression, particularly in individuals who struggle to articulate their feelings verbally. This is especially evident in studies focusing on alexithymia, a condition characterized by difficulty in identifying and describing emotions.

For instance, a study by Akbari, Amiri, and Mehrabi (Akbari, 2021) examined the effectiveness of music therapy in reducing alexithymia symptoms and improving peer relationships among preadolescents. The findings suggested that music therapy had a significant positive effect on reducing alexithymia, thereby enhancing the participants' ability to recognize and express their emotions.

In Appalachia, music wasn't just entertainment, it was a form of storytelling, community building, and emotional release. Families gathered on porches or at church events, singing songs that connected them to their history and to each other. It wasn't just about the notes or the instruments; it was about the shared experience, the togetherness that music fostered.

Incorporating music into therapy, much like laughter, can have transformative effects. It's an opportunity to reach clients on a deeper level, providing comfort and a sense of belonging. Whether it's inviting clients to reflect on songs that hold personal meaning or using music to facilitate emotional expression, it can be a powerful tool in healing. For therapists, recognizing the importance of music in the cultural fabric of Appalachia or any culture can help forge stronger connections with clients. Encouraging clients to engage with music, whether by listening, singing, or playing, can offer an outlet for processing emotions in a way that feels natural and meaningful.

Music and laughter both have the power to transcend pain and hardship. They can be experienced alone, but, as with all things in Appalachia, they are best enjoyed with others. For those seeking connection, healing, and joy, these timeless forms of expression remain as vital today as they were in generations past.

Faith in People and the Healing Process

As a therapist, one of the most important roles we play is to hold faith in our clients, even when they can't yet believe in themselves. In the rugged hills of Appalachia, we've long known the power of belief, whether it's faith in a higher power, trust in family, or the conviction that, no matter how tough the times, "this too shall pass." It's a lesson that resonates deeply with the work we do in therapy. When clients come to us, they often feel broken, hopeless, or lost. Sometimes, the greatest gift we can give them is our unwavering belief that they can change, heal, and grow.

In Kentucky, we have a saying: "It's a mighty poor man that can't get the better of himself." It means that everyone has the capacity to overcome their struggles and rise above their circumstances. But in order for that to happen, someone needs to believe it's possible, especially when the person in question cannot. As therapists, we must be the ones to hold that belief, to have faith in our clients, even when the evidence of change isn't yet clear. This faith, this belief in the possibility of healing, is often what drives the therapy process forward.

I've never been a fan of labels for people. Labels like "alcoholic," "addict," or even a clinical diagnosis can be damaging. I understand the necessity of a diagnosis, particularly when working with insurance, but the problem with labels is that they often reduce a person to their struggles. Labels can reinforce a negative self-image, and for many people, they become a cage. When someone is labeled an addict, it's easy for them to internalize that identity and believe that it's all they'll ever be. And when the world reinforces that label, it can feel impossible to escape.

The same goes for the more casual labels people throw around. I've heard parents call their children "little shits," and it breaks my heart every time. These words stick. Children hear these labels and begin to believe that's who they are. Over time, they live up to the negative expectations placed on them because that's what they've been told to believe. As therapists, we must be cautious about the language we use. Words have power, and when we label someone negatively, we risk reinforcing the very behaviors we want to help them overcome.

In Appalachia, there's another saying: "You catch more flies with honey than with vinegar." In the context of therapy, this means we need to approach people with kindness, encouragement, and belief in their potential. Labels, especially negative ones, are the vinegar; they sour the relationship and limit growth. But faith in someone's ability to heal, that's the honey. It sweetens the process and opens the door to real transformation.

Many times, clients come to therapy without any belief in their own ability to change. They may have been told all their lives that they're not good enough, that they'll never amount to anything, or that they're stuck in their current patterns. Our role as therapists is to hold the belief for them until they can begin to see it for themselves.

I remember a young man named [xvii]Jeremy who came to me for help with addiction. Jeremy had been in and out of rehab programs for years, and nothing had worked. By the time he sat down in my office, he didn't believe he could ever get clean. His family had all but given up on him, and every label you could imagine, addict, loser, junkie, failure, had been thrown his way. But I didn't see Jeremy that way. I saw a young man who was struggling, yes, but also someone who still had the potential for growth.

For months, Jeremy didn't show much progress. He would relapse, miss appointments, and spiral into shame and guilt. But I kept believing in him, and more importantly, I made sure he knew that I believed in him. I didn't judge Jeremy for his setbacks because I knew that healing isn't a straight line. Slowly, something shifted. Jeremy began to come to sessions more regularly. He started talking about his future, about what he wanted from life beyond addiction. Eventually, Jeremy found the strength to commit to recovery, and today, he's sober and building a life that he once thought was impossible.

Another client, a woman named [xviii]Nikki, who had experienced years of abuse, came to me feeling like she had no worth. She couldn't understand why anyone would care about her, much less believe that she had the power to change her life. Nikki's trauma had convinced her that she was broken beyond repair. In her mind, she wasn't just a victim; she was damaged goods. But I refused to see Nikki that way. I knew the power of therapy, and more importantly, I knew the power of her own spirit, even if she couldn't see it yet.

Over time, through gentle support and consistent belief in her strength, Nikki began to see herself differently. She started to realize that she wasn't defined by the labels others had placed on her. She wasn't broken, she was healing. Eventually, Nikki found the courage to leave her abusive relationship, rebuild her self-esteem, and create a life of safety and empowerment. All she needed was someone to believe in her before she could believe in herself.

Therapy is not about quick fixes or instant results. Healing takes time, and the process can be messy and full of setbacks and detours. But at the core of therapy is the belief that change is possible. As therapists, we trust in the process, even when the road is long and winding. We hold the hope for our clients, even when they can't hold it for themselves.

As the saying goes, "Nothing worth having comes easy." This applies to therapy in so many ways. Our clients may struggle, they may lose faith in themselves, and the progress may be slow. But if we continue to believe in them, if we trust in their ability to grow, change will come.

We know the power of talk therapy, of creating a safe space for clients to explore their fears, their hopes, and their potential. When we show our clients that we believe in them, we help them build the courage to believe in themselves. Often, we are the first people in their lives to offer this kind of faith. And that faith can be the catalyst for profound change.

For those learning to become therapists, one of the most important lessons is the power of belief. It's easy to get caught up in the clinical aspects of therapy, diagnoses, treatment plans, and symptom management, but at the heart of the work we do is our belief in people. Clients will often show up in our offices feeling hopeless, but if we hold the belief that they can heal, it will resonate with them.

It's not always easy to maintain that faith, especially when clients seem stuck or resistant to change. But we must remember that therapy is often the first time in their lives that someone is truly listening to them without judgment, without labeling, and with genuine belief in their potential. That belief can spark a transformation, even when progress is slow.

In Appalachia, we have an unspoken belief in the strength of people. We know that life is full of hardship, but we also know that people can weather the storm. In therapy, this belief in the human spirit is essential. As therapists, we must have faith not only in the power of the healing process but also in the resilience of the people we serve. When we trust in our clients, we give them the gift of belief, a gift that can change their lives in ways they never thought possible.

In the end, the labels, the diagnoses, the setbacks, they're all part of the journey, but they don't define it. What defines it is the belief that healing is possible, that people are capable of profound change, and that, with the right support, they can rise above their struggles. That's the faith we must carry with us as therapists, and it's the faith that makes all the difference. "Trust the process"!

Passing It Down

In my birthplace, Kentucky, the passing down of knowledge, heirlooms, and traditions was more than just a ritual; it was a duty. The older generation saw it as their responsibility to ensure that the younger ones knew where they came from, understood the values that guided their family and carried forward the wisdom earned through hard-won experience. This passing down wasn't always about material wealth; it was about preserving the legacy of family and instilling the lessons that had kept generations strong through thick and thin.

One of the most important aspects of this tradition was that it wasn't just the tangible things that were passed down but also the stories, the lessons, and the love that bound families together. Each generation took what they had learned and passed it down, not just to show pride in their heritage but to help the younger ones avoid some of the mistakes they had made themselves. Whether it was a cherished family heirloom, a story about hardship, or a simple piece of advice, these gifts from one generation to the next were the glue that kept families connected, even as the years passed and the world around them changed.

Material objects were often imbued with more meaning than their monetary value. These items became touchstones for family members, reminders of where they came from and the people who loved them. Some of my siblings and cousins were given silver dollars that had the birthdate of their grandparents or great-grandparents engraved on them, a tangible link to their past. Others received pieces of furniture from the family farm, knickknacks that may have had little financial value but carried immense sentimental worth. These items were imbued with the stories of the people who used them, and having them in our homes kept those people close to our hearts.

My grandmothers, [xix]Doreen and Zoni, made a quilt or Afghan for my wife and me when we were married. These quilts weren't just a bedcover; it was a symbol of their love, their hard work, and their care. Every stitch was made with intention, with the hope that it would keep us warm and remind us of the family that surrounded us. My grandmother Doreen was also known for making stuffed bunnies, dolls, and other handmade gifts for our children. My mom, Norma, made stuffed bears. These small creations carried with them the same love and care that they put into everything she did. They weren't store-bought toys but something far more valuable, gifts of time, effort, and love, made by the hands of someone who cared deeply for their grandchildren.

And then there was [xx]Gramps. One of the most prized possessions I received from him was his father's old shotgun. This shotgun had a history, a long, storied past that had seen its fair share of action. It was made with an extra-long firing pin, which made it a little dangerous. One day, when Gramps was young, he and his brother Louis were out hunting for rabbits or squirrels, and they came upon a fence they needed to cross. Louis, without thinking, used the shotgun as a support to get over the fence. His hand grasped the barrel, with his thumb resting right on the end. When the stock hit the ground, the gun went off, and with it went Louis's thumb. I never knew Uncle Louis myself, but from the stories I heard, he was a jolly fellow, never limited by the fact that he only had four fingers on one hand. I've even seen an old family video from the 1950s or early 60s, where Uncle Louis was waving goodbye to the family with that hand, missing a thumb that my shotgun had taken.

That old shotgun, with its stories of hunts and mishaps, remains more than just a family heirloom. It's a piece of our history, a reminder of the quirks and accidents that shaped the lives of the people who came before me. It's a physical connection to Gramps, to his father, and to the land they worked on. And while it might sit on a shelf, rarely used, its presence is a reminder of the lessons, the stories, and the love that have been passed down through the generations.

Louis Wesley and his wife Eva Parker Wesley.
Missing: Louis' Left Thumb

But perhaps the greatest gift that we kids received from our grandparents wasn't something we could hold in our hands, it was the lessons they passed down, the values they instilled in us, and the love they gave so freely. These lessons have shaped who we are and how we approach life, and they are the most valuable inheritance of all.

My grandparents taught us the importance of hard work, of family, and of perseverance. They showed us, through their actions, what it meant to live with integrity and to stand by your word. These were lessons they didn't just tell us; they lived them. Whether it was Gramps spending hours in his garden, growing the food that would sustain us, or Grandma Doreen sitting by the fire, sewing quilts, or making toys for the kids, their lives were an example of dedication, love, and care for others.

One of the most important lessons I learned from them was the importance of passing these values on to the next generation. Just as they took the time to teach us, it's now our responsibility to ensure that our children and grandchildren carry those same lessons forward. This doesn't just happen through words, it happens through actions. The way we live our lives, the way we treat others, and the way we nurture our families are all part of the legacy we leave behind.

I was reminded of this recently when I was at the checkout counter at Walmart with my grandson, [xxi]Landon. We were waiting behind an older lady who was struggling to understand the technology of the card reader to pay for her items. I could see her frustration and confusion growing as she tried to figure it out, so I stepped in to help. But instead of just showing her how to use her card, I decided to use my own credit card to pay for her items. She looked like she didn't have much, and I wanted to give her a little gift. What I didn't realize at that moment was that Landon was standing behind me, watching it all unfold. He was learning a lesson from me that was well worth the $80 I spent on that older lady. I was passing down a legacy of service and love toward others, and Landon was soaking it all in.

There is a deep responsibility that comes with being the older generation. It's not just about giving material items or telling stories but about ensuring that the next generation understands where they come from and what's truly important. It's about passing down not just heirlooms but the values, love, and lessons that have kept families strong for generations.

In our family, the passing down of these lessons often came through simple acts of kindness and care. Whether it was Gramps patiently showing us how to plant a garden or Grandma Doreen making sure we knew how to sew a patch into a pair of jeans, these were more than just skills; they were lessons in self-reliance, resourcefulness, and the importance of caring for the things and people around you.

And while we may live in a different world today, where technology and convenience have replaced many of the old ways of doing things, these lessons are just as important now as they ever were. It's our job to pass them down, to ensure that the next generation doesn't lose touch with the values that made us who we are.

In the end, the greatest gift my grandparents gave me wasn't the quilt or the shotgun, it was their love. The love they showed us in everything they did, from the meals they cooked to the stories they told, is the most enduring legacy they left behind. It's a love that we continue to pass down to our own children and grandchildren, ensuring that the values they taught us live on.

As I look around at the things I've inherited, the quilt, the shotgun, and the stories of Uncle Louis, I realize that these are just symbols of something much greater. They are reminders of the love, lessons, and legacy that my grandparents passed down and that I now have the honor of passing on to the next generation.

It is important that we understand the importance of roots, of knowing where you come from and carrying that knowledge with you. It's not just about the heirlooms or the stories; it's about the love that binds us together, generation after generation. And that, more than anything, is the greatest gift of all.

One of the greatest lessons I've learned from my own family and the generations that came before me is that true happiness doesn't come from what we receive but from what we give. In a world that often measures success by what we accumulate, whether its wealth, possessions, social media likes or honors and accolades, the deeper truth is that fulfillment comes from the act of giving to others. It's not in the taking but in the giving that we find purpose, connection, and joy.

This is a lesson I stress with my clients, particularly those who struggle with depression, dissatisfaction, or a sense of purposelessness. When people feel stuck in their own pain, often the best way to begin healing is to step outside of themselves and focus on others. Giving to others, whether it's time, kindness, or material gifts, can have a transformative effect on how we see the world and ourselves. For many of my clients, I assign homework with this simple instruction: do something for someone else. It could be as simple as helping a neighbor, volunteering at a local charity, or even offering a kind word to a stranger. The result is often the same, what they give comes back to them in the form of increased happiness, gratitude, and a sense of purpose.

This act of giving can also release what is sometimes called a "helper's high." Research has shown that when we help others, our brains release feel-good chemicals, such as endorphins, serotonin, and oxytocin, creating a sense of well-being that's more powerful than any drug (Dossey, 2018). It's no surprise that people who make giving a regular part of their lives report feeling more content and fulfilled. In many ways, this is a key part of the healing process, especially for those dealing with mental health issues. When we shift our focus away from what we don't have and turn our attention to how we can serve others, we find a sense of worth and happiness that material possessions can never provide.

For future counselors, this is a lesson that will serve them well in their own lives and in their work with clients. As therapists, we are in a unique position to offer help and healing to others, and that in itself is a gift. Every time we guide a client through a difficult period or help them see their potential, we experience the helper's high, the satisfaction of knowing that we've made a difference. And this gift doesn't stop with us, it's passed down through the people we help, who in turn share those lessons with others in their lives.

As a professor, I feel this even more deeply. Not only do I get to experience the rewards of helping my clients, but I also have the privilege of training future counselors who will carry forward the lessons I've shared with them. It's a kind of legacy, knowing that the wisdom and guidance I offer will continue to live on in the work my students do with their own clients. In this way, I feel that I can live forever through the acts of kindness, support, and healing that ripple out from my work into the wider world.

In the end, the greatest gift we can pass down to others, whether it's through heirlooms, stories, or acts of kindness, is the understanding that we are all connected and that by giving to others, we find the truest form of happiness. This is why I love my profession as a counselor and professor. Every day, I get to experience the joy of giving, both to my clients and to my students. And in turn, they pass that joy on to others, creating a ripple effect that extends far beyond what any of us can see.

The Unseen Strength

In Kentucky and the South, in general, we have a way of speaking that often seems simple but carries deep wisdom. There's a saying we've passed down through the centuries: "Still waters run deep." On the surface, someone may seem calm, quiet, or even fragile, but underneath lies a deep well of strength and resilience. This is especially true when it comes to vulnerability. Vulnerability often looks like weakness to the untrained eye, but for those of us who've lived through hardship, we know that being open and vulnerable takes more strength than anything else.

Brené Brown, in her research on vulnerability, teaches us that allowing ourselves to be seen and to admit our fears, struggles, and imperfections is one of the greatest acts of courage. She writes that vulnerability is not weakness; it's the birthplace of love, belonging, joy, and creativity. And yet, many of us grow up believing the opposite, thinking that to be strong means to keep our guard up, to never let anyone see the cracks in our armor (Brown, 2012).

In Appalachia, we were taught to be "tough as nails," to "grin and bear it," and to "get on with it" when life got hard. Admitting vulnerability wasn't always encouraged, but underneath all that was a different kind of lesson, one about quiet resilience. You see, in our Kentucky way of life, vulnerability didn't always mean sitting down and spilling your heart. It could be found in the soft acts of asking for help, in trusting someone enough to lean on them, or in simply admitting, "I'm not okay." That kind of openness, especially in a culture that values self-reliance, took a quiet, unseen strength.

In the hills, folks would say, "You need a stiff backbone and a soft heart to get through life." That phrase captures the balance between strength and vulnerability. It's not about having an iron will that refuses to bend, nor is it about being too tender to face the realities of life. Instead, it's about knowing when to stand firm and when to let your guard down, when to press on and when to ask for support.

Vulnerability doesn't mean exposing everything all at once. It's about having the strength to open up, even just a little when the time is right. For many, it's admitting that they're carrying too much on their own shoulders or allowing others to help lighten the load. Vulnerability is also about acknowledging that you don't have all the answers and that sometimes life is too heavy to handle alone, and that's okay.

The phrase "a stiff backbone and a soft heart" reminds us that we can be strong and tender at the same time. It teaches that resilience isn't just about powering through; it's also about knowing when to be vulnerable and when to allow ourselves to soften and let others in.

For many clients, vulnerability feels terrifying. It may seem like opening up to a counselor, or even to loved ones, makes them weak. They've been taught to "pull themselves up by the bootstraps" or to "keep a stiff upper lip," believing that emotions are best kept hidden and dealt with privately. But the truth is, that vulnerability is where healing begins. As [7]Brené Brown says, "You can't get to courage without walking through vulnerability."

In counseling, this is often the hardest step, allowing clients to feel safe enough to be vulnerable and to admit their fears, anxieties, and struggles. It's only by bringing those things into the light that we can begin to work through them. As therapists, we create that space, a kind of "front porch" where clients can come, sit for a spell, and talk without fear of judgment. We're not looking for perfection; we're looking for honesty and openness because that's where the real work happens.

Clients need to understand that showing vulnerability is not a sign of weakness, it's the ultimate sign of strength. When they open up, when they admit they're struggling, they give themselves permission to heal. They allow themselves to be seen and, in doing so, they take the first steps toward true resilience.

There's another saying I like: "You don't know how strong you are until being strong is the only choice you have." Sometimes, it's in moments of vulnerability, when we feel our weakest, that we find our greatest strength. We may not be able to fix everything, but by allowing others in, by admitting our need for support, we find the courage to keep going.

As counselors, one of our most important roles is to model and encourage vulnerability in our clients through self-disclosure. Many people come to therapy with walls built up around them, afraid to let anyone see what's behind them. They may have been taught that vulnerability is dangerous and that it leads to hurt or disappointment. It's our job to show them that, in the right environment, vulnerability is not a threat but a path to healing.

Counselors must be mindful of the delicate balance between encouraging vulnerability and overwhelming clients. Vulnerability is a gradual process. Just as mountain folks don't pour their hearts out right away, clients may need time to feel safe enough to open up. Creating a therapeutic space that feels like a "safe porch" is essential. This means building trust, offering validation, and ensuring that clients

---

[7] In her widely acclaimed TED Talk, "The Power of Vulnerability," researcher Brené Brown explores how embracing vulnerability fosters deeper connections, creativity, and a sense of belonging. This talk, delivered at TEDxHouston in June 2010, has become one of the most viewed TED Talks, highlighting the significance of vulnerability in personal and professional growth. The Power of Vulnerability | Brené Brown | TEDxHouston

know they are heard and seen, no matter how messy or uncomfortable their emotions may be.

For counselors, it's also crucial to guide clients through their vulnerability without allowing them to feel ashamed of it. In fact, we should celebrate their courage every time they take a step toward openness. It's important to remind clients that vulnerability is where change begins, and it's through these moments of openness that they will grow stronger and more resilient.

There's a final saying that fits here perfectly: "If you want to go fast, go alone; if you want to go far, go together." Vulnerability brings us closer together, it allows clients to build deeper relationships with their therapists, with their loved ones, and most importantly, with themselves. Through this process, they are reminded that they don't have to carry everything on their own. They can lean on others, and in doing so, they'll find the strength to go much farther than they ever could alone.

In the end, vulnerability is about quiet strength. It's about knowing when to admit that you don't have it all figured out that you need help, or that you're afraid. It's about being brave enough to sit on that metaphorical front porch and talk things through. Just like still waters run deep, the deepest strength often comes from the quietest moments of vulnerability.

For clients, it's important to remember that vulnerability isn't just something you do once. It's a continual process, and with each step, you grow stronger. By allowing yourself to be seen, by asking for help, and by being open to the possibility of change, you create a path toward healing that's based on honesty and courage.

For counselors, the lesson is clear: create a space where clients feel safe enough to be vulnerable and encourage them to embrace the quiet strength that comes from openness. Vulnerability isn't a sign of weakness; it's one root of resilience. And in the mountains, we know that roots run deep, anchoring us through life's storms and helping us grow stronger with each passing season.

Copperheads Among Us

In Appalachia, you learn early that danger is always lurking. Whether it's the swift current of the creek, a steep cliffside, or the venomous snakes that hide in the brush, you come to understand that the world around you can be treacherous. But the lesson we learn as children is that while we can't avoid danger, we also can't let it stop us from living. "You can't spend your life looking for rattlesnakes under every rock," as the old saying goes. If you do, you'll never get anywhere.

When I was just three or four years old, I had an encounter with one of those hidden dangers, one that taught me a lesson I've carried with me throughout my life. I was standing by a tree, not a care in the world, when I saw my mother's face change. I remember the fear in her eyes as she calmly told me to walk slowly toward her. What I didn't know was inches from where I stood, coiled and ready to strike, was a copperhead snake. Its camouflage had hidden it so well that I hadn't even noticed it.

"You can't make a quilt without a few pricks."

That moment stuck with me, not just because of the danger, but because of the way my mother handled it. She didn't scream, she didn't panic, and she didn't make me feel scared. She simply guided me away from the threat. That's a lesson I've applied not only to my life but also to my work as a counselor. Danger is always around us, but we can't let fear or pain stop us from living fully. Instead, we learn to navigate the dangers, whether they're physical or emotional, and we find a way to keep moving forward.

In Appalachia, there are many dangers that have claimed lives, some of them are sudden and unavoidable, like the horse that kicked my great, great grandpa Elmer Martin, or the fall that killed my Great, Great Grandpa William Washington Elmore. Then there are the dangers that sneak up on you, like the copperhead. But not all dangers are physical. In fact, the emotional and psychological dangers of life can be just as harmful, if not more so. And like the copperhead, emotional pain can be hard to spot until it's right at your feet.

We live in a world where it's natural to want to avoid pain. But as the old saying goes, "No pain, no gain." Pain, whether it's physical or emotional, is a signal from our brain that something is wrong or dangerous. But just because pain is present doesn't mean we should run from it or avoid it altogether. Pain is part of the human condition, and in many ways, it's what teaches us, strengthens us, and ultimately leads us to a more fulfilling life.

Take emotional pain, for example. It's easier to avoid the discomfort of vulnerability, rejection, or embarrassment by staying isolated and never putting ourselves out there. But in doing so, we miss out on all the joys that come from human connection, friendships, love, intimacy, and shared experiences. As the phrase goes, "You can't make a quilt without a few pricks." The same is true for life; you can't have the pleasures without enduring a little bit of pain.

One of the most common issues I've seen in from my clients is the desire to avoid emotional pain. Clients come in feeling anxious, depressed, or overwhelmed, and their first instinct is to pull back, to retreat into themselves, and avoid anything that might hurt them further. But as I often remind them, "You can't avoid the copperheads if you want to get where you're going." Life's dangers are part of the journey, and while it's natural to want to steer clear of them, doing so means you'll never reach your destination.

In therapy, we often talk about the comfort zone, the stretch zone, and the panic zone. The comfort zone is where we feel safe, but nothing grows there. The stretch zone is where we experience discomfort, but it's also where growth happens. Then there's the panic zone, where we're overwhelmed and unable to function. The key to therapy is guiding clients into the stretch zone, where they can feel the discomfort of emotional growth without being pushed into panic.

This approach, often used in exposure therapy, helps clients confront their fears gradually. Exposure therapy involves progressively exposing clients to the very things they fear or avoid, but in small, manageable steps. Over time, the repeated exposure helps desensitize them to the feared object, situation, or emotion, reducing their anxiety and allowing them to engage in life more fully. Whether it's a fear of rejection, intimacy, or vulnerability, the goal is to move clients slowly toward those fears, stretching them just enough to grow but not so much that they become overwhelmed.

While it's essential to guide clients through their fears, we must also recognize when they're stretching too far. If clients are pushed too quickly or exposed to too much emotional pain at once, they can enter the panic zone, where growth halts, and distress takes over. In these cases, it's important to pull back and incorporate techniques like mindfulness, relaxation, and meditation. These practices can help calm the nervous system and bring clients back to a place where they can continue to stretch without breaking.

Mindfulness teaches clients to stay present in the moment, acknowledging their discomfort without letting it overwhelm them. Relaxation techniques, such as deep breathing or progressive muscle relaxation, can ease physical symptoms of anxiety. And meditation offers a way to center the mind and find calm amidst emotional storms. By helping clients use these tools, we allow them to regulate their emotions and continue their journey of growth without falling into the panic zone.

Sometimes this process is slow. Just like walking around a field of copperheads, it takes time to navigate the dangers, and progress can feel painstakingly slow. But step by step, clients move forward, and the fear and pain that once seemed overwhelming begin to fade. "You can't cross the creek without getting your feet wet," but once you've made it to the other side, you realize the journey was worth it.

One of my favorite reminders of how fleeting life is, comes from the film *Dead Poets Society*. Robin Williams' character tells his students: "Carpe diem", seize the day, suck the marrow out of life. That's what we need to do. We can't let fear of pain or danger stop us from living fully. Emotional pain, like physical pain, is part of life, but it's also a part of growth, healing, and ultimately, happiness.

For clients struggling with anxiety, depression, or relationship issues, the temptation is to avoid anything that might hurt them further. But avoidance only leads to more pain. "You can't get the honey without getting stung by the bees." The same is true for life's greatest joys. We need to be willing to face discomfort, take a few emotional hits, and keep moving forward if we want to experience all the richness life has to offer.

For counselors, the lesson here is to recognize that guiding clients toward their goals doesn't mean shielding them from pain. Instead, it's about helping them navigate that pain in a way that leads to growth, rather than pushing them into panic. The work we do is about helping clients move from the comfort zone into the stretch zone, where they can grow emotionally without becoming overwhelmed. We can't avoid the copperheads for them, but we can teach them how to navigate the dangers and keep moving toward their destination.

For clients, the lesson is this: pain is a part of life. It's natural to want to avoid it, but in doing so, you also avoid the pleasures and joys that life has to offer. Whether it's the pain of vulnerability in relationships, the discomfort of stepping out of your comfort zone, or the fear of failure, these are all necessary parts of growth. "You can't dance in the rain if you're afraid to get wet." And sometimes, getting wet is the only way to experience the joy of the dance.

In the end, life is full of copperheads, hidden dangers that can strike without warning. But we can't let those dangers keep us from walking the path. As we navigate the challenges, the pain, and the discomfort, we grow stronger, more resilient, and more fulfilled. The copperheads may be there, but so is the beauty, the joy, and the fulfillment that come from living fully. "Don't let fear rob you of the joy of the journey." There's too much to live for.

A Place to Belong

Resilience is about more than just enduring hardship; it's also about having a place to return to, a foundation that reminds you who you are and where you come from. For me, that place was my grandparents' family farm, a haven of warmth, joy, and connection. It was a place where the hard work of everyday life was balanced with the simple pleasures that come from being surrounded by nature and the people you love.

The farm was a world of its own for my brother, Tony, and me. We would spend hours playing in the creek, catching crawdads and grasshoppers in the high grass, or digging through the rocks to find fossils. The creek felt like an endless source of adventure, its cool waters running over our feet as we searched for hidden treasures. Sometimes, we'd chase the cattle around the fields or lie in the tall grass, staring up at the sky. And in the evenings, we would fill jars with lightning bugs, their soft glow lighting up our rooms as we drifted off to sleep, lulled by the sounds of the farm at night.

But it wasn't just the freedom of the outdoors that made the farm special. It was also the connection we felt to our family, especially our grandparents. I can still picture us sitting on the porch, Tony and I with a pile of corn in front of us, shucking away, while my grandmother prepared beans for canning. As we worked, my grandparents would tell stories of their youth, tales of survival, love, and humor, woven with the same resilience that guided their lives. Those stories were like a thread tying us to the past, reminding us of the values they lived by and the lessons they had learned.

And then there were the gifts as mentioned earlier. My grandpa [xxii]Cortez, with his calloused hands and quiet demeanor, was always creating something from the land around him. He would make us popguns from the branches of elder trees, carefully carving and crafting each one with precision. Or he'd fashion slingshots from a sturdy branch, using an old inner tube and the tongue from one of his worn-out work boots. These weren't just toys, they were pieces of the farm itself, a reminder of the resourcefulness and creativity that came from working the land. I will have that slingshot with the tongue of my grandpa's boot on the wall of my office.

The farm wasn't just a place; it was an anchor. It grounded us, gave us a sense of belonging, and taught us the importance of family. There was something about being there, about feeling the earth beneath our feet and the love of our grandparents, that gave us strength. It was a place where hard work was balanced by moments of joy, where the simple things in life, catching crawdads in the creek, or listening to stories on the porch, reminded us that life's greatest gifts often come from the things that don't cost a dime.

As a therapist, I often think about the importance of having a "base," a place or a community that provides a sense of security and belonging. For many of my clients, finding that base can be the key to resilience. Whether it's a physical place like my grandparents' farm or a strong network of relationships, we all need a foundation that helps us navigate life's storms. It's in those moments when the world feels overwhelming that returning to our roots, whether literal or metaphorical, can remind us of who we are and what we are capable of overcoming.

My grandparents' farm gave me that foundation. It taught me that resilience isn't just about facing hardships; it's about having a place to come back to, a place that reminds you that no matter what happens, you are part of something bigger, something that will always be there to support you. Whether we were catching lightning bugs or shucking corn, those simple acts connected me to the land, to my family, and to a tradition of resilience that has shaped me into who I am today.

In therapy, I often encourage clients to think about their own "base", that place or memory that grounds them. For some, it's a childhood home; for others, it's a person or a moment in time that reminds them of their strength. For me, it will always be that farm, with its creek, its cattle, and the stories of my grandparents echoing through the years, offering me the comfort and wisdom that only comes from knowing you have a place to belong.

The slingshot my grandpa made for me over 55 years ago

Grounding at the Family Farm: A Guided Imagery for Counselors and Clients

This chapter will be a little different. In a previous chapter, I discussed how anxiety can be overwhelming and how it's essential to get grounded before we can move forward toward growth. In therapy, one way we help clients regain that sense of calm and control is through guided imagery. For my counseling students, this chapter will introduce how to use guided imagery effectively with clients. And for clients reading this, the following script is a tool for grounding yourself, releasing tension, and finding peace in the midst of stress.

Guided imagery can be incredibly beneficial (Stefanelli, 2025). It helps clients detach from immediate stress and create a calming space within their mind, a place they can return to whenever life's challenges seem overwhelming. By focusing on all the senses, sight, sound, touch, smell, and taste, it engages the brain in a way that allows both the body and mind to relax. Whether dealing with anxiety, trauma, or just everyday stress, guided imagery provides an accessible, non-invasive way to bring relief.

In this chapter, we will focus on one particular guided imagery exercise. The purpose of this exercise is to help individuals ground themselves in a peaceful, familiar scene. For those of us from Appalachia, places like the family farm hold a special significance. These places offer not just comfort but a connection to our roots, our ancestors, and the land. This script, based on those experiences, is designed to guide you back to that space of peace.

Guided imagery works by leading clients through a vivid mental journey, allowing them to experience a safe and calming environment. It taps into the body's relaxation response, reducing anxiety, lowering heart rate, and creating a feeling of peace. This can be especially helpful for clients who are struggling to focus due to overwhelming emotions. Grounding, the practice of bringing one's attention back to the present moment, helps to interrupt cycles of anxiety or panic. When combined with guided imagery, grounding becomes even more powerful.

For students learning to use this technique, remember that it's not just about reading a script. It's about guiding someone through a personal experience that taps into their sensory memories and emotional connections. Encourage clients to make the imagery their own, adding details that are meaningful to them.

For clients using this tool, I encourage you to set aside time for this exercise. Use it when you feel stressed, anxious, or disconnected, and allow yourself to be fully present in the experience. Let it be a tool to return to whenever you need to ground yourself.

Now, let's walk through the guided imagery script. Feel free to close your eyes and allow the scene to unfold in your mind.

Guided Imagery: A Journey to the Family Farm

Introduction:
Find a comfortable place where you won't be disturbed. Close your eyes and take a deep breath in, letting the air fill your lungs. As you exhale, feel the tension released from your body. Inhale again, drawing in a sense of peace, and as you exhale, let go of any lingering stress or worry. On the next breath, clear your mind, allowing yourself to fully relax. With each breath, sink deeper into calmness and let the following scene unfold.

The Journey:
Imagine yourself walking down the familiar dirt road leading to your grandparents' farm in rural Kentucky. The path is soft beneath your feet, with patches of fossil-filled creek bed gravel crunching lightly as you step. The air is thick with the scent of wild honeysuckle and fresh earth, and the soft breeze carries the gentle mooing of cows from the nearby pasture.

As you approach the farmhouse, you hear the steady rhythm of cows chewing on the grass, their tails swishing lazily to shoo away the flies. You pause at the gate, resting your hand on the cool metal, and breathe in the comforting smell of hay and farm life. Ahead of you, the barn stands tall, its red paint weathered by years of sun and rain, but still as sturdy as ever. You hear the faint clucking of chickens and the occasional thud of hooves inside the barn, where cows stand in the shade peacefully munching on oats and grain.

You decide to explore the barn first. As you step inside, the smell of sweet hay and feed corn fills your nose, and the sound of your feet crunching against loose straw echoes softly. You climb up into the loft, where the hay bales are stacked high, soft and golden. You remember afternoons spent here, leaping from the bales into the soft pile below, your laughter mixing with the gentle lowing of the cows and the rustling of the barn swallows flitting overhead. You run your fingers through the soft, dry hay, feeling its warmth against your skin.

After a while, you head down to the creek. The sun is warm on your face as you walk toward the sound of trickling water. The creek is just as you remember it, the water crystal clear and cool as it flows over smooth stones. You kneel at the edge, feeling the refreshing coolness against your skin as you dip your hands into the stream. You watch minnows dart between the rocks, and with a quick motion, you catch a crawdad, its small claws waving in the air. You laugh, feeling the thrill of the catch before gently letting it go back into the water.

As you move along the creek bed, you find an old, weathered arrowhead lying beside a stone, a treasure that tells a story of a time long past. You run your fingers over its ridges, feeling the smoothness where water and time have worn it down. It's a small but special find, something you tuck into your pocket as a memory of the day.

The sun is beginning to lower in the sky, casting a golden glow over the pasture as you walk with your grandpa through the fields. He moves slowly but surely, his boots sinking slightly into the soft earth. He points out the various trees and plants around you, naming each one with practiced ease. "That's a red oak," he says, tapping a trunk with his walking stick. "And over there, that's goldenrod, good for all sorts of remedies." His voice is steady, calming, and filled with the wisdom of the land. You listen, taking in the knowledge passed down through generations, the smell of rich soil and growing things filling the air.

The woods are cool and quiet as you walk through them together, the crunch of leaves underfoot the only sound. The earthy smell of damp moss and bark surrounds you, and the gentle rustling of the trees above is like nature's whisper. Your grandpa stops to point out a rabbit darting through the underbrush, its soft brown fur blending into the shadows. You feel a deep connection to this place and to him, as if time slows down here and all the worries of the world fade away.

Returning to the Present:
After spending some more time in this peaceful scene, allow yourself to savor the warmth, the sounds, and the scents of the farm. Feel the gentle connection to the land, to family, and to nature. Slowly begin to return to the present moment. Bring with you the peace and calm of the farm, carrying it within you. Take a deep breath in, and as you exhale, feel yourself grounded and refreshed. Wiggle your fingers and toes, gently bringing awareness back to your body. When you're ready, open your eyes, feeling centered, calm, and free from stress, knowing that you can return to this place of peace whenever you need.

Final Thoughts
Guided imagery offers a way to anchor yourself in the present and find peace, no matter the stress or anxiety you face. For counselors, this script can be adapted to fit a client's personal experiences, bringing them closer to a place of comfort and grounding. For clients, it's a tool to use whenever life feels overwhelming, your own personal retreat to the family farm, or wherever your mind finds peace.

Remember, life is filled with challenges and anxieties, but grounding yourself through these techniques allows you to release tension, refocus, and move forward with clarity. "You can't control the wind, but you can adjust your sails." In the same way, guided imagery helps you navigate the emotional storms, find your center, and continue your journey with a little more peace.

Plowing Around the Stump

There's an old saying on the farm that goes, "Life is simpler when you plow around the stump." Anyone who has ever worked the land knows the truth in that phrase. Some obstacles, like a stubborn old tree stump, are just easier to leave alone. Digging it out would take time, effort, and energy that could be better spent elsewhere. So, you adjust. You plow around it, accepting that the stump is part of the landscape, something you'll have to live with. It's the same with past trauma.

Sometimes, in life, it's easier to leave a wound alone, to adjust your path and move forward without digging too deeply into what caused it. For many, the pain of revisiting past trauma can feel overwhelming, like pulling at roots that go deeper and spread farther than you ever imagined. In those moments, plowing around the stump can seem like the best way to keep moving. And sometimes, it is. There are moments when accepting the existence of trauma and learning to live around it is healthier than reopening old wounds.

But just like on the farm, sometimes the stump becomes a bigger problem the longer you avoid it. Maybe its roots are growing and spreading underground, slowly choking off other parts of the land. Or maybe, over time, the stump itself starts to rot and affect the soil around it. In those cases, the hard work of uprooting the stump becomes necessary, even though it's difficult and time-consuming. It's the same with trauma: sometimes, we have to confront it head-on, dig deep into its roots, and face the painful process of healing, even if it takes longer than we expect.

But here's the thing: even after a stump is removed, the roots often remain. They run deep beneath the surface, out of sight but not entirely gone. And every once in a while, a shoot might spring up in the middle of a field where you thought you'd cleared everything. Trauma can be the same. You might do the hard work of healing, uprooting the pain, and finding ways to move forward, but the roots of trauma can remain buried deep within you. Just when you think you've moved past it, a memory or an experience can cause an old wound to sprout again, reminding you that while the stump may be gone, the roots are still there.

This isn't to say that the work of healing is in vain; far from it. Removing the stump and addressing trauma is still important work. It clears the way for growth and allows you to cultivate new things in your life. But it's also important to acknowledge that trauma isn't something we can always fully erase. Its roots are woven into our past, and sometimes, those roots will sprout in ways we didn't expect. The key isn't in pretending those roots don't exist; it's in learning how to manage them when they appear.

Sometimes, it's about learning when to plow around the stump and when to dig it out. Both are valid, and both have their own kind of strength. Knowing which path to take at different times in life is part of the journey of resilience. It's about accepting that trauma is a part of your landscape, but it doesn't have to define you. And when those roots start to sprout again, you'll be better equipped to handle them, knowing that the work of healing is ongoing, not something that's ever truly finished.

There are moments when accepting the existence of trauma and learning to live around it is healthier than reopening old wounds.

In therapy, this is a lesson I often share with my clients. There are times when confronting trauma is necessary, and there are times when it's okay to let it be and focus on the present. The wisdom lies in knowing the difference and in understanding that healing isn't about erasing the past but learning to live with it in a way that allows for growth and peace.

As [xxiii]Sarah's therapist, I remember the day she walked into my office, shoulders hunched and eyes downcast, looking like she carried the weight of the world. Sarah had grown up in the foothills of the Cumberlands, the middle child in a family of five. Her father worked in the coal mines, and her mother, who struggled with her own mental health, rarely offered her the comfort or guidance a young girl needed. Sarah grew up feeling like an outsider in her own home, her father often yelling, her mother emotionally absent, and the small mountain town where everyone knew each other's business, offering little reprieve.

Sarah had buried her childhood trauma for years, focusing instead on building a life far away from her family. She moved to a larger southern town, married, and had two children, but despite the distance, the wounds from her upbringing still festered. In our sessions, Sarah would speak about her constant anxiety and how she felt disconnected from her husband, but she refused to mention her past at first. She would often talk about the resilience people in her hometown were supposed to have, how pride was tied to surviving hard times, and how it was better not to talk about things that hurt.

But as time went on, Sarah opened up about the physical and emotional abuse she experienced from her father, the way he would come home from the mines after a long shift, angry and unpredictable. Her mother would retreat into silence, and Sarah, the most sensitive of the siblings, bore the brunt of her father's moods. It was clear that the trauma had seeped into every aspect of her adult life, affecting her relationships and her sense of self-worth.

Through therapy, we began to unravel her trauma bit by bit. Each time Sarah spoke about a painful memory, the time her father struck her for being too slow to bring him dinner, or the long, lonely nights when her mother sat in silence at the kitchen table, she learned to reframe those memories. She began to see that the shame she carried wasn't hers to bear.

As Sarah processed her trauma, she began to experience a transformation. She told me about a trip she took back to her hometown to visit her mother's grave, feeling a sense of closure rather than dread. She reconnected with her brother, with whom she had been distant for years, realizing he had also carried a burden of pain. Sarah started communicating more openly with her husband, and their relationship grew stronger. The anxiety that had been a constant in her life started to subside. Confronting her past allowed Sarah to reclaim her present, and though the road was long, she became a living testament to the power of healing, even in the heart of Appalachia.

[xxiv]James was a tall, quiet man from a small town in south-central Kentucky, the kind of place where everyone knew you and your worth was tied to your service to your family and community. After returning home from two tours in Afghanistan, James found that the hills he had once found peace in now felt claustrophobic, and the small-town life he had yearned for seemed too quiet. He couldn't escape the noise in his head.

In our early sessions, James rarely spoke about his time in the military. Instead, he talked about how he struggled to be around people, even his wife and kids. He often told me about the days he would sit in the barn for hours, tending to his hunting gear, but not going out to hunt. His family didn't talk about feelings much. In his world, you dealt with hard times by keeping your head down and pushing forward. His father, a logger, had that same attitude, so James never felt it was acceptable to show weakness.

But the nightmares and flashbacks were becoming unbearable. One session, after sitting in silence for several minutes, James finally spoke about the night that haunted him, a convoy ambush that left several of his friends dead. He had never processed it, never spoken about it to anyone, not even to his wife, who had noticed him withdrawing more and more.

In our work together, we used prolonged exposure therapy, revisiting those memories again and again until the emotional sting started to lessen. James was hesitant at first, he feared that talking about the trauma would make things worse. But, over time, he began to see the benefits. His PTSD symptoms started to ease. We also worked on grounding techniques, and James found solace in returning to the activities he had always loved, like fishing in the creek that ran behind his grandfather's old cabin.

James became more open about his struggles, and in a turning point, he joined a therapy group with other veterans from nearby towns. He found that, like him, they had been carrying their burdens alone, believing it was the only way. Sharing his story helped him begin to rebuild his relationship with his family, and for the first time in years, he began to imagine a future free from the ghosts of his past.

Though he still lived in the same quiet town, the silence no longer felt like a trap; it was peace.

When [xxv]Emily came to my office, she was seeking support for anxiety related to her high-stress job as a nurse in a rural Tennessee hospital. Emily grew up in a small southern community where neighbors helped each other but also where trauma was often swept under the rug. She had a difficult childhood, raised by a single mother who worked two jobs to make ends meet and a father who had left when she was just a toddler. She mentioned her tough upbringing in passing but never wanted to dwell on it. "I got through it," she'd say. "Ain't no use digging up old bones."

Emily was fiercely independent, a trait she had learned from her mother, who would always say, "Ain't nobody gonna fix your life but you." This mindset made her wary of revisiting the pain of her childhood. She admitted that she sometimes felt the impact of her past, like when she had trouble opening up in her relationships, but overall, she felt she had moved on. We talked about whether exploring her trauma might help, but Emily was adamant, her focus was on managing her current stress, not revisiting the past.

Instead, we worked on strategies to manage her anxiety in the here and now. Emily found mindfulness techniques helpful, particularly grounding exercises that she could use during long shifts at the hospital. She also found solace in her gardening, a hobby she had inherited from her grandmother. Emily found that being present with her plants helped her stay grounded in the present moment.

Over time, Emily became more at peace with her decision to leave the past in the past. She felt that acknowledging her resilience, rather than reopening old wounds, allowed her to maintain her sense of control and strength. She continued to build a fulfilling life, rooted in the present and focused on the future, knowing that her past shaped her but did not define her.

Another client, [xxvi]Tom, came to therapy not for the trauma of his childhood but for the stress he was feeling as a local business owner in his small rural town. His father, a stoic and often cruel man, had raised him to believe that the only way to survive was through hard work and silence. Tom had grown up in a farming family, and his father was well-known for his temper and heavy hand. But Tom had long since left the family farm, starting his own contracting business and building a life that, on the surface, looked nothing like his father's.

As we began therapy, I noticed that Tom rarely spoke of his childhood, but when he did, it was clear that the memories were painful. However, Tom was firm in his decision not to dig too deep into that part of his life. "It's buried for a reason," he told me once when I gently asked if he wanted to explore how his relationship with his father might still be affecting him. "What's done is done."

Rather than press the issue, we focused on helping Tom manage his work-related stress and his feelings of burnout. We developed practical strategies for balancing his work and personal life, and Tom found comfort in leaning on the support of his wife and children. His life was busy, filled with community events, helping neighbors, and keeping his business afloat, but he found joy in the stability he had created.

Tom's choice not to revisit his trauma was not a form of avoidance, it was a conscious decision that worked for him. He felt that the pain from his past no longer served a purpose in his life and that by focusing on the present, he could continue to build the future he wanted. In our sessions, we often spoke about the satisfaction he found in raising his own children in a loving home so different from the one he had known. His decision to move forward without looking back allowed him to be at peace, knowing that he had broken the cycle without needing to relive it.

Much like on the farm, life is simpler when you learn how to navigate the obstacles, whether by plowing around them or putting in the work to clear them out. Either way, it's about moving forward with resilience and acceptance, knowing that sometimes the roots will remain, but they don't have to stop you from living a full and meaningful life.

In today's therapy world, trauma-informed care has become the default lens through which all struggles are viewed. We are in the midst of a therapeutic fad, where trauma is often seen as the root cause of all distress, and healing is framed as an endless excavation of the past. Trauma-informed care, at its best, helps clients understand their experiences and reclaim their narratives. But at its worst, it can encourage a culture of fragility, where people feel defined by their wounds rather than their resilience.

I believe in balance. Not every hardship requires deep psychological excavation, just as not every tree stump needs to be dug out. There are times when confronting trauma is necessary, and there are times when plowing around it is the healthier, more productive choice. True healing isn't about endlessly processing pain, it's about equipping people to live in the present, build their future, and recognize their own strength. Trauma may shape us, but it doesn't have to define us. The goal of therapy shouldn't just be to help people understand their suffering; it should be to help them move forward.

Living the Sermon

There's a saying that goes, "The best sermons are lived, not preached." It means that actions speak louder than words, that integrity is found not in what we say, but in how we live. In my family, there's no better example of this than my grandfather, [xxvii]Cortez Wesley. He was a man who never felt the need to tell others how to live or what to believe, but he lived his life with such quiet conviction that his actions spoke volumes.

My grandfather owned a [8]tobacco base, as did many people in his community. Tobacco was a way of life for many farmers, a reliable cash crop that provided for families when times were tough. But despite the economic benefits, my grandfather made the personal decision never to grow or use tobacco. He believed that if he made money from it, he would go against his own conscience, especially after seeing firsthand the harm tobacco had caused his own family.

But here's the thing: Gramps never preached to others about his beliefs. He didn't tell his neighbors or friends that they shouldn't grow tobacco or use it. He didn't need to. Gramps believed in living by example. He simply made his choice, quietly and resolutely, and stuck to it. His actions weren't driven by the desire for recognition or moral superiority; they came from a deep, personal conviction.

Even though Gramps never said a word about tobacco to others, everyone in the community knew of his decision. They respected him for it. People would often speak of him as a godly man, someone whose character was above reproach. He was known for his integrity, his hard work, and his commitment to doing what he believed was right, even when it wasn't the easiest path to follow. His life, in many ways, was a sermon in itself, a testament to the power of living out your values, rather than simply speaking about them.

Gramps' choice not to grow tobacco wasn't just about avoiding a crop; it was about standing by his beliefs, even in the face of economic hardship. He could have made money from tobacco, as so many others did. But for him, it wasn't worth the cost to his conscience. And because of that, people saw him not as someone who judged others for their choices, but as someone who stood firm in

---

[8] For much of Kentucky's history, tobacco served as the primary cash crop, significantly influencing the state's economy and the livelihoods of its farming families. In the 1990s, for example, tobacco accounted for approximately 25% of Kentucky's agricultural cash receipts. This high per-acre value meant that many farmers relied heavily on tobacco cultivation for their income. Consequently, choosing not to grow tobacco could have had substantial financial repercussions for these families.

his own. They saw his character in action, and that left a far deeper impression than any sermon ever could.

This lesson that the best sermons are lived, not preached, has stayed with me throughout my life. It reminds me that true integrity comes from consistency, from living in a way that aligns with your values, even when no one is watching. My grandfather didn't need to tell people what he believed or why he made the choices he did. His life was his testimony, and it spoke more powerfully than any words ever could.

As I think about this lesson in the context of resilience and therapy, I realize that it's not about perfection. It's about living authentically, even when it's hard. It's about making decisions that are true to who you are and letting your actions be a reflection of your deepest values. For my grandfather, that meant choosing not to grow tobacco. For others, it might mean something entirely different. But the core of the lesson is the same: live your truth and let your life be the example.

In therapy, I often talk to clients about the importance of living in alignment with their values. It's not enough to say you want to be a better person, to overcome trauma, or to grow in resilience. You have to live it, step by step, choice by choice. And just like my grandfather, sometimes the most powerful changes come not from what we say, but from what we do.

Gramps didn't need to speak a word about his beliefs for people to understand the kind of man he was. His life was his sermon, and through it, he taught me and everyone who knew him that integrity isn't something you wear like a badge. It's something you live, every day, in the quiet moments when no one is watching and in the hard decisions that define who you are.

The Patience of Persistence

In Kentucky, persistence isn't just a virtue; it's a way of life. My grandfather, [xxviii]Cortez Wesley, whom my kids fondly called Gramps, embodied this kind of patience and persistence. He was a man who believed in hard work, the quiet, steady kind that builds something over time. He and my grandmother spent countless hours in their garden, planting, weeding, maintaining, and eventually harvesting the fruits of their labor. That garden was their pride and joy, a source of both food and peace, and they treated it with great care.

But like anything worth having, that garden didn't come without its challenges. One of the biggest came in the form of a persistent groundhog. No matter how much effort Gramps and Grandma put into their garden, this groundhog had a knack for sneaking in and munching on the vegetables they had worked so hard to grow. For Gramps, who had a deep respect for all living things, the decision to take action against the groundhog wasn't an easy one. He didn't like to kill animals, but this particular critter was eating his hard-earned crops, and there was no negotiating with it.

So, after careful thought, Gramps decided it was time for the groundhog to go. But, as with most things in his life, he approached the task with the kind of patience and determination that defined him. Instead of hastily trying to catch or kill the groundhog, Gramps built a blind made of hay bales and stationed himself behind it. There, he would wait. And wait. And wait.

For hours, sometimes whole afternoons, he sat quietly behind the hay bales, scanning the garden and the area near the groundhog's burrow. He had the kind of patience most people could only dream of, an unhurried belief that if he just waited long enough, the moment would come. And finally, after what seemed like endless hours of watching, the groundhog emerged from its hole, hungry and ready to feast on the garden once more.

But Gramps was prepared. With steady hands and a calm focus, he took the shot, ending the groundhog's garden-raiding days. It wasn't something he did lightly, but in his mind, it was necessary to protect what he and Grandma had worked so hard to build.

I often think about that story when I consider what it means to be persistent. Gramps didn't rush, didn't let frustration get the better of him. Instead, he embraced the process, knowing that patience, when combined with purpose, is one of the most powerful tools a person can have. Whether it was protecting his garden or any other challenge in life, he believed in the importance of waiting for the right moment and being ready when it came.

As a therapist, I've come to see the value in this kind of persistence. Often, we want quick solutions and immediate change, but true growth, whether it's in a garden or in ourselves, takes time. It requires patience, and sometimes, it requires sitting in the quiet, uncomfortable space of waiting, knowing that, eventually, the moment for action will come. Gramps taught me that some things, like a well-tended garden or a hard-earned personal breakthrough, are worth the time and effort they take. You just have to be willing to stay the course and be prepared for the moment when the opportunity finally appears.

His story is a reminder that persistence isn't just about action; it's about knowing when to act and when to wait and trusting that with patience, the outcome will be worth the effort.

Education and Connection

Being born in Kentucky, education was a complicated pursuit. It wasn't that my family didn't value learning, but circumstances often demanded that survival come first. For generations, working the land and supporting the family were the highest priorities. My grandparents didn't go beyond the 6th grade, not because they lacked intelligence or ambition, but because poverty and the need to tend the farm always came before schooling. Despite these limitations, the importance of learning was not lost on them. My grandfather, [xxix]Cortez, was a perfect example of this. He was self-taught, a man who loved to read and absorb new knowledge. He may not have had a formal education, but his curiosity about the world never waned.

In this context, I was the first in my family to take education beyond the basics. I was the first to graduate from college, the first to earn a master's degree, and eventually, the first to obtain a doctorate. My mother only went as far as the 9th grade, and my father was the first in his lineage to get a high school diploma. Education, for me, was a path not just toward personal growth but toward honoring the dreams my family had held but hadn't been able to pursue fully. The need to educate myself wasn't just about achieving something for my own sake; it was about expanding the opportunities for my family and showing what could be possible.

But as I climbed the educational ladder, I was always mindful of the values I had been taught growing up. In Appalachia, there are phrases that carry deep meaning, passed down like family heirlooms: "Don't put on airs," "Don't forget your roots," and "Don't get above your raisin." These words have always stayed with me, becoming even more important as I pursued higher education.

In Appalachia, the phrase "don't put on airs" reminds you to stay humble, no matter how far you go in life. It's about authenticity, being true to who you are, and not trying to act like you're better than anyone else just because you've achieved something. As I earned my degrees, I carried this phrase with me, making sure that I didn't lose sight of where I came from or fall into the trap of believing that education made me inherently better than anyone else.

The truth is, the people who raised me, the ones who didn't have the formal education I was able to pursue, were some of the wisest and most capable individuals I've ever known. They taught me about hard work, integrity, and the value of relationships. Education might have given me new tools and perspectives, but it didn't make me superior to anyone. My grandfather Cortez, with his self-taught knowledge, was a perfect example of someone who didn't need formal education to be wise and thoughtful. His curiosity and love for learning were just as valid as the degrees I later earned. I've always tried to live by this lesson:

knowledge is valuable, but it doesn't entitle you to act as though you're better than anyone else.

"Don't Forget Your Roots" This phrase is a guiding principle in Appalachian culture, a reminder to always stay connected to where you come from. For me, earning an education wasn't about leaving my roots behind, it was about expanding on the foundation they provided. My family's sacrifices and their deep commitment to doing whatever was necessary to survive shaped who I am. Even as I learned new things, I never wanted to lose the sense of identity and belonging that came from my upbringing in the hills of Appalachia.

I've always believed that education is a tool for growth, but it should never erase the values and experiences that formed you. The hard work, resilience, and sense of community I learned growing up were the things that sustained me through the long hours of study and the challenges that came with pursuing higher education. It's easy, sometimes, to get caught up in the academic world and forget where you started, but I've always made a conscious effort to stay grounded, to remember that my roots are the reason I was able to grow in the first place.

"Don't Get Above Your Raisin'" This phrase, closely related to the other two, is a call to remain humble and grateful, no matter what success you achieve. "Don't get above your raisin'" means that no matter how far you go in life, you shouldn't forget the values instilled in you by your family and community. It's a reminder that success doesn't mean forgetting the people who helped you get there or the lessons they taught you along the way.

As I earned my degrees and stepped into the professional world, I kept this phrase in mind. My education opened doors for me, but I never wanted it to distance me from the people and the culture that raised me. It was my parents' hard work and sacrifices and my grandparents' resilience that made my education possible. They might not have had formal schooling, but they taught me about grit, kindness, and perseverance, qualities that no degree could ever replace.

In many ways, my educational journey is an extension of the values they passed down to me. My degrees were not just for me, they were for them, too, a testament to the dreams they had, even if they didn't always have the opportunity to achieve them. But I've always known that no matter how many letters come after my name, I am still the person they raised: someone who values humility, hard work, and staying true to their roots.

As I've reflected on my own education and the values I was raised with, I've come to understand that while parents can guide and inspire their children, they are not the sole architects of their children's futures. There is an element of nature at play, innate qualities and characteristics that shape who we become. My family nurtured a love for learning in me, even without formal education, but there was also something inside me that drove me to pursue my studies further. As parents, we can shepherd our children, give them the tools to succeed and teach them the values that matter. But there are forces beyond our control, personality, temperament, and the external influences that shape a child's path.

In the end, my journey toward education has been about honoring the values I was raised with while also recognizing the importance of following my own path. I am deeply grateful for the sacrifices my family made and the lessons they taught me, and I know that my education doesn't separate me from them; it brings me closer. Every degree I've earned has been a way of building on the foundation they laid, a way of expanding the dreams they carried in their hearts but couldn't always pursue.

Those values of humility, integrity, and respect that shaped my educational journey are the same values I've found essential in my work as a counselor. Especially when working with clients from Appalachia, I've come to realize that you cannot approach therapy with an air of superiority or authority. People in these communities are often skeptical of therapy and formal education. They've been taken advantage of by systems they don't trust, and they don't give respect easily, you have to earn it.

Establishing connection with Appalachian clients requires time, patience, and a deep respect for their culture.

This means coming into the therapeutic relationship with the humility to meet clients where they are, to understand their world, and to acknowledge that they are the experts in their own lives. Much like the values I grew up with, it's not about telling people what to do; it's about listening, guiding, and respecting their autonomy. Trust, in this context, is something that's built over time through genuine care and understanding rather than being demanded upfront.

The same is true in the classroom. When working with students, especially those from Appalachian backgrounds, I've learned that they don't need someone lecturing them from an academic pedestal. They need someone who understands the value of hard work, community, and lived experience. They need to see that education doesn't mean forgetting who you are or where you come from, it's about expanding what's possible while staying grounded in the values that shaped you.

In my experience as a counselor, this is a valuable lesson in working with the people of Appalachia. Respect and humility are at the core of building any therapeutic relationship. People from these mountain communities may be slow to trust outsiders, especially if they sense someone is looking down on them. Establishing connection with Appalachian clients requires time, patience, and a deep respect for their culture. Just as the land in these hills requires care to yield crops, so do the people require care to yield trust. You can't rush it, and you can't fake it.

In Appalachia, connection often comes in subtle or indirect forms, shared work, storytelling, and small acts of kindness. It's the offer to help mend a fence, the invitation to a family meal, or the gesture of bringing over fresh vegetables from the garden. These actions are bids for connection, a cultural way of saying, "I'm here, and I care about you." But outsiders, especially those unfamiliar with Appalachian communication styles, can easily miss these cues.

Take the example of a neighbor offering to help you with something around the house. For many Appalachian people, this isn't just about lending a hand; it's an invitation to form a relationship. Rejecting that help might be seen as a rejection of their bid for connection, which could close off further opportunities for trust. As therapists, we need to be aware of these cultural differences. When we miss these subtle bids or dismiss them as unimportant, we miss crucial opportunities to build rapport and trust.

In therapy, it's often not the direct questions that get the most meaningful answers. I've found that listening closely to the stories clients tell, the way they speak about their family, and the small gestures they make are key to understanding their world. We must always be looking for bids for connection, whether they come in the form of a shared story, a self-deprecating joke, or an offer of help.

Appalachians value humility. They are often leery of people who come in with grand ideas or try to prove their expertise right away. To build a therapeutic relationship in Appalachia, it's essential not to "put on airs." When I started my counseling practice, I knew my credentials alone wouldn't earn me respect. I had to earn it through my actions by being authentic, listening deeply, and showing up consistently. We need to remain grounded and humble, no matter how far we've gone in life. As therapists, especially those working with Appalachian clients, we need to remember this. We're not there to "fix" people or impose our ideas on them. We're there to walk alongside them, help them untangle their struggles, and guide them toward their own solutions. Trust is earned through humility and a deep understanding of the people and their values.

In Appalachia, people will test you. They may offer up a story that seems insignificant or ask for help with something small just to see how you respond. How you react to these bids for connection determines whether they'll trust you with more important parts of their lives. It's like planting a seed; you don't see the full harvest right away, but over time, with care and attention, trust begins to grow.

Storytelling is an essential part of connecting with people here. People share stories to make sense of their lives, pass down lessons, and build relationships. As therapists, we can engage with clients through their stories, listening closely, not just for the content, but for what the story represents. In many ways, it's an unspoken bid for connection, an invitation into their inner world.

For example, I remember sitting with a client who shared stories of her family's struggles through the coal mining industry. It wasn't just a history lesson, it was a way for her to convey the pride and resilience that ran through her veins, something she wanted me to understand about her without having to say it outright. By validating her story and reflecting on the values embedded in it, I was able to connect with her in a way that went far beyond surface-level conversation.

As therapists working with the Appalachian community, it's important to let clients tell their stories. Instead of interrupting with solutions or interpretations, we need to listen closely and reflect back what we hear. This not only honors their bid for connection but also helps us understand their values and worldview.

Appalachians are deeply connected to their land, their family, and their history. When someone tells you about their ancestors or talks about their family farm, it's not just idle chatter; it's a way of situating themselves in the world. To dismiss these topics as unimportant is to misunderstand the very fabric of their identity.

For counselors, it's important to recognize the power of place in these conversations. Appalachia is not just a geographical location; it's a cultural identity, a way of life that is deeply ingrained in its people. When we work with clients from this region, we need to respect that identity and understand that it shapes how they see the world.

In therapy, we might ask questions like, "What does home mean to you?" or "How does your family history influence who you are today?" These questions invite clients to reflect on their identity and provide an opportunity for them to make meaningful connections between their past and present.

One of the most valuable aspects of working with Appalachian clients is tapping into their resilience. While many communities in Appalachia have faced hardships, whether through economic downturns, health issues, or generational trauma, the people here are incredibly strong and resourceful. They have learned to rely on themselves, their families, and their communities to survive and thrive.

However, it's important to remember that while Appalachian people are resilient, they do not want to be viewed as powerless or pitiable. They take great pride in their strength, and they want that to be acknowledged in any relationship, especially a therapeutic one.

For clients, this means that therapy should focus on empowerment. It's about recognizing the inner strength they've carried through difficult times and helping them harness that strength to move forward. Therapy should not be about rescuing them but about supporting them in rediscovering their power.

Appalachian people have a deep-rooted sense of identity, community, and family. By understanding these cultural nuances and accepting their bids for connection, we can foster meaningful therapeutic relationships that not only respect their heritage but also support their growth and healing.

One of the best educators I've known was a colleague and good friend, an accomplished Black man who taught counseling courses in Eastern Kentucky. He had a wealth of experience, not only in the field of counseling but also in navigating difficult conversations about race, culture, and identity. His presence in the classroom was striking, not just because of his knowledge but because of his passion for helping students see the world through a broader lens.

One semester, while teaching a multicultural counseling course, he found himself at a pivotal moment, one of those unscripted opportunities where real education happens, where the lesson isn't in the syllabus but in the space between students' words. A student in class, a young woman from a small Appalachian town, confidently stated, "I don't see race." Others in the class nodded in agreement. From their perspective, this wasn't a political statement or an attempt to deny racial differences. It was, in their minds, a declaration of shared humanity, a way of saying, "I judge people by their character, not by the color of their skin."

Rather than recognizing this statement as a bid for connection, a way for these students to express their own understanding of race and culture, my colleague immediately pushed back. "Of course, you see race," he said, his voice firm. "We all do. It's impossible not to." He proceeded to lecture on the importance of acknowledging racial differences, systemic issues, and the impact of privilege. While everything he said was valid and deeply informed, his approach unintentionally shut down the conversation rather than opening it up.

From the students' perspective, their professor had dismissed their lived experience outright. What they heard was not an invitation to learn but a challenge, one that put them on the defensive. Instead of engaging in dialogue, they dug in their heels, feeling as though they were being told their own understanding of the world was not just incomplete but outright wrong. A wall went up. The classroom, which had been a place of exploration and exchange, suddenly became a battlefield of opposing perspectives.

After that day, my colleague noticed a shift. The same students who were once eager to participate became hesitant and guarded. They listened but didn't engage in discussion. They weren't openly disrespectful, but they had emotionally checked out. He had lost them, not because his message was wrong, but because he hadn't earned their trust first. Instead of meeting them where they were, he imposed an academic truth on them before they were ready to receive it.

This story is a powerful example of how education, especially in counseling, requires humility, patience, and connection. In Appalachia, people are deeply tied to their values and experiences. They don't respond well to being told what they "should" believe, but they do respond to relationships built on trust. If my colleague had first acknowledged their bid for connection, validating that their desire to see people beyond race came from a well-intentioned place, he might have been able to guide them toward a deeper understanding. Instead of telling them they were wrong, he could have asked, "Tell me more about what you mean when you say you don't see race." He could have helped them explore the complexities of their perspective rather than shutting it down.

The lesson here isn't just about race; it's about how we approach difficult conversations in education and therapy. If we come in swinging, eager to correct before we connect, we lose the opportunity to teach. But if we listen first, acknowledge where people are coming from, and build trust, we have the chance to guide them toward deeper understanding. My colleague, an excellent educator, learned a hard lesson that day: sometimes, the best way to teach isn't to confront but to connect first and guide second.

In both counseling and education, the lessons of "not putting on airs," "not forgetting your roots," and "not getting above your raisin'" remain vital. Whether I'm working with a client facing challenges or teaching a student who is unsure about the value of education, I remember that it's not just the degrees that matter; it's the character, the humility, and the respect that we bring to each encounter that truly makes a difference. These values, deeply rooted in my Appalachian upbringing, continue to guide me, reminding me that the work I do is not just about sharing knowledge but about building trust, honoring the past, and helping others find their own path forward.

The Legacy of My Ancestors

As I reflect on my life and career, it's impossible to separate my role as a therapist and counselor educator from my roots in Kentucky. The land, the people, and the values I grew up with shaped my approach to working with clients and students alike. But my connection to the past goes even deeper than my immediate family and upbringing. It stretches back through generations, all the way to my 6th great-grandmother, Sarah Boone, the sister of the legendary Daniel Boone.

Growing up, I knew I was connected to Daniel Boone, a name synonymous with exploration, resilience, and survival. As a child, the stories of his courage and frontier spirit were part of the tapestry of Appalachian lore that surrounded me. While Daniel Boone's name is known far and wide, it's his sister, Sarah Boone, my 6th great-grandmother, who adds a more personal connection to my family's history. The Boone family's strength, adaptability, and courage in the face of adversity were qualities that were passed down through the generations. And while I didn't grow up on the frontier in the same sense that Daniel Boone did, those qualities found their way into the fabric of my life and the work I do today.

Daniel Boone is often remembered as a pioneer, a man who forged new paths through uncharted lands, guiding settlers and ensuring the survival of those who dared to journey into the wilderness. His life was one of perseverance, grit, and unwavering determination, qualities that resonate deeply with the people of Appalachia. The Boone family, like many others in the region, had to rely on their resourcefulness and inner strength to survive the harsh conditions of frontier life. It was a life that demanded not just physical endurance but emotional and mental resilience.

Daniel Boone, from a picture by J. W. Berry

These same qualities have shaped my own journey, both personally and professionally. As a therapist, I see resilience in my clients every day. Many of the people I work with have faced significant challenges, from generational poverty to trauma and addiction. Their struggles often stem not just from individual hardship but from systemic barriers, family legacies, and cultural expectations. In therapy, we often talk about resilience, but it's important to recognize that resilience is not just about "bouncing back." It's about adapting, growing, and finding ways to thrive despite adversity.

In working with clients, particularly those from Kentucky, Appalachia or similar backgrounds, understanding the concept of intergenerational resilience is crucial. Many clients have inherited not only strength but also hardship, cycles of poverty, trauma, and emotional suppression. As therapists, we can do many things to help. First, we need to reframe the narrative. Instead of focusing solely on trauma and hardship, we help clients identify the strength that has been passed down to them. This strength-based approach shifts the focus from victimhood to empowerment. Ask clients, "What strengths have been passed down in your family? What qualities have helped you survive?"

Secondly, encourage the exploration of personal and family identity. Many clients feel disconnected from their roots or carry shame about their background. Helping clients explore their family legacy can be a source of pride and healing. Clients can create a "family resilience map" identifying values, traditions, and strengths that have helped their family through difficult times.

Finally, we can bridge generational gaps. Appalachians, like many cultural groups, often carry a deep respect for their ancestors but also struggle with evolving social expectations. In therapy, we can help clients honor their past while creating their own future. For example, clients can explore how they can "carry forward" the strengths of their ancestors while breaking free from unhealthy cycles such as rigid gender roles, emotional suppression, or generational poverty.

Just as Daniel Boone helped carve paths through uncharted lands, my work as a counselor and educator feels like a continuation of that legacy. Counseling, especially in regions like Appalachia, is still met with skepticism by many. There are cultural barriers that make therapy seem unnecessary or even foreign to some people in the area. Many still believe in "handling things on their own" rather than seeking professional support.

For therapists working in these communities, it is crucial to build trust and demonstrate that therapy is not about weakness but about harnessing inner strength. Many clients see therapy as an intrusion rather than a resource, a cultural barrier that must be approached with care. For me, I am intentional about using culturally relevant language – Instead of framing therapy as "getting help," it may be more effective to talk about it as "figuring things out together" or "strengthening what's already there."

It is also about respecting autonomy while offering guidance. Much like a pioneer guide, the role of the therapist is not to dictate but to walk alongside clients, helping them navigate challenges while reinforcing their ability to make their own choices.

I also integrate storytelling and metaphors, which I will talk about more later. Many Appalachian families, including my own, pass down wisdom through storytelling. Using narrative therapy techniques, clients can reclaim their personal stories in a way that emphasizes resilience. For example, I might ask them, "If your life were a story passed down, what would you want the next generation to learn from it?"

Historically, therapy has focused too much on individual pathology rather than social context. Many clients are misdiagnosed, over-medicated, or placed in rigid treatment models that do not account for their cultural background. As therapists, we must challenge over-diagnosis and quick fixes. Many Appalachian families are skeptical of therapy because they see children being labeled and medicated instead of being taught discipline and resilience. Instead of immediately diagnosing, we should explore environmental and behavioral factors first.

We should empower clients instead of pathologizing them. Too often, we focus on what's wrong with a client instead of what's right. Appalachian resilience means that many clients already have problem-solving skills, therapy should enhance these, not override them.

Finally, when working with families, teach parenting and resilience skills, not just offer medication. One of the greatest disservices modern mental health care has done is abdicating our responsibility to teach parents how to shape their children's behavior. Instead of simply prescribing medication for ADHD or behavioral issues, therapists should guide parents in authoritative parenting techniques that reinforce responsibility, discipline, and self-regulation.

As I sit with clients in therapy or stand before my students in the classroom, I am mindful of the fact that I am not just doing this work alone. I carry with me the strength of those who came before me: my family, my ancestors, and my community. When I talk to clients about finding their own inner resources, I am speaking from a place of understanding. I know what it's like to draw strength from those who came before, to stand on the foundation that they built.

The Boone family's legacy isn't just about exploration, it's about survival, and in my work as a therapist, I help people not just survive but thrive in their own lives. Therapy is its own form of pioneering, navigating the emotional wilderness, carving new paths forward, and reclaiming the strengths that have always been there.

Through my connection to these ancestors, I have learned that life is about more than just survival; it's about growth, discovery, and leaving a legacy of strength for those who come after us. That's what I hope to do in my work every day as I walk the path of both my Appalachian roots and the Boone family's enduring legacy.

The Counselor as the Sin Eater

The practice of the sin eater is one that hails from the old country of Europe and took root in the hills of Appalachia, deeply entwined with the region's folklore and beliefs. A sin eater was called upon when a person passed away to symbolically consume their sins so the departed could rest in peace. The sin eater, often an outsider or someone on the margins of society, would partake in eating bread cakes shaped as coffins or bodies laid upon the deceased's body, taking on their unresolved guilt and shame, freeing the soul from its earthly burdens.

A Welsh funeral of 1814, showing the custom of passing food across the body of the deceased to the sineater. Engraving by I. Havell for The Cambrian Popular Antiquities, Public Domain

Though the practice of the sin eater has long faded from modern life, the symbolism remains deeply powerful, especially for those of us who work in counseling. In many ways, a professional counselor can be seen as a modern sin eater, not in a literal sense, but in the way they help clients confront and release the emotional burdens they carry. As counselors, we become vessels for our client's guilt, shame, and unresolved trauma. We sit with them in their darkest moments, helping them to process and let go of the things that weigh on their souls. Like the sin eater, the counselor doesn't judge or condemn but instead serves as a conduit for release and healing.

Counseling, much like the role of the sin eater, allows a person to unburden themselves. A client comes to a counselor with years of accumulated guilt, shame, and unresolved issues, looking for someone to help them make sense of it all. While we don't "consume" their sins, we do hold space for them to express those deep-seated emotions, to release them in a safe, non-judgmental environment. This act of witnessing, of holding space for their pain, can feel like a symbolic cleansing, much like the ritual of the sin eater.

However, unlike the sin eater of old, the counselor's role isn't to bear the burden forever. Instead, we facilitate a process where the client can learn to release the weight themselves, finding resolution and peace through therapy. In this way, the counselor is not a permanent vessel for their clients' suffering but rather a guide, helping them move forward without the chains of the past binding them.

[xxx]Freda came into therapy with deep feelings of shame rooted in her childhood. She had grown up in a household where her parents, though well-meaning, placed unrealistic expectations on her. Whenever she failed to meet their standards, she was met with guilt and emotional withdrawal. This burden carried into adulthood, manifesting in perfectionism and the constant feeling that she was "not enough."

Through counseling, Freda began to share the painful memories she had been too ashamed to confront. As her therapist, I acted as her witness, allowing her to speak about the things she had been holding inside for so long. Much like the sin eater of old, I took in her shame, not by absorbing it, but by allowing it to be spoken aloud in a safe, accepting space. The act of putting her emotions into words, of having them heard and validated, was the first step toward letting them go.

Over time, Freda began to reframe her experiences. She no longer needed to carry the burden of guilt imposed by others. Together, we worked to release those feelings, empowering her to reclaim her sense of self-worth. The therapy process mirrored the symbolic role of the sin eater, providing a way for her to unburden herself of the weight she had carried for years.

[xxxi]John came into therapy burdened with a deep sense of guilt over the death of a close friend. Years ago, his friend had passed in a car accident that John narrowly survived. Though the accident wasn't his fault, John had spent years believing he could have done something to prevent it. This survivor's guilt haunted him, affecting his relationships, his work, and his ability to enjoy life.

In our sessions, John struggled to articulate the depth of his guilt. As we worked through his trauma, I became a vessel for the stories he couldn't tell anyone else. He spoke of his friend, the accident, and the weight he had carried since that day. As his counselor, I allowed John's guilt to be expressed fully, without judgment or dismissal, helping him to understand that it wasn't his responsibility to hold onto that pain forever.

Over time, John was able to release some of the guilt he had carried. He didn't forget his friend or diminish the loss, but he learned that holding onto the guilt wasn't honoring his friend's memory, it was keeping him from living his own life fully. Like the sin eater, I helped John process and release the burden, allowing him to move forward without the overwhelming weight of guilt pressing down on him.

The counselor's role, like that of the sin eater, is to be present for the difficult emotions our clients struggle to release. We help them work through the emotions they struggle to process alone, whether it's regret over past mistakes, the invisible scars left by hardship, or the lingering weight of unhealed wounds and fractured relationships. By creating a space for these emotions to be expressed, acknowledged, and ultimately released, we allow our clients to move forward with lighter hearts and clearer minds.

In this way, the ancient practice of the sin-eater finds a modern parallel in therapy. Counselors today offer a form of symbolic release, not by absorbing the burdens of others as the sin-eater once did, but by helping clients process and let go of the emotional weight they no longer need to carry. Through this process, clients find healing, resilience, and the strength to move forward.

As therapists, we often become emotional caretakers, bearing witness to pain, grief, and trauma. While the sin-eater was a relic of the past, the role they played, taking on the suffering of others, mirrors the emotional toll of therapeutic work. The difference, however, is critical: the sineater had no outlet for what they absorbed, whereas we, as therapists, must be intentional about releasing what we take in. If we do not, we risk carrying that weight until it overwhelms us.

This is why self-care is not just an afterthought in our profession; it is essential. We cannot help others if we neglect our own well-being. Our health, our relationships, and our own emotional resilience must be priorities, not luxuries. Without nurturing our own roots, we risk withering under the emotional weight of our work. Like a tree with shallow roots, if we are not grounded and cared for, we will eventually topple.

John Coffey, the mystical figure from [9]"*The Green Mile*, understood this all too well. His ability to absorb the pain of others came with a cost, if he didn't release it, it would make him sick. Therapists face a similar reality: we must have healthy ways to process and let go of the emotional burdens we encounter, or we risk being consumed by them.

---

[9] In Stephen King's novel *The Green Mile* and its 1999 film adaptation, John Coffey is portrayed as a mystical, Christ-like figure with the supernatural ability to absorb and transfer pain, illness, and suffering from others. His ability to "take it back" mirrors the archetype of the sin-eater, a figure in folklore and religious tradition believed to take on the sins or burdens of others, often at great personal cost. Coffey's gift, while miraculous, also isolates him, as his power is misunderstood and feared by those around him. His fate reflects the tragic burden of carrying the pain of others, ultimately leading to his wrongful execution despite his innocence.

Empathy is at the heart of good therapy. A therapist who can connect deeply with their clients, who can truly feel the pain and sorrow that others carry, is often the most effective. But this empathy comes with a price. We often find ourselves getting alongside individuals in the depths of their despair, walking with them through their darkest moments. While this is vital to our role as therapists, it can also rub off on us, leaving us drained, emotionally fatigued, and sometimes even physically unwell.

One of the most difficult aspects of being a therapist is the inability to simply "turn off" empathy. A good therapist doesn't just listen to the stories of their clients; they feel them. They experience the emotions that their clients are feeling, sometimes to a profound degree. And while this is part of what makes therapy effective, it can also make it deeply challenging.

I remember one client in particular whose story was so raw and painful that it kept me awake for nights. [xxxii]Bethany had experienced horrific trauma at the hands of someone she trusted, and the weight of her suffering was almost unbearable to witness. As Bethany recounted her experiences, I felt tears welling up in my eyes. I knew that I needed to be strong for her, to guide her through the healing process, but her story was so overwhelming that it has stayed with me even now. There were nights I couldn't sleep, replaying Bethany's words in my mind, trying to figure out how I could best help her.

Another time, I worked with a client named [xxxiii]Cari, who had recently lost a child. The grief she carried was so heavy, so palpable, that it felt as though the air in the room thickened every time she spoke. I sat with Cari through her sobs, through her silence, and through her anger. After those sessions, I would return home feeling emotionally drained, as if I had lived through the loss myself. The pain of her story clung to me, and I found it difficult to shake.

These experiences are not unique to me; every therapist, at some point, will encounter clients whose stories are so painful, so raw, that they leave a lasting mark. And while we cannot, and should not, avoid these moments of deep connection, we must be mindful of how they affect us.

As therapists, we are tasked with holding space for the emotional turmoil of others, but we cannot do this effectively if we neglect our own well-being. We are, after all, human, and like everyone else, we have limits. If we do not care for ourselves, we risk burning out, becoming disconnected from our work, and ultimately being less effective for the clients who depend on us.

Self-care for therapists is not a luxury, it's a necessity. We must learn to nurture our own roots to ensure that we are grounded and healthy, both emotionally and physically. Just as we guide our clients toward healing, we must guide ourselves toward balance and well-being.

Here are a few lessons I've learned about self-care as a therapist:

First, it's essential to set boundaries between work and personal life. While empathy is a gift in therapy, we cannot carry the weight of our client's stories with us 24/7. It's okay to leave the work behind at the end of the day, to take time for ourselves and our families, and to focus on our own lives. As much as possible, establishing clear boundaries between work and personal life helps to prevent emotional burnout.

Second, we often encourage our clients to seek support from loved ones, friends, and professionals. As therapists, we must do the same. Whether it's through supervision, consultation with a peer therapist, or personal therapy, having a space to process our own emotions and experiences is crucial. There is no shame in seeking help; we are, after all, human. Having trusted colleagues or a therapist to talk to allows us to release the emotional burden that builds up over time.

Next, self-care is not just about resting; it's about engaging in activities that bring joy, relaxation, and meaning to our lives. Whether it's spending time with family, hiking in nature, reading a good book, or pursuing a hobby, these activities help us recharge. For me, spending time with my family is a source of deep renewal. Being surrounded by loved ones, sharing laughter, and enjoying the simple moments of life helps me feel grounded and whole.

Finally, the mind and body are interconnected, and when we neglect one, the other suffers. As therapists, it's important to take care of our physical health. Regular exercise, healthy eating, and adequate sleep are essential components of self-care. Physical well-being has a direct impact on our emotional and mental health, and it helps to counteract the physical toll of stress and emotional labor.

Being a therapist is a unique calling. We walk alongside people in their darkest moments, and that takes a toll. But we cannot pour from an empty cup. We cannot truly help others if we are depleted ourselves. In many ways, taking care of ourselves is part of taking care of our clients.

One of the most important lessons I've learned as a therapist is that self-care isn't selfish. It's a way of preserving the energy and compassion we need to be effective in our work. Just as a sineater would take on the burden of sin, therapists take on the emotional weight of their clients. But unlike the sineater, we must also find ways to release that burden, to cleanse ourselves so that we can continue to help others.

In many ways, the best therapists are those who feel deeply. We cannot simply turn off our empathy or shield ourselves from the pain of others. But while that pain can be heavy, it doesn't have to consume us. By nurturing our own roots through self-care, support, and boundaries, we ensure that we can continue to grow, both as professionals and as human beings.

In the end, our clients need us to be whole. They need us to be present, engaged, and compassionate. And we can only be those things if we take the time to care for ourselves, to nurture our own lives, and to seek out the people and activities that sustain us. Only then can we offer our clients the guidance and support they truly deserve.

Fresh from the Garden

When it comes to therapy, there's a world of difference between good therapy and masterful therapy. Both can be effective, but just like food, there's a significant difference between the canned and the fresh. Imagine walking into a kitchen. A can of vegetables on the shelf can certainly nourish a family, especially in the cold winter months when nothing is growing. But there's nothing quite like the taste of a fresh Kentucky beefsteak tomato picked straight from the vine, or a bite of cooked sweet corn just shucked from the cob. If you've ever eaten something right out of my grandfather's garden, you'd know what I mean. That fresh, flavorful experience can make you wonder why you ever settled for canned food in the first place.

This analogy applies just as well to counseling. In therapy, we have "canned" approaches, techniques, and interventions that have been tested, standardized, and packaged neatly into evidence-based treatments. These approaches can be extremely helpful and are often essential, providing a consistent level of care. Like canned vegetables during a long winter, evidence-based treatments can nourish those who need it most, providing essential mental health care that is proven to work.

But there is something that sets the master therapist apart from the good therapist, and it's the difference between serving canned vegetables and offering something fresh from the garden. The best therapists don't rely solely on these canned, cookie-cutter approaches. Instead, they are able to bring creativity, freshness, and adaptability into their work. They pull from a vast array of knowledge, experience, and empathy to create something that feels personal, alive, and tailored specifically to the individual in front of them.

Make no mistake: evidence-based treatments have an important role in the world of counseling. These "canned" therapies, such as Cognitive Behavioral Therapy (CBT), Dialectical Behavior Therapy (DBT), and Solution-Focused Therapy, are grounded in research and have been shown to be effective across a variety of populations and issues. They provide a reliable framework, giving counselors a clear path to follow and helping clients feel confident that the approach has been tested and validated.

For counselors in training, learning these evidence-based treatments is crucial. These therapies provide the foundational skills every counselor needs, offering techniques and interventions that can help clients make progress. Just as canned vegetables provide vital nutrients during times of scarcity, these therapies can feed the masses, helping a wide range of clients who may be struggling.

However, while evidence-based treatments are necessary, they are not sufficient to become a master therapist. The true art of counseling lies in knowing when to step outside the confines of these approaches and bring something fresh, creative, and personalized to the table.

What sets master therapists apart is their ability to tailor therapy to the unique needs of each client. Like a chef who selects ingredients fresh from the garden, the master therapist knows how to take their knowledge of evidence-based practices and apply it in a way that feels custom-made for the individual. They are not confined to one approach or one technique; rather, they pull from a deep well of experience and intuition, blending interventions to fit the client's personality, culture, and specific challenges.

For example, just as I've shown in this book with the people from Appalachia, the master therapist knows how to adapt therapy to meet the cultural, emotional, and personal needs of each client. In Appalachia, where storytelling, metaphor, and nature play significant roles in daily life, a master therapist might integrate these elements into the therapeutic process. They might use metaphors of gardening, farming, or weather patterns to help clients understand their emotional experiences. They might draw on the client's connection to the land or family history to create a sense of grounding and healing. This ability to customize therapy based on the individual's cultural background, life experience, and emotional needs is what makes therapy feel "fresh" rather than "canned."

The best therapists are not bound to a single modality. They know that while Cognitive Behavioral Therapy might work well for one client, it might feel too rigid for another. They are able to seamlessly move between approaches, drawing on humanistic techniques in one session, trauma-focused interventions in the next, and mindfulness-based practices when needed. This flexibility allows therapy to be responsive, meeting the client where they are and helping them move forward in a way that feels organic and intuitive.

Counseling is both a science and an art. The science is important, it gives us the evidence, the research, and the techniques that have been proven to work. But the art of therapy comes from the ability to use these tools creatively, to bring them to life in a way that feels deeply personal and relevant to the client sitting across from you.

Master therapists don't throw out evidence-based treatments, but they don't rely on them exclusively either. They recognize that therapy is not a one-size-fits-all solution. It's a living, breathing process that requires flexibility, adaptability, and a deep understanding of human nature. Just as a master gardener knows when to prune, when to water, and when to let things grow on their own, the master therapist knows when to offer structured interventions and when to allow space for the client to lead the process.

This is where the therapeutic alliance becomes so important. The relationship between therapist and client is one of the most significant factors in whether therapy is successful. A master therapist builds this relationship with care, using their empathy, intuition, and creativity to connect with clients on a deep level. They understand that therapy is not just about delivering techniques or following a manual; it's about creating a space where clients feel safe, seen, and understood.

For clients looking for the best therapist for their needs, it's important to consider more than just the therapist's qualifications or theoretical orientation. While evidence-based practices are essential, the true mark of an excellent therapist is their ability to adapt their approach to fit you. Just as there's a difference between canned food and fresh produce, there's a difference between therapy that feels standardized and therapy that feels alive, creative, and deeply personal.

Clients should look for therapists who are not only knowledgeable but also flexible, creative, and willing to go beyond the standard approaches when necessary. A therapist who can balance the science of evidence-based practice with the art of intuitive, personalized care is likely to offer the kind of transformative experience that leads to real, lasting change.

In summary, there's a place for "canned" approaches in therapy, just as there's a place for canned food in our diets. But if you've ever tasted a fresh Kentucky beefsteak tomato or a sweet ear of corn straight from the garden, you know that nothing beats fresh. The same is true in therapy. Evidence-based treatments provide essential nutrients, but the most satisfying, transformative therapy comes from master therapists who know how to cultivate fresh, creative, and personalized interventions that speak directly to the client's heart.

Social Impact from the Hills

Being born in Kentucky and having the blessing of living and working with the people of Appalachia, stories were woven into the very fabric of who we all were. The land, the people, and the struggles all shaped our understanding of the world. One story that always stuck with me was about my first cousin, three times removed, Edgar Bruce Wesley. In his autobiography (Wesley E. B., Too Short the Days, 1966) wrote about growing up just like many around him did, surrounded by the beauty and hardship of rural Kentucky. But there was something different about Edgar, something shaped not just by the landscape but by an experience that would stay with him for the rest of his life.

Edgar was just a boy when he witnessed a hanging, a [10]legal hanging, sanctioned by the state. But it wasn't the execution itself that haunted him; it was the reaction of the people in the hills around him. Word had spread quickly that a Black man was going to be hanged, and for many, it became a spectacle. A dark excitement rippled through the community as people gathered, eager to witness the execution. The bloodlust was palpable, with crowds expecting a public display, some even hungry for vengeance.

But the sheriff, a man with more decency than most, saw the gathering storm. Instead of feeding the crowd's desire for a show, he quietly moved the time of the hanging to 6:30 in the morning before the crowds could descend on the scene. By the time the mob arrived, expecting to witness the event, it was over. The people were furious, angry that they had missed their chance to watch a man die. The frustration quickly grew into a near-riot, with many in the crowd yelling and pushing, their bloodlust turning to rage. Edgar, standing with his father at the edge of the crowd, took it all in. He saw the hatred, the excitement for violence, and the raw anger that bubbled up when they were denied their spectacle. That moment never left him.

Witnessing the mob that day in the hills of Barbourville, Kentucky, planted a seed in Edgar, a deep understanding of the power of human behavior, both the good and the ugly. But more than that, it gave him an unshakable belief in justice, fairness, and the idea that people could, and should, rise above their baser instincts.

---

[10] Jesse Fitzgerald, a black man, was executed by hanging in 1907 in Barbourville, Kentucky, for the murder of Mrs. Robert Broughton. Following his execution, his skeleton was preserved and utilized as a teaching specimen in the biology department at Union College. Over time, it became an unofficial mascot, displayed in a cabinet and occasionally brought out during sports events. This information is documented in Union College's 1945 Stespean Yearbook, among other resources.

Those principles would shape the rest of his life and, in turn, would influence social studies education across America.

In time, Edgar left the community of Bethelridge, Kentucky, and his teacher education at Union in Barbourville to pursue even higher education. But even as he earned his degrees and stepped into the world of academia, he carried the lessons of Appalachia with him. He understood people in a way that books and classrooms couldn't teach. He had seen firsthand how the desire for violence and vengeance could sweep through a crowd, and he knew that education was the key to tempering those instincts, to helping people think critically about the world around them and the choices they made.

Edgar became a prominent figure in social studies education, and his work laid the foundation for much of what we take for granted today. His textbooks on *Teaching the Social Studies* (Wesley, 1952) (Wesley E. B., 1958) were not only seminal works in the field; it was a roadmap for how to teach students about the complexities of human behavior and society. He believed deeply that education wasn't just about memorizing facts; it was about preparing young minds to engage with the world thoughtfully and ethically. His early experience with the mob at the hanging had shown him how dangerous ignorance and unchecked emotions could be. Education, he believed, was the way to prevent those forces from gaining the upper hand.

One of Edgar's greatest contributions (Shermis, 1978) was his work with the National Council for the Social Studies (NCSS). As president of the NCSS in 1935, he organized the council's first independent annual meeting, a milestone that gave educators a place to come together and share ideas. He also helped establish *Social Education*, the journal that would become a cornerstone for teachers across the country, providing them with resources and insights to better their practice. Edgar's Appalachian roots were always with him, guiding him as he fought to create an educational system that didn't just teach facts but cultivated understanding, empathy, and justice.

But Edgar didn't stop there. He understood that the world was growing more connected, and he believed that students needed to learn about global issues, not just those within their own country. After World War II, he launched the Program of Information on World Affairs in collaboration with the *Minneapolis Star*. The program provided schools with resources on contemporary global issues, encouraging students to think beyond their immediate surroundings. Edgar knew that education had to prepare young people for a world that was much larger and more complex than their own backyards, an idea that echoed the lessons he'd learned in the hills, where survival often depended on understanding forces much larger than yourself.

When I think about Edgar, I don't just think of him as a distant relative who made his mark in education. I think of him as an example of Appalachian resilience and the power of personal experience to shape a life. He took that moment as a boy, standing on the edge of a mob hungry for violence, and turned it into a lifelong mission to educate and uplift. He understood that the best way to fight the darkness he had seen was with knowledge, empathy, and a commitment to justice.

In my work as a therapist, I often sit with clients who feel overwhelmed by the struggles they face. I think of Edgar then, how he saw the best and worst in people and used that experience to become better, not bitter. It's a lesson I carry with me: that hardship doesn't have to define us, but it can shape us into something stronger. Edgar knew that education was more than a tool; it was a shield against ignorance and cruelty. His life, his work, and his belief in the power of knowledge remind me every day that we can rise above our circumstances, no matter how dark the world around us may seem. That's the gift Appalachia gave him, and through him, it's the gift he gave to the world.

The Gift of Kindness

One story passed down through my family, capturing the spirit of Kindness, comes from my great-great-grandfather, [xxxiv]Shelby Martin. It's a story about the power of human connection and how integrity and respect can bring unexpected rewards, including the bond of a lifelong partnership.

Shelby was still a young man when this tale took place. While traveling, he came across an old man who had fallen ill, struggling to survive. At a time when resources were scarce, and most people barely had enough for themselves, Shelby didn't hesitate. He took the frail man back to his home, cared for him, and nursed him through his illness. Shelby wasn't looking for anything in return; he did it because it was the right thing to do.

The older man, deeply moved by Shelby's kindness, wanted to show his gratitude. Knowing he had little to offer in material wealth, he made an offer rooted in the customs of the time. He told Shelby that if he ever desired a wife, he could seek the hand of one of his daughters in marriage. It's important to understand that this wasn't a transaction, nor was the daughter simply given away. This gesture of trust came from a deep understanding of Shelby's character. The old man knew Shelby would honor and care for his daughter just as he had cared for him.

Of course, the daughter had her say in the matter as well. In those days, arranged marriages were not uncommon, but they were built on mutual respect, especially when parents had observed the good character of the suitor. When Shelby later sought out the daughter, she agreed, knowing that her father's judgment of Shelby's integrity was sound. Their marriage grew into a happy and fulfilling union, which may not have been founded on romantic love at first, but on mutual respect, kindness, and shared values, the very traits that sustain a lifelong partnership.

This story, passed down through generations, is a powerful reminder of the importance of character and integrity in building meaningful relationships. The love that formed between Shelby and his wife grew out of an act of kindness and the respect he showed for her family, setting the tone for their partnership.

Reflecting on Shelby's story, I can't help but think about my own journey with [xxxv]Dawn, my wife. Before I ever asked her out on a date, I first "dated" her father, Norman Fisher. I knew that before I could even think about winning Dawn's heart, I needed to win over her parents. I took her father out, spending time with him, talking, and proving my character. I wanted to show him the same respect I intended to show his daughter because I knew that gaining his trust would be the foundation for my relationship with Dawn.

In many ways, this mirrored the example set by Shelby Martin generations before. Just as Shelby sought to honor the trust placed in him by the father of his future bride, I wanted to demonstrate to Dawn's father that I was someone who would respect and care for his daughter. It wasn't just about seeking permission, it was about showing, through my actions, that I was a man of integrity and that I would treat her with the respect and care she deserved.

These acts of respect, whether Shelby's act of compassion toward the old man or my effort to build a bond with Dawn's father, remind us that relationships are built on a foundation of trust, character, and kindness. Shelby's story, and my own, are reminders that true partnership comes not from what we say but from how we live and show respect for others.

Shelby's story is not just a personal or family lesson; it holds profound implications for therapists and clients alike. Kindness is more than a moral virtue; it is a transformative force that can enhance emotional well-being, foster stronger relationships, and even aid in psychological healing.

In counseling, kindness manifests in multiple ways: in the therapeutic alliance, in a client's self-compassion, and in the way individuals engage with others in their lives. Counselors can use the lessons of kindness to help clients build healthier relationships, strengthen self-worth, and foster resilience.

Many people struggle with self-criticism, shame, or a sense of unworthiness. Shelby's story teaches us that acts of kindness toward others and ourselves can shift our emotional landscape. Research has shown that kindness increases serotonin levels, the neurotransmitter associated with feelings of happiness and well-being (Lyubomirsky, 2005). Even small acts of kindness, offering help, expressing gratitude, or practicing patience can create a ripple effect in improving mental health.

Often, clients treat themselves with far less kindness than they extend to others. Therapists frequently encounter clients who engage in negative self-talk, believing they are not "good enough" or unworthy of love. Encouraging self-kindness, treating oneself as one would treat a dear friend, can be a powerful intervention. Dr. Kristin Neff's research on self-compassion highlights how practicing kindness toward oneself can decrease anxiety, depression, and emotional distress (Neff, 2011). One exercise I have used is asking clients can write a letter to themselves from the perspective of a kind and understanding friend. This practice can help reframe negative self-beliefs and encourage self-compassion.

Shelby's story demonstrates that trust, integrity, and kindness form the bedrock of deep relationships. Clients struggling with relationship conflicts often focus on what they are lacking or how they've been wronged. Instead, therapists can guide them toward kindness-based interventions such as encouraging them to perform one small act of kindness for their partner, friend, or family member daily. This can be as simple as leaving a kind note, expressing appreciation, or offering a listening ear. Over time, this practice strengthens bonds and shifts the emotional climate of relationships.

For my counselors in training, the foundation of effective therapy is the therapeutic alliance, a relationship based on trust, empathy, and nonjudgmental acceptance. Simply being present for a client, listening without interruption, and offering genuine understanding is an act of kindness that fosters healing. Clients learn from the behavior of their therapist. When therapists demonstrate warmth, patience, and encouragement, they provide a model for how clients can engage in kinder interactions with themselves and others. For example, if a client is struggling with feelings of guilt or failure, a therapist might gently ask, "What would you say to a friend who was feeling the same way?" This reframe invites the client to engage with self-kindness. I also have had my clients engage in a "kindness experiment" where they perform intentional acts of kindness over a week. Ask them to journal their experiences and reflect on how these actions impacted their emotions and relationships.

Kindness is not just a sentimental ideal; it is a practical and powerful tool for personal growth, emotional healing, and relationship building. Shelby Martin's story reminds us that kindness has the power to change lives, not just for the one receiving it but also for the one offering it. Whether in counseling, relationships, or daily interactions, kindness fosters connection, trust, and resilience. In therapy, kindness is woven into the fabric of healing, offered through compassionate listening, self-acceptance, and acts of goodwill that ripple outward.

As therapists, we must ask ourselves: How can we help our clients embrace kindness as a tool for growth? And as individuals, we can ask ourselves: How can we bring more kindness into the world, knowing that it has the power to change not only our lives but the lives of others? Kindness, after all, is one of the greatest gifts we can give, to others, to our clients, and most importantly, to ourselves.

Our Brother's Keeper

In the hills of Appalachia, family wasn't just something you were born into, it was something you worked to protect, to nurture, and to guide. The sense of responsibility didn't stop at the edges of your own well-being. It extended outward, encompassing every sibling, every cousin, and every member of the family who needed care and support. This idea of being "our brother's keeper" was not just a saying; it was a way of life passed down through generations, as evident in the stories from my great-great-grandfather, W. P. Martin, who wrote about his parents' philosophy of raising their children.

My Great, Great grandfather, William Perry "W.P." Martin

W. P. Martin's parents had a clear program for rearing their family, a plan that emphasized responsibility, care for others, and education. The eldest child in the family, as Martin described, was given a unique role. The firstborn was trained in the arts of household management and, more importantly, was groomed to be a helper, a role model for the younger children. As the eldest, W. P. Martin remembered how the responsibility of being his brother's keeper was impressed upon him at an early age. This wasn't a burden to him, though; rather, it was a privilege and a duty that shaped him into the man he would become.

When children did wrong in their household, punishment wasn't immediate. Their parents appealed to their conscience, trusting that the children would learn right from wrong through reflection and understanding. This method of parenting, more focused on guiding through example than chastising with harsh words or actions, often achieved the desired result. Martin himself recalled that he had never been whipped by his father, not because he was perfect, but because his father's trust and guidance were usually enough to bring about obedience.

This sense of trust extended beyond discipline and into every aspect of their lives. Their parents trusted them in both business and pleasure, giving them opportunities to prove their trustworthiness. It was through this foundation of trust and responsibility that the children learned how to manage not only their own lives but also the well-being of those around them.

The responsibilities of home duties flowed naturally from the older children to the younger ones. This sense of continuity, where each child was taught to look after the one who followed, created a system where every member of the family had a role, not just in household chores, but in the emotional and moral support of one another. This wasn't a practice unique to the Martin family; it was a way of life for many families in Appalachia. Being your brother's keeper was a value passed down, celebrated during family reunions, and lived out through the choices they made in daily life.

One of the greatest responsibilities of parenting, as Martin's story illustrates, was the protection and education of children. The Martin family, despite their poverty and limited resources, placed an immense value on education. Though their ancestors were largely illiterate, W. P. Martin's parents made it their mission to provide their children with every opportunity for learning. The eldest son was given the chance to gain an education, and in turn, he became the teacher for his younger siblings. Education was a family affair, with the older children helping the younger ones learn, instilling in them a love for knowledge and the responsibility to uplift one another.

Even though they had little material wealth, Martin's parents taught their children about the riches of love, kindness, and service. Their poverty did not prevent them from helping others in need. Though they didn't have much money, they gave what they could through acts of service, teaching their children that being one's brother's keeper meant extending love and support to others in the community as well. This lesson of mutual care and responsibility was not just a duty but a reflection of the deep love that bound the family together.

Being your brother's keeper, as Martin's story shows, is about more than just taking care of others. It's about creating a foundation of trust, responsibility, and mutual support that can be passed down through generations. But in today's fast-paced, technology-driven world, many of these foundational values are being replaced with distractions, social media, video games, and a lack of direct family involvement.

Parenting today requires a balance between structure and warmth, what we call authoritative parenting (Baumrind, 1967). Authoritative parents set firm boundaries, provide guidance, and expect responsibility, much like W. P. Martin's parents did. However, they also offer warmth, support, and open communication. This parenting style has been shown to produce children who are more confident, responsible, and emotionally healthy compared to permissive or authoritarian parenting approaches (Steinberg, 2001).

Counselors can help parents recognize that children thrive when they feel a sense of belonging and responsibility within the family unit. Teaching children to contribute at home, just as older siblings once did in Appalachian families, fosters independence and emotional maturity. Parents can be encouraged to implement structured roles for their children, such as household responsibilities and mentoring younger siblings, to reinforce responsibility and care.

Excessive time on social media and video games can erode real-world relationships and diminish children's ability to develop empathy and responsibility. Therapists can guide families in creating "technology-free zones" where meals, conversations, and shared activities take precedence over screens. Encouraging parents to model healthy digital habits by prioritizing direct interactions with their children fosters stronger emotional connections.

The Martin family's discipline method, appealing to a child's conscience rather than immediately punishing, aligns with modern therapeutic techniques like Cognitive Behavioral Therapy (CBT) (Beck, 1978). Instead of punitive measures, parents can guide children through reflective conversations: "How do you think your actions impacted others?"; "What could you do differently next time?"; or "How would you feel if you were in their place?" This technique teaches children self-awareness and moral reasoning, leading to lasting behavior change rather than short-term obedience.

The tradition of older children teaching younger ones reflects a time-honored model of education and mentorship. Today, families can reintroduce this through simple habits such as encouraging older siblings to help with homework, involving children in storytelling that emphasizes family values, or prioritizing family discussions over passive entertainment.

Many of the problems families face today stem from disconnection between parents and children, between siblings, and within communities. Counselors can help families rebuild the "village" mentality, where responsibility, mentorship, and support are woven into daily life. Counselors can guide parents in developing family traditions that foster connection, such as weekly story-sharing nights, gratitude circles, or community service activities. Rather than resorting to punishment, parents can teach emotional intelligence through kindness-based discipline, encouraging children to reflect on their actions, take responsibility, and make amends. Parents struggling with children's behavioral issues often look for quick fixes (e.g., screen time to pacify emotions). Instead, counselors can help them develop engagement-based solutions through encouraging hands-on activities like cooking, gardening, or volunteering. They can also encourage using family meetings to discuss concerns rather than relying on punitive measures.

Unfortunately, as counselors, we have sometimes contributed to the problem by shifting the focus away from parental responsibility and behavioral shaping. In many cases, instead of equipping parents with the skills to guide and discipline their children effectively, we have leaned too heavily on overdiagnosis and medication as quick fixes. While some children certainly benefit from clinical interventions, the growing trend of labeling normal childhood struggles as disorders without first exploring environmental and behavioral solutions has weakened parental authority and problem-solving skills. True change requires effort from families, not just prescriptions. As counselors, we must reclaim our role in supporting parents, helping them develop the confidence, tools, and strategies to shape their children's behavior rather than outsourcing discipline to medication alone.

As W. P. Martin's story illustrates, the role of family is not simply to protect; it's to guide, to teach, and to nurture the bonds that keep us close. Today, with the rise of digital distractions and passive parenting, we risk losing the traditions that kept families strong for generations.

By reviving authoritative parenting, limiting screen time, and fostering real-world engagement, we can ensure that children grow up with the values of responsibility, kindness, and trust. In the end, being our brother's keeper is not just about family; it's about building a stronger, more connected future for all.

As W. P. Martin's story illustrates, the role of family is not simply to protect; it's to guide, to teach, and to nurture the bonds that keep us close. Through his parents' "program" of organized parenting and moral guidance, he learned the true meaning of being his brother's keeper. And through the generations, that lesson has become a cornerstone of our family's values. In my own life and work, I've tried to carry those lessons forward, understanding that the love, trust, and care we offer others are the greatest gifts we can give.

The Apple Doesn't Fall Far, or Does It?

There's an old saying we often hear: "The apple doesn't fall far from the tree." It suggests that children inherit their parents' characteristics and that their actions and behaviors are largely shaped by the environment they grew up in. It's a phrase often used to explain why people are the way they are, pointing to their family as the source of their character and choices. But there's another phrase, equally well-known in Appalachia: "Don't judge someone by their kin." This saying advises caution, reminding us not to assume a person's character based on their family alone. Taken together, these two phrases offer a valuable lesson about assessing character and understanding the many influences that shape a person.

As a therapist and a parent, I've spent a lot of time thinking about these sayings and the nature vs nurture debate. On one hand, it's true that children are often shaped by their parents' values, behaviors, and choices. In many cases, you can see a clear connection between how a parent lives and the actions of their children. You might say the apple doesn't fall far from the tree when you see a child who mirrors their parents' work ethic, kindness, or even their struggles. There's truth in the idea that family creates a powerful influence, shaping our earliest understanding of right and wrong, success and failure.

But it's just as true that we shouldn't judge a person solely based on their family. As the saying goes, you can't assume that a person is a reflection of their kin until you get to know them for who they are. A child raised in difficult circumstances may choose to live a life radically different from their parents, while a child raised in privilege and love may take a path that seems at odds with their upbringing. People are complex, and while family plays a role in shaping us, it's not the only influence in our lives. As a therapist, I've seen firsthand how children grow up in families that may not reflect who they become, shaped instead by other mentors, experiences, and even by the forces of nature itself.

As parents, we often feel the weight of responsibility for who our children become. We see ourselves as shepherds, guiding our children, teaching them values, and showing them how to navigate the world. And to a large extent, that's true. We are their first teachers, the ones they look to for guidance and protection. But we aren't sculptors, crafting them into perfect versions of ourselves or molding their every decision. In truth, much of parenting is about guiding rather than controlling, about offering wisdom without dictating every choice.

There's an element of nature that plays a significant role in a child's development, and it's a role over which we have very little control. Some children are born with natural temperaments that influence how they respond to the world. One child may be naturally curious and adventurous, while another is more cautious and reflective. These traits are part of who they are, shaped not just by upbringing but by their own inner wiring.

As much as we try to steer them, children are exposed to influences beyond their parents, teachers, friends, experiences, and the wider world all contribute to who they become. We do our best to instill values and set examples, but there's a limit to the control we have over the outcomes of their lives. It's in this delicate balance that the two sayings, "The apple doesn't fall far from the tree" and "Don't judge someone by their kin", come together.

In therapy, I often work with people who feel defined by their families, for better or worse. Some clients feel pressure to live up to the expectations of their parents or to follow a path that's been set out for them. Others work to distance themselves from family legacies that they feel don't represent who they are. The truth, as I've come to see it, is that while family shapes us, it doesn't define us completely.

When assessing someone's character, it's important to take the whole picture into account. Yes, the apple may not fall far from the tree. There are many cases where a person's behavior or values closely align with those of their parents, and this can be both a positive and a negative thing. You might see a person who shares their parents' generosity, or you might see someone repeating the mistakes their parents made. But we can't stop at that observation alone. To truly understand a person, we have to look beyond their family to their own choices, actions, and experiences.

"Don't judge someone by their kin" reminds us that people are more than their family's story. I've seen children who rise above difficult family circumstances, breaking cycles of addiction, violence, or neglect to live lives that reflect their own values. I've also seen people struggle to escape the weight of their family's reputation, even when they've lived lives of integrity and responsibility. It's not fair to assume that just because someone comes from a certain family, they will act a certain way. Each person is responsible for their own actions, and their character is often a blend of influences, both from within and beyond their family.

The tension between these two sayings also speaks to the ongoing debate about nature versus nurture. As parents, we can provide a nurturing environment, but we cannot entirely shape who our children will be. They are born with their own unique blend of traits and their own way of responding to the world. Some of this is inherited, but much of it is individual to them. The role of parents is to shepherd, to guide, to provide the tools and values for children to navigate life. But it's up to the children, influenced by the world around them and their own internal compass, to decide who they will become.

As I reflect on these two sayings, I see that both hold truth. We shouldn't be quick to judge a person based solely on their family because each person is a unique individual shaped by a variety of influences. At the same time, it's undeniable that family plays a powerful role in shaping our early years. But ultimately, the measure of a person's character comes from their actions, their choices, and the way they live their life, whether they follow in their family's footsteps or blaze their own path.

Samantha came to therapy struggling with addiction, something that had haunted her family for generations. Her father had battled alcoholism, and his father before him had been the same. Growing up in that environment, Samantha had learned to cope with the chaos by escaping into her own world. By the time she was a teenager, she was experimenting with drugs, trying to numb the pain of her family life. By her twenties, addiction had taken hold, and she found herself repeating the very cycle she had witnessed growing up.

[xxxvi]Samantha initially believed that "the apple doesn't fall far from the tree." She felt that her fate had been sealed, that addiction was something inescapable for her family. Her identity was so intertwined with her family's struggles that it seemed impossible to break free. She feared that no matter what she did, she was destined to follow in her father's footsteps.

Through counseling, Samantha slowly began to untangle herself from her family's legacy. Together, we explored her beliefs about addiction and the way it had shaped her view of herself. We worked on separating her identity from the behaviors and choices of her father, recognizing that while her family's history had influenced her, it didn't have to define her. She started to see that while the apple might not have fallen far from the tree, it didn't mean she couldn't choose a different path.

Samantha began attending support groups for addiction and worked hard on building new coping mechanisms. Through therapy, she discovered the strength to create new boundaries with her family and distance herself from the cycles that had held her back for so long. She learned that while her upbringing had shaped her experiences, it didn't have to dictate her future.

As Samantha broke the cycle of addiction in her family, she also came to understand that "don't judge someone by their kin" was just as true. Her actions, her choice to seek help, to live a sober life, were her own, and she was determined to build a life that reflected her values, not the patterns of her past. Samantha's journey was about recognizing that while family influences are powerful, each person has the capacity to choose a new direction.

[xxxvii]Joe's life took a drastic turn when a series of poor decisions landed him in jail. In his mid-twenties, he had been swept up in a lifestyle that was far removed from the values his parents had worked hard to instill in him. Growing up, Joe's parents had emphasized honesty, responsibility, and hard work. But in his young adult years, Joe got involved with the wrong crowd and made choices that led to his arrest. By the time he came to therapy, he had served his time, but he was struggling to rebuild his life.

Joe felt ashamed of his actions and disconnected from the values he had been raised with. He believed that his time in jail had undone the foundation his parents had laid for him, and he worried that he had lost their respect. He felt that he had failed his family and was unsure how to regain their trust or his own sense of self-worth. He told me, "Don't judge someone by their kin. My parents did everything right, and I still messed it up."

In therapy, we worked to shift Joe's perspective. While he had made mistakes, his parents' values had never left him. Those foundational principles, honesty, responsibility, and integrity, were still within him, waiting to be reclaimed. Joe slowly began to see that his time in jail didn't erase the good he had been taught. Instead, it offered him an opportunity to realign himself with the values he had grown up with, to take responsibility for his actions, and to live a life that honored the lessons his parents had instilled in him.

Over time, Joe reconnected with his family and leaned into the strength they offered. He realized that "The apple doesn't fall far from the tree" had another layer of meaning for him; while his actions had led him astray, the character his parents had nurtured in him was still there. He wasn't defined by his mistakes but by his ability to learn from them and move forward with integrity. Joe rebuilt his life by taking ownership of his choices, making amends where needed, and finding a renewed sense of purpose in the values his family had given him.

These two examples illustrate the tension between the phrases. Samantha's story shows how a person can break free from harmful family cycles and choose a different path, proving that our families don't define us entirely. Joe's journey, on the other hand, demonstrates how someone can return to the foundational values they were raised with, even after losing their way. Both stories reflect the complexity of human character and the many influences, family, personal choices, and external circumstances that shape who we become.

In summary, as parents and as individuals, we can guide and inspire, but we must also recognize the limits of our influence. Our role is to create a foundation for our children and to offer them the tools to live with integrity and compassion. The rest, their choices, their paths, is theirs to shape. Whether the apple falls close to the tree or rolls far away, it is the strength of the roots that matters most.

Empowerment Over Powerlessness

Addiction is a deeply personal and complex struggle, and no two journeys to recovery are the same. But when it comes to treating addiction, the model we choose to guide individuals toward healing can make all the difference in their success. In Appalachia, many addiction treatment programs have adopted the 12-step model, which has become a cornerstone of recovery programs across the country. At its heart, the 12-step approach encourages individuals to surrender, to acknowledge their powerlessness over addiction, and to place their trust in a higher power. While this model has helped countless people recover, I've long held a belief that it doesn't align with the spirit of the people of Appalachia.

Living in rural Kentucky and working in areas of Eastern Kentucky, West Virginia, Virginia, and Tennessee, I saw firsthand the resilience of the people who live there. Life in Appalachia isn't easy. It's a place where hardship is met with grit, where survival often requires a fierce determination to pull from inner strength you didn't know you had. The people of Appalachia don't see themselves as powerless. In fact, many would say it's precisely their ability to tap into their inner reserves of strength that has allowed them to overcome generations of poverty, isolation, and hardship.

This is why I've always felt that the 12-step model, with its emphasis on powerlessness, is at odds with the culture and values of the Appalachian people. While surrender might work for some, for many people in this region, the idea of giving up control feels foreign, coming from the upper society of the [11]Oxford Club. My people spent their lives relying on their ability to survive, to make do with what they have, and to push through adversity. Asking them to embrace powerlessness can feel like stripping away the very essence of what has kept them going for so long.

My philosophy of addiction treatment is grounded in the belief that recovery is not about surrendering to powerlessness but about discovering the power within.

---

[11] *The Oxford Group was a Christian fellowship movement founded by Lutheran minister Frank Buchman in the early 20th century. The group emphasized personal transformation through self-examination, confession, restitution, and reliance on God's guidance. Their core principles, honesty, purity, unselfishness, and love, served as the foundation for Alcoholics Anonymous (AA) when Bill Wilson, one of AA's co-founders, was introduced to the group in the 1930s. Many of AA's key concepts, including the idea of surrendering to a higher power and the practice of sharing one's struggles openly, were influenced by the Oxford Group's teachings. Over time, AA evolved into its own distinct program, shifting away from its explicitly religious roots to become more inclusive to people of all spiritual backgrounds.*

For people in Appalachia, recovery needs to be framed as a journey of empowerment, of reconnecting with the inner strength that has been buried under the weight of addiction. Instead of focusing on what has been lost, I believe treatment should focus on what remains: resilience, strength, and the ability to overcome challenges.

In my experience, people from Appalachia respond better to treatment models that emphasize self-reliance, personal responsibility, and inner strength. The 12-step model's external locus of control, which asks individuals to turn over their will to a higher power, can feel disempowering to people who have spent their lives fighting to maintain control over their circumstances. Instead, I advocate for a model that helps individuals take back control and reminds them that while addiction may have taken much from them, it hasn't taken everything.

I've seen many addiction treatment programs fail in Appalachia because they try to impose a one-size-fits-all model that doesn't take into account the unique culture of the region. The 12-step model, with its emphasis on surrender and external guidance, doesn't resonate with people who pride themselves on self-sufficiency. In the mountains, people have always had to pull from their own strength to survive, whether it's tending to a farm, raising a family, or getting through a hard winter. They've learned not to wait for someone else to solve their problems but to dig deep and find their own solutions.

The concept of powerlessness, which is central to the 12-step model, feels foreign to many in Appalachia. The idea that you must admit defeat and surrender to something outside of yourself can feel like a betrayal of the very resilience that has sustained generations of mountain families. It's not that people here don't believe in a higher power, faith runs deep in the region, but they also believe in their own ability to overcome. For them, recovery needs to be about reclaiming their power, not surrendering it.

In my work as a therapist, I've seen how important it is to meet people where they are, to understand their culture, and to respect the values that have shaped their lives. For people in Appalachia, that means creating a treatment model that emphasizes strength, resilience, and personal responsibility. Instead of telling individuals that they are powerless, I encourage them to recognize the power they already possess: the power to choose, the power to change, and the power to reclaim their lives from addiction.

A strength-based recovery model focuses on empowering individuals to take control of their own healing. It doesn't deny the importance of community or spiritual guidance, but it places the individual at the center of their recovery. This model recognizes that addiction is not a moral failing, but it also doesn't strip people of their agency. Instead of asking them to surrender, it asks them to step up, to take responsibility for their recovery, and to tap into the strength that has always been a part of who they are.

In Appalachia, this approach resonates more deeply with people who have spent their lives relying on their own strength. It honors their resilience while providing the tools and support needed to navigate the complex journey of recovery. By focusing on empowerment rather than powerlessness, this model aligns with the cultural values of self-reliance, perseverance, and personal responsibility that are so deeply ingrained in the people of the mountains.

Appalachia has a long history with substances that offer an escape from the challenges of life. Decades ago, moonshine was a part of the culture, a homemade escape from the hardship of daily life in the hills. But as times have changed, so too have the substances that plague the region. The old moonshine stills have been replaced by meth labs, and where moonshine was once the drink of choice, now the region faces the scourge of opioids like OxyContin and fentanyl.

"If You Find Yourself in a Hole, the First Thing to Do Is Stop Digging."

The opioid crisis has hit Appalachia hard. West Virginia, Kentucky, and Tennessee have some of the highest rates of opioid addiction and overdose in the country. A 2019 report indicated that West Virginia had the highest overdose death rate in the United States, at 52 deaths per 100,000 people, nearly three times the national average (Appalachian Regional Commission, 2019). The Appalachian region has been particularly vulnerable to addiction due to a combination of economic hardship, high unemployment rates, and limited access to quality healthcare.

Just as moonshine was once a symbol of the region's defiance and resourcefulness, today's meth labs and opioid addiction represent a new kind of rebellion against the hardships of life in the mountains. But where moonshine was often a communal effort, passed down through generations of families, the current drug crisis is tearing families apart, leaving behind a trail of devastation that reaches deep into the heart of Appalachia.

[xxxviii]Martha was raised in a small town in Appalachia, where faith and family were the cornerstones of life. By her mid-twenties, addiction had taken over her life, but her challenges went far deeper. For years, she had endured an abusive marriage. Her husband controlled every aspect of her life, her finances, her movements, and even her access to treatment. When Martha first tried to get clean through 12-step programs, she felt hopeless and defeated. The 12-step model, with its focus on powerlessness, mirrored the abuse she was experiencing at home. "How can I recover if I have to admit I'm powerless when I already feel powerless every day of my life?" she asked during one of our sessions.

For Martha, the idea of surrendering to something outside herself felt not only wrong but dangerous. The 12-step model's external locus of control reinforced the helplessness she had been feeling in her abusive relationship. She had already been told by her abuser that she had no control over her life. A treatment program that asked her to give up what little power she had left felt like it could be deadly.

When Martha came to me, she was on the verge of giving up. But we worked together to find a different path, one that focused on taking back control of her life rather than surrendering it. Through a strength-based model of recovery, Martha began to reconnect with the inner resilience that had kept her going through years of domestic violence. She found the strength not only to leave her abusive husband but to take her children with her and start over.

This model allowed Martha to see that while addiction had taken much from her, it hadn't taken everything. She still had the power to protect herself and her children. She found housing, secured a job, and began rebuilding her life. By embracing her inner strength rather than focusing on her perceived powerlessness, Martha was able to move out of a dangerous situation and create a new life for her family. Her journey to recovery was not about surrender; it was about empowerment, and it saved her life.

[xxxix]Jake, like so many others in the region, had been caught up in the opioid crisis. After a work-related injury, he was prescribed OxyContin, and before long, he found himself addicted. He had tried several 12-step programs, but they never seemed to stick. He felt that the meetings were asking him to give up control, to admit that he couldn't overcome his addiction on his own. But Jake had spent his entire life being self-reliant, fixing his own problems, and standing strong through adversity. The 12-step model just didn't align with his sense of self.

When Jake came to me, we began to explore a different approach, one that focused on reclaiming his power rather than surrendering it. We worked on building his sense of agency, helping him recognize that while addiction was a formidable challenge, he had the inner strength to face it head-on. Jake found success in this strength-based approach, learning to rely on the same self-reliance that had gotten him through other hard times in his life. It wasn't about giving up control, it was about taking it back, one step at a time.

These examples illustrate how a strength-based model of addiction recovery can resonate more deeply with the people of Appalachia. By honoring their resilience and empowering them to take control of their recovery, we can offer a more effective path to healing, one that aligns with the spirit and strength that have always been a part of the mountains.

The hills of Appalachia are rich with sayings that capture the essence of life and its lessons, passed down from generation to generation. These bits of mountain wisdom might seem simple, but they hold deep truths about navigating life's challenges. When applied to the context of addiction treatment, they offer practical insights and powerful reminders about choices, consequences, and empowerment. For clients and counselors alike, these phrases reflect the core belief that we have the power to change our circumstances if we are willing to take responsibility and make wise decisions.

Three phrases stand out in particular: "When you wallow with the pigs, expect to get dirty," "Always drink upstream from the herd," and "If you find yourself in a hole, the first thing to do is stop digging." Each of these sayings highlights a key aspect of addiction treatment and recovery, emphasizing empowerment and self-awareness rather than powerlessness.

"When You Wallow with the Pigs, Expect to Get Dirty." This old saying is about choices and consequences. In life, the company we keep and the environments we immerse ourselves in have a profound impact on who we become. If you choose to surround yourself with negativity, toxic influences, or people who encourage destructive behavior, it's only a matter of time before that behavior rubs off on you. In the context of addiction treatment, this saying serves as a powerful metaphor for clients who find themselves stuck in harmful patterns.

Many people struggling with addiction are caught in a cycle where their social environments reinforce their substance use. Whether it's a group of friends who use drugs together, family members who enable unhealthy behaviors, or environments where substances are easily accessible, staying in these spaces makes it nearly impossible to break free. "Wallowing with the Pigs" is about recognizing that if you remain in a dirty, destructive environment, you will get dirty, too.

For clients, this means looking honestly at the people and places they surround themselves with. Are they conducive to recovery, or are they pulling them back into addiction? It's not about blaming others but about recognizing that we have the power to choose where we spend our time and who we allow into our lives.

For counselors, this phrase is a reminder to encourage clients to take ownership of their environments. Empowerment in addiction treatment often starts with helping clients realize that they have the agency to change their surroundings. They don't have to continue "wallowing" in environments that are hurting them. With support, they can make choices that promote their well-being, even if that means leaving behind people or places that were once central to their lives.

"Always Drink Upstream from the Herd" In Appalachia, this saying is about making smart decisions, especially when it comes to avoiding contamination. Drinking upstream from the herd means finding clarity and purity away from the mess of the crowd. It's a reminder that just because everyone else is doing something doesn't mean it's right for you.

In addiction treatment, this phrase speaks to the importance of avoiding the unhealthy influences that everyone else may be participating in. Often, people struggling with addiction find themselves following the crowd, whether that's continuing to use substances because it's normalized in their social circles or engaging in behaviors that aren't aligned with their own recovery goals simply because "everyone else is doing it." Drinking upstream is about finding your own path, one that's free from the contamination of the crowd and leads to a healthier, clearer future.

For clients, this means learning to trust their own instincts to make choices based on what's right for them rather than following the crowd. Recovery is often a path that requires stepping away from the familiar, from the herd, and finding a new direction. It's about understanding that what's best for the group may not be what's best for them, and that's okay.

For counselors, the message here is to help clients recognize their unique path to recovery. Everyone's journey is different, and what works for one person might not work for another. By encouraging clients to "drink upstream," we help them find clarity in their own lives, away from the influences that led them to addiction in the first place. This is about empowerment, showing clients that they have the ability to choose their own path, even if it means going against the grain.

This piece of Appalachian wisdom is straightforward and powerful: if you're in a bad situation, continuing to do the same thing that got you there won't help. The first step to getting out is to stop making things worse. In the context of addiction, this saying is a wake-up call for clients who are stuck in a cycle of self-destructive behavior. It's easy to keep digging deeper, whether that's through denial, excuses, or continued substance use, but at some point, you have to stop.

For clients, this is about recognizing that they have the power to stop digging. It doesn't mean they'll immediately climb out of the hole they're in, but stopping the behaviors that are making things worse is the first critical step. In addiction treatment, this might mean recognizing when denial is keeping them stuck, when they're blaming others for their situation, or when they're engaging in behaviors that sabotage their recovery. The hole won't get any deeper if they stop digging, and that's the beginning of the way out.

For counselors, this saying is about helping clients take that first step, stopping the behaviors that are hurting them. It's not about overwhelming them with the enormity of the task ahead but about empowering them to make one key decision: stop the actions that keep them trapped. From there, we can work together to find a way out.

All three of these Appalachian sayings point again to one central theme: empowerment. They remind us that we have choices, even in difficult circumstances, and those choices matter. In addiction treatment, the message of empowerment is crucial. Too often, the focus is on powerlessness, on the idea that individuals struggling with addiction have no control over their lives. But that perspective can be harmful. It reinforces the idea that people are at the mercy of their circumstances rather than agents of their own change.

As therapists and counselors, we must shift the narrative. Yes, addiction is powerful, and yes, recovery is challenging, but people are capable of making choices that lead to healing. Empowerment in addiction treatment means helping clients see that they have the ability to change their environments, choose healthier influences, and stop the behaviors that are keeping them stuck.

These Appalachian sayings are simple, but they're grounded in the wisdom of people who understood that life is about choices. When you wallow with the pigs, expect to get dirty. So, choose to step out of the mud. Always drink upstream from the herd; don't follow the crowd blindly but find your own way to clarity and health. And if you're in a hole, stop digging because that's the first step toward climbing out.

Recovery is possible, not because people are powerless, but because they are powerful. They have the strength to make better choices, to change their lives, and to overcome the obstacles before them. And as counselors, it's our job to help them see that power within themselves, to believe in their ability to heal, and to support them as they take those steps toward a brighter, healthier future.

The Family of Destiny

Destiny was our firstborn, and from the moment she entered our lives, she brought light and joy to our home. She was a delight to her mother and me; she was cute, precocious, and full of personality. Like most firstborns, she challenged us as new parents in ways we couldn't have predicted. Her stubborn streak made us quickly realize that raising a child required not just love but patience, creativity, and sometimes a bit of humor.

I remember one of our early lessons in parenting: trying to teach Destiny the importance of picking up after herself. As a young child, she loved playing with her toys and blocks, but when it came time to clean up, she wasn't always eager to cooperate. We would tell her, "If you bring your toys out, you always need to put them away." But as any parent knows, telling a child something doesn't always make it happen.

So, we got creative. I remember how we would turn the task of picking up her blocks into a game, inventing a "block monster" who loved to eat blocks and needed to be fed. We'd take the large block bag and pretend it was this hungry creature, and most of the time, Destiny would delight in feeding the block monster until all of the blocks were picked up. But there were times when even the block monster trick didn't work, and we had to discipline her in a way she could understand at her age.

Destiny, like most children, wanted our full attention. If she thought we weren't truly listening to her, she would grab our faces in her small hands, and with all the seriousness she could muster, she'd say, "Oook at me… Oook at me!" She wasn't going to let us get away with half-hearted attention. She needed to know that we were fully present with her.

This need to be heard and understood is universal. It's not just children who demand our attention; it's something we all crave. Destiny, even as a little girl, was no different. She wanted her parents' attention, and she was determined to get it. And as I think about it, I realize that this need is deeply embedded in our work as counselors.

One memory that sticks out to me is a conversation Destiny had with us when she was around three or four years old. She had just returned from Sunday School and wanted to process a lesson she'd learned about heaven. Her teachers had explained that heaven was a wonderful place and that you could go there when you die. Destiny, like most children, had a vivid imagination and was constantly trying to piece together how the world worked.

I remember seeing the wheels turning in her little head as she pondered the idea of heaven. She liked the sound of heaven, but the idea of dying didn't sit well with her. Finally, she asked, "Instead of dying, can we just take the car there?"

That question stopped us in our tracks. How do you answer a child who's grappling with the big questions of life and death? She was too young to understand the complexities but too smart to brush them off. We were left speechless because her question wasn't something we could just explain away. It required understanding, respect, and a thoughtful response. Dang, I still don't know the answers to some of these questions!

These stories about Destiny have stuck with me, not just because they remind me of my daughter's childhood but because they carry valuable lessons for my work as a counselor. At its core, counseling is about seeing and hearing our clients, truly seeing them, not just skimming the surface of their experiences. Like Destiny demanding that we "look at her," clients come to us with the same need: to be heard, understood, and seen for who they are, without judgment.

Just like Destiny grabbing my face and saying, "Oook at me," our clients often seek our undivided attention. In our fast-paced world, people are used to not being fully heard. Many of them come into therapy not necessarily for answers but for the experience of being understood and validated. As counselors, it's our job to listen deeply, not just to the words they say but to the emotions behind those words. Destiny wanted us to understand the world from her perspective, and in many ways, our clients want the same thing. They need us to enter their world without imposing our own judgments or solutions.

When Destiny asked about driving to heaven instead of dying, I could have given her a complicated theological answer, but she wouldn't have understood it. Sometimes, the best thing we can do as counselors is to admit that we don't have all the answers. Clients, like children, appreciate honesty and respect more than a well-rehearsed explanation. When we acknowledge that some questions don't have easy answers, it opens up space for exploration and growth. We don't need to know everything; we just need to be present and willing to walk alongside our clients as they navigate their own questions and struggles.

Destiny, like most children, didn't need a long explanation about why she should pick up her blocks. What she needed was the experience of doing it herself, of being guided and supported as she learned. In therapy, the same principle applies.

Clients don't change because of the ideas we share with them; they change because of the experiences they have with us. Whether it's the experience of being heard, of confronting painful emotions, or of trying new behaviors in a safe environment, it's these lived experiences that lead to transformation.

Destiny's question about heaven wasn't just a cute moment; it was an example of how children and clients process information at their own level. As counselors, we need to meet clients where they are, emotionally, intellectually, and experientially. Trying to force clients to see the world through our lens doesn't help them grow. Instead, we need to respect their perspective, even if it's different from our own, and guide them gently toward insight and change.

The lessons from Destiny's childhood remind me that therapy isn't about giving clients all the answers or fixing their problems for them. It's about creating a space where they can explore their own questions, make their own discoveries, and grow in their own time. Sometimes, as counselors, we simply need to sit with them in the uncertainty, offering empathy and understanding without judgment or haste.

Just as Destiny wanted us to see her and take her seriously, our clients want the same. They want to know that their thoughts, feelings, and experiences matter. And just like we learned to be patient and creative with Destiny, we must bring those same qualities into our work with clients

In the end, it's not about having the perfect answer or the right solution. It's about being present, offering a safe space, and guiding clients toward the answers they already have within themselves. Like watching a child grow and learn, the transformation in therapy comes not from what we tell them but from what they discover through their own experiences, supported by a therapist who sees them fully and respects the journey they're on.

Legacy of Family Loyalty

Family is the cornerstone of my Kentucky life. From the smallest moments to the most dramatic acts of heroism, the ties that bind us run deep, and they have long served as the backbone of trust, protection, and loyalty. One story that illustrates this family bond happened on a summer day at Nolin Park, near the Nolin River Dam, close to Mammoth Cave, Kentucky, a place where my mother's side of the family had lived for generations. It was at a family reunion that [xli]Brittany, my second to eldest daughter, saved her younger brother Milo, reinforcing a lesson that has always been central to Appalachian values: family looks out for one another.

Milo, being the adventurous type, wandered too far into the swift currents of the river. It didn't take long before he was swept off his feet, struggling to keep his head above water. Without a moment's hesitation, Brittany jumped into the water, not caring about the danger to herself. She grabbed Milo, and with the combined strength of her will and his determination, they both made it safely back to shore. That day, Brittany became Milo's hero, and in true Kentucky fashion, family once again proved to be the foundation of survival.

But this instinct to protect family, especially in the face of danger or adversity, isn't unique to our generation. It's something that has been passed down through the stories, struggles, and sacrifices of our ancestors.

The Carroll Family Coat of Arms from Ireland.

The deep bond within our family can be traced back to the old country of Ireland. My mother's family, the Carroll's of the O'Carroll clan, had long carried with them a distrust of authority, which was deeply ingrained in their identity. This distrust stemmed from the centuries of conflict between the Irish people and the

British government. Many families, including my own, brought these attitudes with them to rural Kentucky, where they would continue to view the government with suspicion, a sentiment only reinforced by local experiences.

One such story of betrayal involved my great-granduncle [xlii]Forrest, who was killed by a sheriff at the site of a moonshine still. Forrest was no outlaw, but like many Appalachian families, he relied on moonshine as a means of survival in tough economic times. Moonshining, especially after the Civil War, was more than just a way to make a living; it was an act of defiance against a government that had long taken more than it gave.

In 1924, Forrest's son Earl had taken a job working on a farm owned by a young man named Ray Priddy. Ray, like many others struggling during the Great Depression, decided to make moonshine to earn enough money to buy fertilizer for his spring crops. He assured Forrest that this would be a one-time thing, just enough to get by. Despite Forrest's warning that he didn't want his son Earl involved, Ray persisted, and on the night they were set to draw off the "first shots" of moonshine, they asked Forrest to bring supper to the still site.

That night, Forrest arrived at the still with a small bottle, intending to fill it with moonshine as part of a joke they planned to play on Forrest's nephew, Everett Carroll. But while he was filling the bottle, a sheriff and his deputy moved in on the operation. Earl hid behind a barrel while Ray ran and was shot in the chest. Forrest, standing up with nothing but a bottle in his hand, was shot and killed by the sheriff. The sheriff later claimed he thought the bottle was a gun, but the truth of that claim was questionable. The local newspaper, the *Glasgow Times*, referred to the incident as a "shootout," yet no mention was made of any guns being present on my family's side.

The senseless killing of Forrest further deepened the family's already-rooted distrust of law enforcement and government authority. Lije, another family member, went to Brownsville to see if anything could be done to hold the sheriff accountable, but his efforts were in vain. Like so many other tragedies in Kentucky history, Forrest's death was written off as just another casualty of law enforcement overreach in a poor, forgotten region.

This incident wasn't just a story of personal loss; it was a tale that echoed the generations-long distrust of authority that had been passed down from Ireland. For the Carrolls and other families like them, the government wasn't something to be trusted. This mistrust would only be further reinforced when, decades later, the government seized prime farmland to create Nolin Lake, uprooting graves and displacing families without proper compensation. Once again, the Carrolls were left feeling betrayed by the very authorities who were supposed to protect them.

The distrust of the government also manifested in the way families handled their own disputes. In Appalachia, when someone wronged a family member, they didn't wait for the authorities to step in. The family was the authority. Nightriders, as they were often called, were local men who took justice into their own hands, especially in matters of protecting the family. If a husband abused his wife, her brothers and cousins would show up in the dead of night to deliver swift, silent retribution. There was no room for second chances when it came to hurting a loved one.

This kind of vigilante justice wasn't always about violence; sometimes, it was about sending a message and ensuring that the perpetrator knew the consequences of crossing a family. In a world where the law couldn't always be relied upon to protect the vulnerable, family stepped in. It was a harsh but effective system. It created a culture of accountability where trust and protection were paramount.

These stories, whether it's Brittany saving Milo from the river, Forrest being killed at the moonshine still, or the legacy of nightriders, are more than just family tales. They are part of a cultural narrative that teaches us about loyalty, protection, and the importance of family bonds. As counselors, especially when working with clients from Appalachian backgrounds or other tight-knit communities, it's essential to understand the central role that family plays.

In Appalachia, trust doesn't come easily, especially not with outsiders or institutions. For many families, the only people they can truly rely on are their kin. Understanding this cultural context is crucial when working with clients struggling to trust counselors, the government, or any authority figures. For these clients, building trust is a slow process, one that requires patience and genuine care. It is often through the counselor-client relationship, much like family relationships, that healing and growth take place.

While family can be a source of immense strength and support, it can also create complex dynamics that make therapy challenging. Loyalty to family can sometimes prevent clients from setting healthy boundaries, especially when that loyalty is ingrained in cultural identity. Counselors need to help clients navigate these dynamics, understanding when family is a source of resilience and when it may be a barrier to personal growth.

For many Appalachian families, distrust of authority is passed down through generations, rooted in real historical betrayals, like the killing of Forrest or the exhumation of family graves for Nolin Lake. This mistrust can manifest in therapy, as clients may be wary of counselors who represent systems they've been taught to distrust. Therapists working in this context must be aware of this cultural legacy and take the time to earn their clients' trust.

Just as Brittany saved Milo from drowning, the family often acts as a lifeline for those in distress. In times of crisis, clients may turn to their families for support, even when those relationships are strained. As counselors, we can help clients strengthen these bonds or establish new ways of connecting with family members. Whether its helping clients repair broken relationships or guiding them to set boundaries, the role of family in healing should never be underestimated.

The story of Brittany helping Milo is more than just a tale of sibling love and courage. It's a reflection of the deeper values that run through Appalachian life:

loyalty, protection, and the enduring strength of family. Whether it's jumping into a river to save a loved one or standing up against government oppression, the family is the cornerstone of trust in this region.

As counselors, we must recognize the importance of these family bonds while also understanding the challenges they can present. Our role is to help clients navigate the complexities of family loyalty and distrust of authority, helping them find balance, healing, and personal growth. In the end, just as Brittany reached out to save Milo, we, too, must extend our hands to those who are struggling, offering support and guidance as they navigate the swift currents of life.

Blood Is Thicker Than Water

Family is the foundation of who we are, shaping our identities, values, and relationships. It's where we find unconditional love, support, and often the most difficult challenges we'll ever face. In my work as a therapist and educator, I've seen countless families struggle, fracture, and heal through life's transitions. But my deepest understanding of the importance of family comes from my own experience with my youngest child, Milo.

[xliii]Milo has always been precocious, creative, and wonderfully unique. From the time he was small, I encouraged all my children to find their own path in life, to dare to be different, and to explore the world in ways that made sense to them. In many ways, Milo was just following my advice when he made a major decision as an adult. Yet, despite my words of encouragement over the years, when the time came for this life transition, it was incredibly difficult for me and Dawn, his mother.

This wasn't just a difficult time for us as parents, it was a shockwave that reverberated throughout our entire family. Milo's decision challenged our understanding of everything we thought we knew about our child and about ourselves. It's one thing to tell your children to find their way, but it's another thing entirely to face the reality when their path leads them somewhere you weren't prepared to go.

Milo, true to his nature, sought guidance and support during this transition. He entered therapy and, in Milo's wisdom, asked me to join him. As a close-knit family, it was natural for him to want our support, but I wasn't as fully supportive at the time as I should have been. This life transition was overwhelming for me, and I struggled to navigate my feelings as a father while also being the board chair of the Kentucky Board of Licensed Professional Counselors and the founding Dean of the School of Counseling at the University of the Cumberlands.

It was a humbling experience to sit in therapy, not as the expert, but as a parent trying to understand and support my child. Milo invited me into his therapeutic process, hoping we could bridge the gap that had opened between us. During one of our sessions, Milo shared how much he loved me and how nothing could ever change that love. He also asked me to accept his decision and to fully support him on this journey. I expressed my own love for him and my deep commitment to our relationship, but I wasn't yet at a place where I could offer the full support he was asking for. The changes happening were too new, too unexpected, and I was still coming to terms with them.

Then, the therapist offered a piece of advice that could have shattered our family. Looking at Milo, the therapist suggested that he might need to seek support from another family if we, his parents, couldn't provide the acceptance he needed. Hearing those words was like a knife to the heart. I couldn't believe what I was hearing. After 18+ years of love, care, and family bonds, the idea that Milo should seek support from others instead of working through the complexity of our family dynamics felt incredibly wrong.

It's true that major life transitions create resistance, and resistance can be difficult to handle. However, what the therapist failed to recognize is that resistance is often a natural part of change. It takes time for families to process, adapt, and ultimately embrace new realities. Suggesting that Milo push us aside rather than giving us the time to work through our emotions and reach a place of understanding could have torn our family apart for decades.

Thankfully, Milo didn't take that advice. He didn't walk away from his family. Instead, he gave us all the time and space we needed to work through our feelings and come to a place of mutual acceptance. As a family, we could negotiate the complexities of this transition, not by separating but by leaning into the love we had for one another. We worked through our differences, had difficult conversations, and ultimately grew closer through the process.

Family isn't perfect. It's messy, complicated, and sometimes painful. But what makes a family so powerful is its ability to endure. Blood truly is thicker than water. The bonds that tie us together are not easily broken, and when we are given the time to navigate our struggles, those bonds become even stronger. Milo's transition was a major challenge for our family, but today, I am incredibly proud of who he has become.

Through this experience, I've learned that family is about more than just support during the easy times. It's about staying connected through the difficult times, the moments of resistance, and the challenges that force us to grow. It's about recognizing that while acceptance may take time, love is constant. Our roots run deep, and those roots, family, love, and loyalty, are worth protecting and nurturing, even in the face of change.

In reflection, I'm grateful that we didn't take the therapist's advice to sever ties in the face of difficulty. We were given the opportunity to grow together as a family, and today, I'm proud to say that we are stronger for it. Milo's courage and perseverance through this transition have been remarkable, and the love we share as a family has only deepened as a result.

This experience reaffirmed for me the importance of family and the enduring strength of those bonds. No matter how much things change, no matter how hard it gets, family is a place where love, time, and understanding can always prevail. In the end, it's that love that carries us through the hardest transitions and allows us to emerge stronger together.

Never Bored

In today's society, boredom is a common complaint, but growing up in Kentucky, boredom was a concept that seemed almost foreign. Children and adults alike always had something to do, there was never an idle moment. Whether it was exploring the woods, playing in creeks, taking care of animals, or helping with household chores, there was always something to engage the body and mind. Family time was sacred, and religion also played a significant role in shaping daily life. The combination of hard work and meaningful connection left little room for boredom or dissatisfaction.

Children, especially, were never at a loss for things to do. There were wide-open spaces for running, climbing, and discovering new adventures. Nature was the playground, and chores were a natural part of growing up. From feeding the animals to tending gardens, children learned responsibility early, and those tasks gave them a sense of purpose and pride. In contrast, today's children often live in a world dominated by screens, constantly seeking stimulation but rarely finding satisfaction. In Appalachia, satisfaction came from the simple things, connection to the land, to family, and to the rhythm of life.

Parents, too, were always busy. They worked hard, whether it was on the farm, in the home, in town or in the mines. Yet they also found time to enjoy life and each other. There was a balance between labor and play. Church socials, family gatherings, and simple evening conversations on the porch were common, and they provided opportunities for intimacy, connection, and joy. There was a deep bond between partners, a bond that went beyond just raising children or getting through the day. It was about being a team, a partnership rooted in mutual respect, love, and intimacy.

In my counseling practice, I see a stark contrast to this. Modern life seems to be filled with distractions, but it is also filled with dissatisfaction, particularly in relationships. Our culture is often hyper-focused on sex, with advertising, entertainment, and social media all pushing the message that sexuality is at the core of happiness. Yet, ironically, many couples in therapy report that they have stopped having sex long before old age or health issues even come into play. Many have resorted to substitutes, pornography, masturbation, and emotional detachment, trying to fill the void that a once-loving relationship used to satisfy.

Masturbation can be a healthy outlet, but it should never replace the deep, intimate connection that a person shares with their partner. In my sessions, I've seen how many people turn to these substitutes not because they want to but because they've lost the closeness that should naturally come from being in a committed relationship. In contrast, when I look at the lives of my Kentucky ancestors, I see couples who didn't just survive; they thrived in their relationships. They worked hard and loved deeply, with an intimacy that ran deeper than physical attraction. They understood that life's greatest joys were shared, whether that was raising children, tending the farm, or sharing the intimacy of their marriage bed.

People often make the mistake of viewing the Appalachian lifestyle as backward or unsophisticated. But when you look deeper, you find a culture that understood the secret to happiness far better than modern society does. While the rest of the world today seems obsessed with pleasure-seeking and fleeting distractions, people in the mountains of Appalachia found contentment in their families, in their faith, and in their relationships. Intimacy between couples wasn't something that was easily cast aside. The partnership was everything, and it was nurtured through the ups and downs of life.

When I look at my family tree, I can't help but notice the sheer size of my ancestors' families. My grandparents, great-grandparents, and even earlier ancestors often had 10, 14, or even more children. [xliv]John "Turkey" Green Watson, one of my grandfathers, was a Civil War veteran who married three times. His first wife, Piety Ann Carmen, bore him over ten children, including Elizabeth Serena Watson, who married W.P. Martin, as mentioned earlier. After Piety Ann passed away, Turkey remarried, this time to Charlotte "Lotty" Cundiff, and had another five or six children. When Lotty passed, Turkey, at the age of 73, married his third wife, Quintella Carman, and fathered yet another child, Eva Watson, when he was nearly 80 years old. Eva lived until 2009 and was one of the last daughters of a Civil War veteran.

George "Turkey" Green Watson, Quintella and Eva Watson

It's clear to me that my ancestors were not only hard workers, but they were also deeply connected to their spouses. They found joy and satisfaction in the intimate partnership of marriage, and that bond extended to raising children and building a life together. While today's couples often give up on intimacy for reasons that seem less significant than health or age, my ancestors found ways to keep that part of their relationship alive and thriving, even when life was difficult.

Turkey Watson's life alone tells a story of love, resilience, and vitality. Despite the hardships of war and the loss of two wives, he continued to seek companionship and love, even into his later years. His marriage to Quintella Carman when he was in his seventies and the birth of his daughter Eva when he was almost 80 shows a man who believed in the power of love and family. His story isn't just one of procreation; it's a testament to the idea that love and intimacy can endure throughout life, no matter how old we become or how many challenges we face.

When I work with couples today, I often reflect on the values that my ancestors embodied: hard work, commitment, intimacy, and love. I see many couples who have given up on these things, resigning themselves to lives of isolation even while living under the same roof. In Appalachia, people understood the importance of their partner, not just as a co-parent or fellow laborer, but as a true helpmate, someone with whom life's joys and struggles could be shared.

As a therapist, I try to help couples rediscover that connection. It's not about recapturing youthful passion but about reigniting the bond that once held them together. Intimacy, in all its forms, is an essential part of a healthy relationship, and it's worth fighting for. When couples lose that connection, they often look elsewhere for satisfaction, but the truth is that the deepest fulfillment comes from the love shared between partners.

In reflecting on the lives of my ancestors, I see a wisdom that many couples today have forgotten. Love is not something that fades away with time, it's something that can grow deeper when nurtured. My Appalachian ancestors may not have had the luxuries or distractions of modern life, but they had something far more valuable: a deep understanding of what it means to love and be loved, to work and play together, and to find joy in the simple, intimate moments of life. And that, perhaps, is the real secret to happiness.

Grandma Doreen and Grandpa Cortez Wesley

Resilience in War and Conflict

Resilience is a quality deeply embedded in the culture of Appalachia. It's not just about surviving hardships but about persevering with strength, determination, and a sense of purpose. This quality has been passed down through generations, particularly in times of war and conflict, when both physical and emotional endurance were put to the test. As I reflect on the legacy of resilience in my family and in the people of Appalachia, I'm reminded of the incredible stories of those who served their country, faced immense hardships, and emerged stronger for it.

From my great-granduncle, Daniel Boone, who fought for the survival of the American frontier during the Revolutionary War, to my great-granduncle Lewis Carroll and John "Turkey" Green Watson who served the Union in the Civil War, to my great-uncle Kenneth Martin fighting in the Battle of the Bulge during WWII and liberating prisoners from Nazi concentration camps, and to my cousin Dwight D. Eisenhower, one of the most influential military leaders and presidents in American history, and finally my uncle Truman Carroll a decorated Vietnam war veteran, the spirit of resilience in war has shaped the legacy of my family and the people of Appalachia. These stories illustrate not only the bravery of individual soldiers but also the enduring strength of the Appalachian people and their commitment to service, family, and country.

Though ^{xlv}Daniel Boone is often remembered for his exploits as a trailblazer and pioneer, his role as a soldier during the Revolutionary War is equally significant. Boone served as a Lieutenant Colonel in the Virginia militia, and his experiences in wartime highlight the resilience and strategic mind of a man who was no stranger to hardship.

During the Revolutionary War, Boone was stationed at Boonesborough, a frontier settlement he had helped establish in Kentucky. The settlement was under near-constant threat from British forces and their Native American allies. Boone's knowledge of the land and his experience as a frontiersman made him an invaluable leader during these dangerous times. In 1778, Boone was captured by Shawnee warriors allied with the British while hunting for salt to preserve food for the settlement. This could have been the end for most men, but Boone's resilience and tactical thinking helped him survive.

Boone not only earned the respect of his captors during his time with them but also escaped after four months in captivity, traveling more than 160 miles on foot to warn Boonesborough of an impending attack. His return to the settlement wasn't just a personal victory, it helped save countless lives. Under his leadership, the settlers were able to prepare for the attack and ultimately defend Boonesborough against a siege that lasted more than nine days. Boone's resilience during this time wasn't just physical; it was mental and emotional as well. His ability to endure captivity, escape, and lead his people in a time of war illustrates the profound strength that defined his character.

Even after the war, Boone faced numerous personal challenges, including financial ruin and the loss of land he had fought so hard to settle. But through it all, he remained a symbol of resilience, never giving up on his vision or his belief in the frontier life. Boone's experience as a soldier and a leader during the Revolutionary War is a testament to the endurance and strength that have become hallmarks of Appalachian character.

Another powerful example of resilience in my family comes from my great-grandfather, [xlvi]John "Turkey" Green Watson, a U.S. Civil War veteran who fought for the Confederacy. Watson's life was marked by war, loss, and hardship, yet he persevered and built a large family that would carry on his legacy of resilience.

Turkey Watson served during one of the most tumultuous times in American history. He joined the army at the courthouse in Adair County, Kentucky. There, he became one of the Wild Riders led by Frank Lane Wolford. The Wild Riders fought at the Battles of Wildcat Mountain, Mill Springs, and Perryville, but mostly they guarded Kentucky railroads, bridges, and supply depots. Confederate cavalry, including General John Hunt Morgan and his raiders, kept the Union forces in Kentucky constantly on guard and in pursuit. However, the Wild Riders would eventually take down Morgan and end his scourge in Kentucky. The Civil War tore families apart, especially in Kentucky, devastated communities, and left scars that would take generations to heal. For Watson, as for many soldiers, the war wasn't just about fighting on the battlefield; it was about surviving the emotional and physical toll it took on him and his family. After the war, Turkey Watson faced the struggles of Reconstruction, navigating a divided and deeply wounded state and nation.

Yet despite these challenges, Watson built a family and a legacy that spanned generations. He married three times, fathered children into his seventies, and remained a figure of strength and endurance in his community. His story of perseverance, like that of many Appalachian soldiers, speaks to the deep well of resilience that allowed him not only to survive but to thrive in the face of adversity. Even after enduring the devastation of war and loss, Watson remained focused on rebuilding his life and ensuring a future for his children.

John "Turkey" Green Watson

One story that stands out as a testament to both the personal and familial resilience in war is that of my second great-uncle, [xlvii]Lewis Miles Carroll. A soldier fighting for the Union Army during the Civil War, Lewis found himself in one of the bloodiest and most devastating conflicts in American history. He fought valiantly at the Battle of Chickamauga, but like many others during that battle, his fate took a tragic turn when he was captured as a prisoner of war by Confederate forces.

After his capture, Lewis was sent to the notorious Andersonville prison in Georgia. Andersonville was infamous for its horrific conditions. Overcrowded and undersupplied, it became a death trap for thousands of Union soldiers. Diseases like dysentery, scurvy, and typhoid ravaged the prison, and Lewis became one of its many casualties, succumbing to dysentery after enduring months of suffering.

Despite the dire conditions, Lewis managed to send a final letter to his family before he passed. My mother, Norma, recalls seeing the original letter encased in glass when she was young. Though the original has since been lost, I still have a copy of this precious letter. It serves as a powerful reminder of the love Lewis had for both his family and his country. Even in the face of unimaginable suffering, he reached out to express his devotion to his family and to ensure that they knew of his enduring love for them. His legacy, preserved in that letter, became a symbol of the Carroll family's resilience and the sacrifices made for the United States.

Lewis Miles Carroll's life and death are a testament to the power of family ties and the deep connection that Appalachian soldiers often had to their loved ones. His final act, sending that letter, reminds me of the strength and courage it took not just to endure the hardships of war but to continue loving and thinking of others even in his darkest moments.

Another powerful story of wartime resilience comes from my cousin Dr. Larry Kenneth Martin, who shared with me a deeply personal memory about his father, Cpl. Arnold Kenneth Martin. Like many Appalachian boys of his generation, Arnold left the farm fields of Kentucky and answered the call to serve in World

War II. Appalachians have long been known to serve in high numbers in the armed forces; patriotism, duty, and sacrifice running deep in our hills and hollers. In fact, statistics confirm that the Appalachian region has contributed more soldiers per capita than nearly any other part of the country during major conflicts.

Cpl. Martin didn't talk about the war for decades, which was not uncommon for men of his generation, especially those who had seen unspeakable things. But in his final years, while living in a nursing home in Louisville, he quietly shared a story with his son that had been locked away in silence for more than 70 years. Looking over at Larry one day, he said in a hushed voice, "You know, near the end of the war, we found one of those camps, and we set them free."

Larry realized instantly what he meant. His father had helped liberate a Nazi concentration camp.

Later research confirmed that Arnold Kenneth Martin had been part of the 8th Infantry Division, which, alongside the 82nd Airborne Division, liberated the Wobbelin Subcamp in northern Germany. The camp had held over 5,000 prisoners in horrific conditions. Bodies were stacked four and five feet high. The few survivors left were so starved that they could barely eat the rations offered by U.S. soldiers. The stench of death was so pervasive that the U.S. Army ordered local townspeople to walk through the camp and assist in burying the dead.

Uncle Kenneth never forgot what he saw. For most of his life, he buried that memory, never mentioning it, not even to his sons, with whom he shared countless hours on their family farm in Kentucky. But in his 90s, after taking part in an Honor Flight to Washington D.C. and then back to Louisville, where he finally received the welcome home he was never given after the war, uncle Kenneth started opening up. That single trip may have unlocked the door for a long-buried story to finally find its way into the light.

Larry recalled the details of their daily time together, of a father and son bound by fieldwork and familiarity, yet never speaking of the horror his father had witnessed. That was the resilience of men like my uncle Kenneth, not just to endure trauma but to carry it quietly while still building a family, working the land, and giving to their communities.

This story, like so many in Appalachia, reflects a quiet strength passed from one generation to the next. A strength forged in hardship, tempered by duty, and softened by the unbreakable bonds of family and place.

[xlviii]Dwight D. Eisenhower, a cousin of mine through his connection to Sarah Boone, Daniel Boone's sister, offers another powerful example of resilience in the face of war. While Eisenhower is best known for his role as the Supreme Commander of the Allied Expeditionary Forces during World War II and later as the 34th President of the United States, his leadership was forged in the fires of conflict.

Eisenhower's rise to prominence during World War II was marked by his ability to navigate the complexities of war with calm, strategic thinking. Tasked with coordinating the Allied invasion of Normandy on D-Day, Eisenhower faced enormous pressure. The success or failure of the entire operation and the world rested on his shoulders. Yet, despite the weight of the world's expectations, Eisenhower displayed the resilience that had been passed down through generations of his Appalachian ancestors.

Eisenhower's ability to balance the demands of leadership with compassion for his soldiers made him one of the most respected military leaders in history. After the war, he continued to serve his country as president, guiding the nation through the post-war years with the same resilience and steady leadership that had defined his military career.

His connection to the Boone family only deepens my understanding of how deeply rooted resilience is in our lineage. Eisenhower, like Daniel Boone, faced adversity head-on and used his leadership to inspire and uplift those around him. His legacy, both as a military leader and as a president, continues to be a testament to the strength and endurance that define the Appalachian spirit.

Dwight D. Eisenhower on June 5, 1944 - DDE speaks with paratroopers of the 101st Airborne Division just before they board their planes to participate in the first assault of the Normandy invasion.

One of the most decorated veterans in my family is my uncle, [xlix]Truman Carroll. His service during the Vietnam conflict is a testament to the extraordinary courage and resilience that runs deep in the Kentucky spirit. During his time in Vietnam, Truman received two Silver Stars, four Bronze Stars, and two Purple Hearts, among other commendations, for his bravery and dedication to his fellow soldiers.

One of his Silver Stars tells a particularly remarkable story of gallantry in the face of danger. The official citation reads:

"The President of the United States of America, authorized by Act of Congress July 9, 1918 (amended by an act of July 25, 1963), takes pleasure in presenting the Silver Star to Sergeant Truman D. Carroll (ASN: US-51942671), United States Army, for gallantry in action while engaged in military operations involving conflict with an armed hostile force in the Republic of Vietnam. Sergeant Carroll distinguished himself by exceptionally valorous action on 19 February 1968 while serving as a rifleman with Company A, 1st Battalion, 12th Cavalry Regiment, 1st Cavalry Division (Airmobile), during a search and destroy mission near Long Quang, Republic of Vietnam. When his unit became heavily engaged with a large enemy force, Sergeant Carroll exposed himself to the hostile fire as he personally assaulted and destroyed an enemy bunker. His courageous action contributed greatly to the successful completion of his unit's mission. Sergeant Carroll's gallant action was in keeping with the highest traditions of military service and reflects great credit upon himself, his unit, and the United States Army."

In this moment of incredible danger, my uncle's bravery was on full display. He could have stayed back and avoided the intense firefight, but instead, he charged forward, putting his life on the line to protect his fellow soldiers. This is the essence of resilience and courage, facing fear and danger head-on, not for personal glory, but out of a sense of duty and commitment to others. Truman's actions that day helped secure the success of his unit's mission and saved the lives of many men who depended on him.

Truman's military career didn't just reflect a single act of bravery; it was filled with moments where his resilience shone through. His other metals further attest to the sacrifices he made during his service in Vietnam. The Vietnam War was a brutal conflict, testing the physical and mental endurance of every soldier who served there. The conditions were harsh, the enemy relentless, and the stakes were always life and death. For Truman, however, the war became a defining moment of his life, and he rose to the challenge with bravery and honor.

His medals tell the story of a man who faced some of the most challenging circumstances a soldier can endure and yet never wavered in his resolve. Truman, like so many soldiers from Kentucky, carried with him the values instilled in him by his upbringing: hard work, loyalty, courage, and a sense of duty. These values, deeply rooted in the Kentucky way of life, gave him the strength to persevere, even when the odds were stacked against him.

Truman's legacy is not just one of personal bravery but of the broader Appalachian spirit that continues to define the region's approach to hardship and conflict. His actions remind me of the countless men and women from Appalachia who, like him, have answered the call to serve their country with honor and resilience. Whether it was on the battlefields of Vietnam, the Revolutionary War, or the Civil War, the people of Appalachia have always risen to meet the challenges before them with courage and strength.

The stories of resilience in war and conflict, as exemplified by my ancestors and countless Appalachian soldiers, highlight the incredible capacity of the human spirit to endure hardship. However, resilience is not the absence of suffering. War leaves emotional and psychological scars that can persist long after the battlefield is left behind. The weight of combat, exposure to loss, survivor's guilt, and reintegration into civilian life can all create lasting mental health struggles. As therapists, we have a duty to not only honor the resilience of veterans but also to help them process their pain, heal from trauma, and reclaim a sense of purpose.

Counselors need to understand combat trauma and PTSD. Many veterans return home carrying the invisible wounds of post-traumatic stress disorder (PTSD), moral injury, and survivor's guilt. These conditions can manifest in flashbacks, nightmares, and hypervigilance. It can create emotional numbness or detachment from loved ones, difficulty trusting others or reintegrating into civilian life. It can also manifest itself in depression, anxiety, and substance use as coping mechanisms.

As counselors, we must provide trauma-informed care that acknowledges both the biological impact of trauma on the brain and the emotional complexities that veterans face. Cognitive Processing Therapy (CPT) and Prolonged Exposure Therapy (PE) may also help veterans reframe traumatic memories and gradually reduce avoidance behaviors. Eye Movement Desensitization and Reprocessing (EMDR) can assist in processing deeply ingrained traumatic memories. Finally, narrative therapy allows veterans to rewrite their stories, integrating their experiences in a way that fosters resilience rather than shame.

Counselors also need to address moral injury and survivors' guilt. Beyond PTSD, many veterans struggle with moral injury and the psychological distress of violating deeply held values during war. This may involve actions taken in combat, witnessing suffering, or struggling with decisions made under duress.

The therapeutic process may involve making meaning of these experiences. Veterans must be given space to explore what their service meant to them, how they can process regret, and how they want to define their post-war identity. Therapy can also involve guided reflection and letter writing. Writing letters to fallen comrades or to their younger selves can help address unresolved grief and survivor's guilt. Finally, therapists can encourage acts of service. Many veterans find healing through mentorship, volunteering, or advocacy work, allowing them to channel their experiences into something meaningful.

For the Appalachian veteran, there are many unique cultural considerations that need to be addressed. Many veterans from Appalachia share a strong sense of duty, loyalty, and self-reliance, which can make seeking mental health treatment challenging. They may view therapy as a sign of weakness rather than strength. Many times, family- and faith-based coping strategies are prioritized over professional help, making the work we do much more difficult. Finally, stoicism and emotional suppression may lead to untreated PTSD, depression, and substance use disorders.

As therapists working with Appalachian veterans, we must frame therapy as an extension of their resilience rather than an admission of weakness. We need to use strength-based language. Instead of saying, "You need therapy," frame it as, "Let's build a plan to strengthen the skills you already have."

We also need to consider incorporating faith and community support into therapy. There are many veterans who benefit from spiritual counseling, peer groups, or veteran mentorship programs. Engaging the family in the process may also prove to be beneficial. The tight-knit, family-centered nature of Appalachian culture means that healing is often most successful when loved ones are involved.

The impact of war is not limited to the veteran, it affects spouses, children, and extended family members as well. Intergenerational trauma is trauma that can be passed down through families, affecting relationships, parenting, and emotional well-being. Many veterans struggle to emotionally reconnect with family members after returning home, creating tension in marriages and parent-child relationships.

Interventions may include Couples Counseling by helping spouses understand PTSD, reintegration challenges, and emotional communication techniques.

Parenting support can also be helpful by teaching veterans how to reconnect with their children after deployment and how to balance discipline with emotional presence. Sometimes, psychoeducation may also play an important role because educating families on the emotional and neurological impact of war can foster compassion and patience during the healing process.

My goal in working with veterans is often to find purpose after service. Many veterans struggle with loss of identity after leaving the military. Their role in service gave them structure, purpose, and camaraderie, and adjusting to civilian life can feel disorienting. By offering career counseling, veterans can set new goals, explore meaningful careers, and find fulfillment outside the military. I also like to encourage creative expression through writing, music, art, and storytelling. These can be powerful tools for veterans to process and share their experiences. I also use existing peer support networks. Many veterans find healing through groups like Team Rubicon, the Wounded Warrior Project, or veteran storytelling programs.

The resilience of my ancestors, Daniel Boone, Lewis Miles Carroll, John "Turkey" Green Watson, Arnold Kenneth Martin, Dwight D. Eisenhower, and Truman Carroll, demonstrates that war does not just test physical endurance but also the depth of emotional and mental strength. Yet resilience does not mean enduring in silence.

As therapists, we must help veterans integrate their experiences into a meaningful narrative, one that honors their sacrifices without leaving them trapped in trauma. By providing trauma-informed care, moral injury support, family interventions, and purpose-driven counseling, we can guide veterans through their own emotional battlefield and help them reclaim a life filled with connection, meaning, and peace.

Just as my ancestors forged new frontiers in the face of adversity, therapy can be a new frontier for healing. It is not about erasing the past but about finding a way forward with honor, strength, and purpose.

Uncle Truman Carroll (left) with the mohawk haircut, in Vietnam.

The Power of Appalachian Women

The strength of Appalachian women is something that cannot be overstated. These women possess a deep well of resilience, courage, and an indomitable spirit passed down through generations. I grew up surrounded by such strong women… my grandma Doreen, Grandma Zoni, my mom, Norma, and my wife, Dawn Wesley. Each of them demonstrated a quiet but unyielding strength, providing not just for their families but for their communities as well. They navigated life's challenges with grace, grit, and wisdom that was often learned the hard way.

Grandma [l]Doreen was the backbone of her family. She raised her children with firm love and a strong sense of responsibility. Though life on the farm was never easy, she knew how to stretch every resource to make sure her family never went without. Whether it was putting up vegetables from the garden or making clothes last through countless seasons, she did what needed to be done. But it wasn't just about survival; Grandma Doreen also found ways to make life beautiful. She'd craft quilts with her own hands, each stitch representing love and care. Those quilts were more than just blankets, they were heirlooms, imbued with the legacy of family and tradition, passed down to future generations.

Then there was Grandma [li]Zoni, a woman who could see right through you, even though she was nearly blind. She had a way of understanding people that wasn't taught in books. It was intuition honed by experience. Zoni was sharp and full of wit, quick to offer a piece of wisdom wrapped in an Appalachian idiom or a joke that could leave you laughing for days. But her wisdom wasn't all humor, she embodied the kind of strength that came from faith and family. Her life wasn't easy either, but she believed in taking things one day at a time, always putting her family first and never shying away from hard work.

My mother, [lii]Norma, inherited that same strength from her mother. She balanced work, family, and faith with an ease that seemed effortless, though I know it wasn't. She instilled in us a sense of purpose and connection to our family, our community, and to nature. My mom believed in the importance of passing down values and knowledge, knowing full well that those lessons would shape our futures.

And then there's [liii]Dawn Wesley, my wife and a therapist herself, who has spent years guiding individuals and families through trauma, mental illness, and relationship issues. She is a woman of strength, using her deep empathy and therapeutic skills to help others find healing. Dawn's ability to navigate the delicate balance of work and family is a testament to her resilience. She has helped countless clients through difficult times, just as she's helped guide our own family through life's challenges. Dawn's work in the field of counseling has had a profound impact, particularly in working with families, couples, and individuals struggling with mental health issues. Her role as a therapist reflects the same enduring spirit that Appalachian women have displayed for generations, one that sees adversity and rises to meet it with love, patience, and determination.

Their stories are not unique to my family. The hills and hollers of Appalachia are full of strong women who have kept their families and communities alive through sheer will and determination. In fact, the strength of Appalachian women extends far beyond family farms and home kitchens. This is best exemplified by two of the most famous women in America in 1944: [liv]Rose Monroe, known as "Rosie the Riveter," and [lv]Venus Ramey, Miss America.

Both of these incredible women grew up only nine miles apart in Pulaski County, Kentucky; Rose from Science Hill (population 600) and Venus from Eubank (population 300). My great-aunt Velma Mullins, who graduated from Waynesburg High School in 1941 with Venus Ramey, had a front-row seat to Venus's rise to fame.

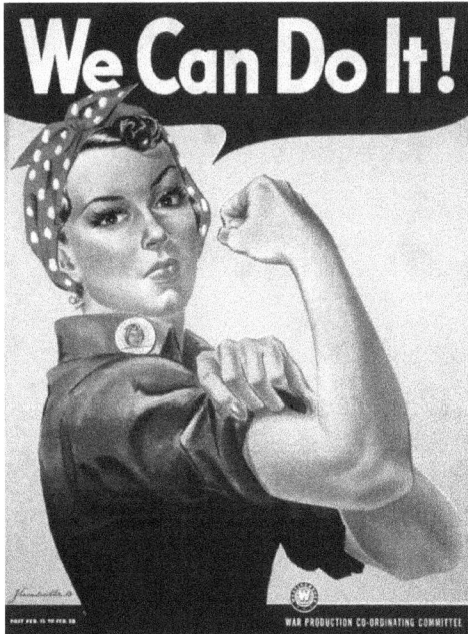

Rose Monroe, known as "Rosie the Riveter,"

Venus went on to become Miss America in 1944 during one of the most tumultuous times in American history, World War II. She embodied the spirit of American women who were stepping into new roles, both on the Homefront and in the public sphere. Venus moved to Washington, D.C., to work in the war effort, using her fame to sell war bonds and inspire countless young women. Bomber planes were named after her, and her face became iconic during a time when the nation desperately needed hope and optimism.

Issue #2 of *Miss America* from 1944 featured a photo cover of the real Miss America, Venus Ramey, in uniform as Miss America, a superhero appearing in American comic books published by Marvel Comics.

Similarly, Rose Monroe became the face of "Rosie the Riveter," a symbol of women stepping into traditionally male-dominated jobs in factories while men were off fighting the war. Together, Rose and Venus represented a shift in the national consciousness, showing the country that women were not just capable but essential to the survival and success of the nation.

The interconnectedness of their lives and the small Kentucky towns they came from is remarkable. My great-uncle[lvi]Kenneth Martin learned of Venus becoming Miss America while stationed in Germany during the war. He was clearing a small German town of combatants, entered a house, and saw a magazine with Venus on the cover. To him, it was a poignant reminder of home in the midst of war, a touch of familiarity in a world turned upside down.

The strength of women like Rose and Venus, combined with the quiet resilience of women like my grandmothers, my mom, and my wife Dawn, is a testament to the power of Appalachian women. These women were/are the backbone of their families, communities, and, in many ways, the entire region.

Appalachian women, like my grandmothers, mom, Dawn, and women like Rose Monroe and Venus Ramey, teach us about resilience. They faced the harshest conditions, whether it was war, poverty, or the isolation of rural life, but they did so without complaint, always with their eyes set on the future.

In therapy, resilience is often a central theme. For counselors, understanding the strength that comes from these lived experiences is crucial. It is important to recognize that, especially in Appalachia, many women are raised with the understanding that they are the glue holding their families together. They are often taught to be self-sufficient and to persevere, no matter the challenge. However, this doesn't mean they don't need support. Even the strongest women need someone to lean on, and therapy can be a space where they feel heard and validated.

Seventy-five percent of therapists today are women and carry the tradition of caregiving into their profession. Women are the backbone of the therapeutic community. Just as Appalachian women kept their families going during the toughest times, female therapists like Dawn kept the profession strong by offering support, empathy, and guidance to those in need.

For clients, the stories of these women can serve as a reminder that they are not alone. The struggles they face are not unique, generations before them have faced similar hardships and come out the other side stronger. Resilience is in their DNA, and they can draw upon the strength of their ancestors as they navigate their own challenges.

The women of Appalachia, whether they are grandmothers, mothers, therapists like Dawn, or public figures like Rosie the Riveter and Miss America, have paved the way for future generations. Their resilience, strength, and wisdom continue to guide us today. In the face of adversity, they have shown time and time again that, while life may be hard, it is also full of beauty, connection, and love. As counselors, we can learn from these women by embodying the same compassion and resilience they displayed in their own lives. For clients, their stories offer hope, reminding them that no matter how difficult life may seem, they, too, can rise above their circumstances and find strength within themselves and their communities.

Honoring Our Kin Beyond Life

In Appalachia, the reverence for family doesn't end with life, it carries on long after death. This respect for the dead is woven into the fabric of Appalachian culture, a reminder of where we came from and a tribute to the lives of those who shaped us. One of the most powerful displays of this respect can be seen during funeral processions. Unlike in many other places in the country, where traffic keeps moving or barely slows down, in Appalachia, when a funeral procession passes by, everyone pulls over. Whether you're a family member or a stranger, it doesn't matter. Traffic halts and people step aside to pay their respects, honoring the life that has passed. This small yet significant gesture reflects a deep understanding that death is not something to be rushed past, it's a moment to acknowledge, a life to remember.

Growing up, I witnessed this countless times, and it always moved me. There's something sacred about the act of stopping, of taking a moment out of your day to show respect for someone you may not have even known. It speaks to the tight-knit nature of Appalachian communities, where family and neighborly ties run deep. Even in death, people are not forgotten, and even in grief, they are not alone. The community recognizes that the loss of one person affects us all, and for that, we pull over and honor the departed.

Another reflection of this deep respect for our people is the care that goes into preserving and tending cemeteries. In many Appalachian communities, the graves of loved ones are more than just markers of where they rest, they are tended with the same love and attention that people gave them in life. Cemeteries are regularly visited gravestones cleaned, and flowers laid upon the resting places of ancestors. It's not uncommon to find that cemeteries in Appalachia are often larger and more well-kept than playgrounds or recreational spaces, a testament to the priority given to family and heritage.

I have often seen churches with vast cemeteries that outsize their playgrounds, and that observation speaks volumes. The people of Appalachia know where they come from, and they honor that connection by maintaining the places where their kin rest. This act of care serves as both a memorial and a continuation of a relationship that does not end with death. The gravestones of ancestors, carefully maintained and decorated, stand as lasting tributes to their lives and legacies.

For me, this tradition is especially meaningful when I visit my family cemetery in Bethelridge, Kentucky. Many of my family members are buried there, my father, my paternal grandparents, and great-grandparents, and I know that one day, I will join them. This knowledge doesn't bring sadness but rather a sense of belonging. It's comforting to know that when my time comes, I will rest alongside those who came before me, in a place that is cared for by those who remain.

My grandpa, Cortez, with his sister and tall cousin, visiting an old cemetery in a cow pasture in Adair Co., Kentucky

The cemetery at Bethelridge holds more than just the remains of my loved ones; it holds our family's stories. Every time I walk among the gravestones, I'm reminded of the lives that shaped mine, their sacrifices, their love, and their resilience. The cemetery serves as a reminder that family is eternal and that even in death, our connection remains. And as long as someone tends to the gravestones and keeps the stories alive, that connection will never fade.

In the Appalachian tradition of honoring the dead, there's a valuable lesson for us all, one that I often share with my clients. The way we treat others, especially our elders, is a reflection of the way we will one day be treated. It's an old lesson but one that holds true across generations: *what we sow, we reap.* If we show respect, care, and love for those who came before us, we set an example for those who will come after us.

Just as we tend the graves of our ancestors, we must tend to the living relationships we have with our elders and those who rely on us. If we care for our family and show them love and respect, we teach our children and the younger generation the importance of those values. In turn, when we reach old age, we can expect to receive the same care and respect. It's a cycle that nourishes not only individual relationships but entire families and communities.

In my counseling practice, I often meet people who feel disconnected from their families or are struggling with a sense of neglect. One of the most valuable lessons we can learn from our heritage is that caring for others, particularly our elders, is an investment in our own future. The respect we give today is the respect we will receive tomorrow. This is true not just for family relationships but for all human connections. By honoring those who came before us, we build a legacy of love and respect that will carry on long after we're gone.

In Appalachia, the respect for our past kin, our people, is intertwined with the legacy they leave behind. It's not just about tending to graves; it's about remembering the people who filled those lives. The annual decoration days, when families gather to clean and adorn the graves of their loved ones, are more than just tasks, they're rituals of love. Stories are retold, memories are shared, and in those moments, the dead live on.

These traditions show how deeply Appalachian families value the importance of legacy. To some, cemeteries may seem somber or grim, but to many in the hills, they're hallowed grounds where the past, present, and future meet. The gravestones stand as silent reminders of the lives lived, and the care given to them speaks volumes about the importance of family, not just in life but in death as well.

I often reflect on how, in today's fast-paced world, this sense of connection to our roots is increasingly rare. In many places, gravesites are neglected, and the dead are forgotten. But in Appalachia, the importance of honoring our ancestors is a living tradition. Our cemeteries are not forgotten places but sacred spaces that remind us of who we are and where we come from.

In many ways, the Appalachian respect for their past kin reveals a deeper truth about life. Death is not viewed as a final goodbye but rather as a continuation of the relationship between the living and the dead. Through the act of remembering, tending graves, and telling stories, we keep our loved ones alive in our hearts and minds. There is a reverence in these acts that transcends the physical world, reminding us that family is forever.

This sentiment is beautifully reflected in many Hispanic cultures, particularly in Día de los Muertos, a tradition that celebrates and honors the spirits of ancestors. As depicted in the Disney movie *"Coco"*, the belief that "as long as we remember them, they remain with us" resonates deeply with Appalachian traditions of storytelling and tending to family graves. In both cultures, the past is not something to be forgotten, but rather woven into the fabric of the present, ensuring that the legacy of our ancestors continues to guide and inspire us."

To me, this is one of the most beautiful aspects of Appalachian culture. Even as generations pass, we continue to honor the dead, ensuring that their lives, and their lessons, are never forgotten. We tend to their graves, we pull over for funeral processions, and we remember. And in that remembrance, we preserve not only their legacy but our own.

In this way, family who have passed are not simply laid to rest and forgotten. They are part of the living landscape, honored through our actions and cared for by their descendants. It is a reminder that while life may be fleeting, family endures. And when our time comes, we will rest among those we loved, in a place where our legacy will be honored and our lives remembered.

In a world that often feels disconnected and transient, the Appalachian reverence for the dead provides a powerful example of the importance of roots, continuity, and respect for those who came before us. It's a tradition I hold dear and one I will carry with me, knowing that one day, I, too, will be remembered in the same way in the peaceful hills of Bethelridge.

By living a life that honors those who came before us, we plant seeds of respect, love, and care that will one day grow and bear fruit in our own lives. And just as we reap what we sow, the care we give to others will come back to us, ensuring that we, too, are remembered and respected when we are gone. This, perhaps, is the greatest lesson of all.

The Appalachian tradition of honoring the dead is more than a cultural practice, it is a therapeutic act of connection, healing, and identity. In modern counseling, many individuals struggle with grief, disconnection, and unresolved familial wounds. The Appalachian emphasis on remembering and honoring ancestors offers a framework for helping clients process loss, identity, and intergenerational healing.

Modern grief counseling often focuses on closure, but Appalachian traditions remind us that grief is not about severing ties with the deceased; it is about continuing the relationship in a different way. The idea that we "keep our loved ones alive" through memory and tradition aligns with contemporary grief theories that advocate for maintaining a continuing bond with the deceased rather than letting go completely (Klass, 1996).

To do this, we can encourage our clients to engage in rituals of remembrance, such as visiting a loved one's grave, telling stories, or maintaining a family tradition in their honor. We may want to introduce narrative therapy techniques and helping clients reframe their grief by integrating their loved one's influence into their ongoing life story. And for those clients struggling with unresolved grief, letter-writing therapy can be effective, guiding them to write letters to deceased loved ones to express lingering emotions and find meaning in the loss.

Many individuals can struggle with intergenerational trauma, where the emotional burdens can be passed down through families due to hardship, war, poverty, and displacement. However, just as trauma can be inherited, so too can resilience. The tradition of honoring our kin reinforces the idea that we are part of a larger story... that our strength is built on the strength of those who came before us.

Some interventions I use in my practice include family genograms and legacy mapping. This can help clients explore their family history, identifying patterns of resilience alongside struggles. This can help reframe negative family legacies into sources of strength. I also use storytelling where I encourage clients to learn and share family stories as a way to connect with their ancestry and find deeper meaning in their identity. Finally, it is important that we use culturally affirming counseling. Many clients, particularly those from rural backgrounds, feel disconnected from modern mental health models. Integrating cultural traditions of honoring ancestors can be a bridge to deeper healing.

As a therapist, we may also need to address existential anxiety and fear of death.

Many individuals, especially those disconnected from cultural traditions, struggle with existential anxiety, the fear of mortality, and the uncertainty of what comes after death. In contrast, many cultures, such as that of the Appalachian and Hispanic traditions of continuing relationships with the dead, provide a comforting framework: death is not the end but a transition into memory and legacy.

I often encourage my clients to try and make meaning by asking them to consider how they want to be remembered and what legacy they wish to leave behind. I will introduce life-review therapy, where clients reflect on their most meaningful experiences, ensuring their life story is shaped with purpose and connection rather than regret. I may ask them to write their own epitaph.

The Appalachian reverence for ancestors is more than tradition, it is a deeply therapeutic practice that provides meaning, connection, and healing across generations. In therapy, we must recognize that grief is not about letting go; it is about carrying forward. By integrating remembrance into our lives, we honor not only the past but also our own emotional well-being.

As therapists, we can guide clients in rediscovering the value of legacy, the power of storytelling, and the healing found in cultural traditions. Whether through Appalachian rituals, Día de los Muertos, or personal acts of remembrance, honoring the dead allows us to stay connected, find strength in our roots, and cultivate resilience for the future.

Come and Sit for a Spell

In mountain and rural life, we've always known the value of slowing down and spending time with people. When someone would come by the house, we'd say, "Come and sit for a spell," inviting them to rest, talk, and share whatever was on their mind. There was no rush, no agenda, just the simple act of being present with each other. In many ways, this is the greatest gift we can give, to truly spend time with someone, listen to them, and show them that we care.

As counselors, this is what we do. Our counseling offices should feel like a front porch, a place where anyone can come by, sit down, and talk for a while. We believe in the power of talk therapy, the idea that healing and change happen through conversation, understanding, and time. We're not looking for a quick fix or a magic pill. Real change takes time, and it often involves hard work, patience, and a willingness to dig deep into the issues that have brought someone into therapy.

Time is one of the most valuable things we can give our clients. In a world that moves too fast, where everyone is looking for instant gratification, the counseling process slows things down. It's a space where people can come in, sit down, and just be. They can talk about what's bothering them, explore their feelings, and work through the things that are holding them back.

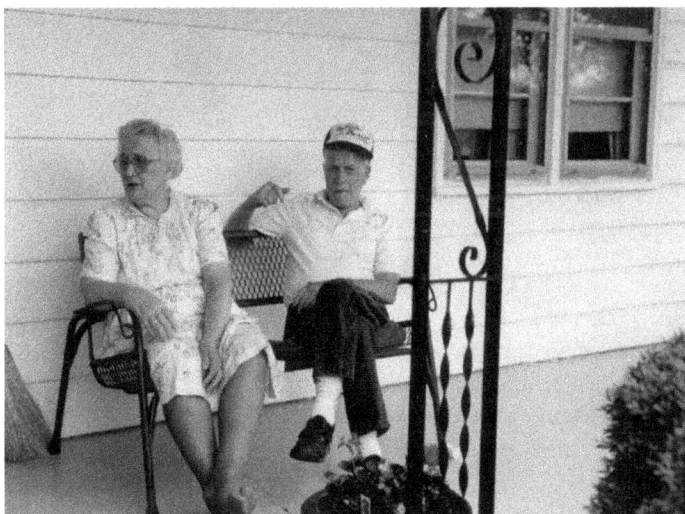

Grandma Doreen and Grandpa Cortez Wesley on the porch of the family farm.

There's an old saying that I remember that goes: "You can't rush a good thing." Healing is one of those good things that you can't rush. Too often, clients come to therapy looking for a quick solution. They've been told that a pill will fix their depression, that medication will take away their anxiety, or that there's an easy way to get over their problems. But the truth is, while medication can help some people, it's not the answer for most. And sometimes, in our rush to find a solution, we overlook the deeper issues that are at the root of a person's struggles.

Let me be clear: medication has its place. Some clients truly need antidepressants, mood stabilizers, or medication-assisted treatment for addiction. For certain individuals, these medications are lifesaving, allowing them to function and manage conditions that would otherwise be debilitating. But in many cases, we're too quick to jump to medication as the first solution, looking for the quick fix without taking the time to understand the underlying issues.

This is especially true in cases of depression, anxiety, and addiction. For example, some clients struggling with depression may seek out medication to help them feel better, only to find that the medication dulls their feelings, both the lows and the highs. This might solve the problem of feeling deeply sad, but it can also take away the joy in life, leaving clients in a place of emotional mediocrity. In cases where depression is linked to relationship or sexual issues, the use of antidepressants can complicate things further by reducing sexual desire, making the root issue even harder to address.

The same is true for anxiety, insomnia, and even addiction treatment. Some clients may look for a pill to take away their anxiety or help them sleep at night, but these solutions often treat the symptoms without addressing the deeper issues that cause the anxiety or insomnia in the first place. When clients become dependent on these quick fixes, they sometimes find that their problems worsen over time.

As counselors, we need to advocate for real, lasting solutions instead of just covering up the symptoms. This means encouraging our clients to do the hard work of therapy, to sit with the discomfort, and to face the underlying issues head-on. It means taking the time to build trust, explore emotions, and work through problems slowly and deliberately.

Change is hard. It takes time to unlearn unhealthy patterns, to shift behavior, and to develop new ways of thinking and being in the world. As therapists, we understand that therapy is not a one-size-fits-all approach. Some clients will need medication or harm reduction strategies for addiction, and those are valid and necessary tools for many people. But for most, the path to healing lies in doing the hard work of therapy, talking through their issues, exploring their emotions, and facing the difficult truths they've been avoiding.

For clients dealing with relationship issues, for example, it's easy to look for a quick fix, like medication, to treat the symptoms of dissatisfaction, sexual problems, or communication breakdowns. But these issues are rarely solved by medication alone. Real healing comes from addressing the deeper emotional and relational dynamics that have caused the problems in the first place. Couples counseling, individual therapy, and open communication are often the most effective ways to restore connection and intimacy.

Similarly, with anxiety or insomnia, it's tempting to look for a pill that will make the problem go away. But in many cases, anxiety and insomnia are signals that something deeper is wrong, whether it's unresolved trauma, stress, or emotional imbalance. Therapy can help clients explore what's underneath the surface and address the root causes, rather than just treating the symptoms.

Be Patient, Be Present. For those of us in the counseling profession, the most important thing we can offer our clients is our time and presence. It's not about rushing to fix them or giving them a quick solution. It's about sitting with them in their pain, offering a safe space for them to talk, and helping them find their own path to healing.

Counselors should approach each session with patience and empathy, understanding that real change takes time. We need to encourage our clients to stick with the process, even when it feels slow or difficult. We must remind them that healing isn't linear, and that setbacks are part of the journey. By being consistent, compassionate, and supportive, we create the space for our clients to do the hard work of therapy.

It's also important for us to advocate for a wellness approach that emphasizes holistic care. This means considering all aspects of a client's life, mental, emotional, physical, and social, and working with them to find solutions that promote overall well-being. While medication may be part of the solution for some clients, it's essential that we also focus on lifestyle changes, coping strategies, and personal growth as part of the healing process.

For clients, my advice is this: don't be afraid to take the long road. Healing doesn't happen overnight, and there are no quick fixes for the things that matter most. If you're struggling with depression, anxiety, or addiction, it's important to take the time to understand what's really going on beneath the surface. Medication might help, but it's not a substitute for doing the deeper work of therapy.

Be patient with yourself. Change is hard, and it's normal to feel frustrated when things don't get better right away. But remember, just like sitting on a front porch and talking things out takes time, so does healing. Trust the process, and trust that your therapist is there to walk alongside you, offering support and guidance.

Most importantly, invest in yourself. Therapy is an investment in your future, your relationships, and your overall well-being. It's a place where you can come and sit for a spell, talk things through, and work toward real, lasting change. While it may be tempting to look for a quick fix, the true rewards come from doing the hard work of self-exploration and personal growth.

In our fast-paced world, it's easy to look for the quick solution to life's problems. But just like in the mountains, where sitting on the porch for a spell and talking things out took time, true healing takes time too. As counselors, we know that lasting change doesn't come from a pill or a quick fix. It comes from patience, persistence, and the willingness to do the hard work of therapy.

By offering our clients the gift of time, we help them find real solutions to their problems, not just temporary relief from their symptoms. And for clients, the message is clear: invest in yourself, take the long road, and trust that with time, support, and effort, you can create the lasting change you seek.

Fair to Middlin'

In rural Kentucky, when someone asked how you were doing and you were feeling alright, not too bad but not great, the answer would often be "fair to middlin'." It was a humble, honest way of saying that things were fine, but there was room for improvement. That phrase sticks with me because it reflects a truth that's common to most of us, life isn't always perfect, but it doesn't have to be terrible, either. Most people aren't struggling with severe mental illness every day, but they do face common struggles with stress, anxiety, depression, and the challenges that come with navigating relationships, work, and purpose.

As counselors, we often find that many of our clients are like that, fair to middlin'. They're not in crisis, but they're not thriving either. They come to us counselors not because they're in a deep mental health crisis, but because they need support, guidance, and sometimes just a place to be heard. For most clients, counseling isn't about being treated for a mental illness; it's about seeking counsel and finding a trusted place to talk through life's challenges and gain perspective. It's about finding that support, advice, and encouragement that, in generations past, we might have sought out from our elders, mentors, or a member of the clergy.

I think about my mom, [lvii]Norma, or my grandpa, Cortez, when I reflect on what counseling should look like. They were not trained therapists, but they had a gift for making people feel cared for and heard. I can still talk to my mom about anything, knowing that even if she doesn't have all the answers, she would listen without judgment. Same for Gramps, he accepted people just as they were, meeting them where they stood. Sometimes that's all anyone needs, a compassionate ear and the assurance that someone cares.

Grandpa, Cortez Wesley, holding my baby brother Tony and me crouching beside him. You may notice the round red mark on my grandpa's forehead; this is where I placed a suction cup toy that I would place on him that left a mark. Christmas 1965.

In today's world, counseling has taken on an almost clinical tone that can make it feel more like a diagnosis and prognosis than a conversation. We've moved away from seeking counsel as a natural part of life and instead view it as something to be reserved for when things go terribly wrong. That mindset makes it harder for people to reach out for help when they need it most.

Counseling should be more about seeking counsel rather than seeking "counseling" in the traditional sense. We need to normalize asking for help in areas where we're struggling, whether it's stress from a job, issues in a relationship, or questions about our life's purpose. It doesn't always have to be about diagnosing a mental illness, it can be about finding someone to talk to, someone who listens like my mom or Grandpa Cortez, with kindness and acceptance.

For students wanting to become therapists, this is a crucial point to understand. Most of the clients you'll work with aren't going to be battling severe mental illness every day. They'll come to you because they're "fair to middlin'", dealing with life's everyday challenges, feeling stuck, or just needing a bit of guidance. Your role is to offer that space of understanding and support, helping them to find their own solutions without jumping to a medical or pathological label.

This is where the wellness model of counseling comes into play. Unlike the disease model, which focuses on diagnosing and treating mental illness, the wellness model emphasizes strengths, potential, and personal growth. It's about working with clients where they are and helping them become the best version of themselves, rather than seeing them as sick or broken.

When we approach counseling from a wellness perspective, we focus on holistic health, mental, physical, emotional, and social. We help clients explore all aspects of their lives, looking at how their relationships, work, lifestyle, and personal habits contribute to their overall well-being. We're not just trying to eliminate symptoms; we're helping clients build resilience, develop coping strategies, and improve their quality of life.

Take addiction issues, for example. Too often, addiction is treated from a disease model that emphasizes powerlessness and surrender, particularly in the case of the 12-step approach. But as I've discussed in a previous chapter, this model doesn't always align with the spirit and resilience of the people of Appalachia. In contrast, a wellness model of addiction treatment focuses on empowerment. It recognizes that people have strengths and capabilities that can be drawn upon to overcome addiction. It's not about seeing someone as an "addict" or labeling them with a lifelong disease, it's about helping them rediscover their inner strength and build a life worth living, free from addiction and cured from a perpetual label.

For clients dealing with more common mental health issues like depression, anxiety, or adjustment disorders, the wellness model is especially valuable. Depression and anxiety are part of the human experience, and while they can be debilitating at times, they aren't necessarily lifelong illnesses. They're often responses to stress, loss, or change, and with the right support, most people can recover and move forward.

Counseling students must learn to recognize these common issues without over-pathologizing them. Not every client who feels sad or overwhelmed is clinically depressed. Not every person who feels anxious needs to be diagnosed with an anxiety disorder. As a therapist, it's important to meet clients where they are, assess their needs, and focus on their strengths rather than jumping straight to a label.

For example, when working with a client experiencing an adjustment disorder, it's not about diagnosing them with something severe; it's about helping them navigate a life transition, like a new job, a move, or a relationship change. It's about providing practical tools, offering encouragement, and helping them see that they're capable of handling the change, even if it feels overwhelming at the moment.

In many ways, counseling should feel more like a conversation with a trusted elder than a clinical intervention. When I sat with Gramps, I never felt like I was being analyzed or diagnosed. He was just there, listening, offering his perspective, and making me feel understood. The same with my mom. That's what clients need from us as counselors: someone who listens deeply, someone who accepts them just as they are, and someone who can offer support without judgment.

This doesn't mean that clinical skills aren't important. As therapists, we need to be well-trained in assessment, diagnosis, and treatment planning. But those tools should serve the larger goal of helping clients grow and thrive, not define their experience or limit their potential.

For students aspiring to be therapists, my advice is simple: don't lose sight of the human aspect of counseling. Yes, you'll learn about diagnostic criteria, treatment modalities, and clinical skills, and all of that is important. But don't forget that your clients are people first, not problems to be solved. Approach each person with the kind of care, respect, and compassion that my grandpa showed me. He may not have had all the answers, but he knew how to listen, and that's sometimes the most important thing you can do.

As you step into your role as a counselor, remember that you're not just there to diagnose and treat, you're there to offer counsel, support, and guidance. You're there to help people navigate life's challenges, to show them their own strength, and to walk alongside them as they find their way.

In the end, most of us are just "fair to middlin'", not perfect, not broken, but somewhere in between. And that's okay. Our job as counselors is to meet people where they are, help them get to where they want to be, and remind them that they have everything they need within themselves to thrive.

Fishing for Change

One thing you quickly learn about my people, and most people really, is that nobody likes being told what to do. It's not in our nature. When someone tells you to do something, your first reaction is often to dig in your heels and say, "I'll do it when I'm good and ready, not when you tell me." That independent spirit is strong, especially in mountain folks and rural communities who've spent their whole lives making their own way in a world that doesn't always make it easy. There's a deep sense of pride in being able to say, "I did it on my own."

As therapists, we come up against that same resistance. No one likes being told how to fix their life, and for many of our clients, especially those from rural communities, the second you start telling them what to do, they'll shut down or push back. It's human nature to go on the defense when you feel like someone's trying to take control of your life. That's why, as counselors, we have to be careful not to play into that resistance. Our job isn't to tell clients what to do, it's to guide them toward their own solutions in their own time, using their own values.

I often think of counseling like fishing. You can't just throw a hook in the water and expect the fish to jump on it. You have to be patient, find the right spot, and use the right bait. Sometimes, it's a slow process, waiting for that nibble, but when you know your craft, you have the confidence that it'll come. In therapy, the lure we're using is the client's own values, and when they start biting, the change that follows is not because we forced it but because they decided it was time to reel themselves in.

One of the most valuable tools I've found for working with clients, especially those who are resistant to change, is Motivational Interviewing (MI) (Miller, 2023). This approach aligns perfectly with the Appalachian mindset because it doesn't involve pushing or telling the client what to do. Instead, it's about guiding clients to find the answers themselves, using their own values and beliefs to motivate them toward change. MI is like a dance, where you follow the client's lead but gently steer them in the direction, they need to go without them even realizing it.

Mountain people, with their rugged independence, often want to fight back when they feel cornered. But MI teaches us not to fight against this resistance but to roll with it. If a client is ornery or resistant, I don't push back. I listen. I learn their values, the things that really matter to them, and I use those values to help them move in the direction of change. Often, they don't even realize that, over time, I'm slowly guiding them toward a better place, one step at a time.

I like to think of it as rolling with the punches. Just like in life, where we don't always have control over what comes at us, in therapy, we don't always have control over how clients respond to our guidance. But instead of getting knocked down by their resistance, we roll with it, using it as part of the journey toward change. It's a subtle, artful way of getting clients to see the value in moving forward without feeling like they're being told what to do.

In MI, one of my favorite techniques for handling resistance is something called amplified reflections. When a client expresses what's called "sustain talk", statements that suggest they're comfortable just where they are and not interested in changing, I take what they say and amplify it. For example, if a client says, "I'm just not sure I can quit drinking," I might respond, "So, it sounds like you're completely unwilling to try cutting back at all."

This exaggeration of their words usually catches clients off guard. Nine times out of ten, they'll respond by saying something like, "Well, that's not exactly what I meant. I think I could cut back, but I'm just not sure how." Now, all of a sudden, the client is arguing against their own resistance, and change talk begins to emerge. They've gone from sustain talk to talking about the possibility of change, all because I've nudged them to reflect on their own words.

This is where the fishing analogy comes in. It's like casting out my line with a favorite lure, one I know has worked well before. I don't yank the line the second I feel a nibble. I let the client work with it, slowly but surely, until they're ready to reel themselves in. The beauty of this approach is that the client believes the change is their idea. And, in a way, it is, because I've simply guided them to recognize what's already inside them.

There's a simple but powerful truth in the saying, "If you find yourself in a hole, the first thing to do is stop diggin'." This applies to so many of the clients we work with, especially those stuck in patterns of behavior that aren't serving them anymore. Whether it's addiction, unhealthy relationships, or self-destructive habits, many people continue digging deeper into their problems because they're afraid to stop, look up, and face the reality of where they are.

In therapy, part of our job is to help clients stop digging. Through MI, we can help clients recognize the hole they're in without making them feel ashamed or hopeless for being in it. Instead of pointing fingers and telling them what they need to do, we gently guide them to see that continuing down the same path will only make the situation worse. And when they're ready, we help them find a way to climb out, step by step, using their own strengths and values as the ladder.

While reflections are one of the most effective ways to move clients from sustain talk to change talk, MI offers several other techniques that are just as powerful.

One of the core techniques in MI is OARS, which stands for Open-ended questions, Affirmations, Reflections, and Summaries. These are the building blocks of MI and help create a safe, supportive environment for clients to explore their thoughts and feelings.

Open-ended questions invite clients to share more about their experiences. Instead of asking, "Do you want to quit smoking?" (a question that invites a yes or no answer), you might ask, "What are your thoughts on quitting smoking?" This opens the door for clients to explore their feelings more fully. Affirmations involve recognizing and acknowledging the client's strengths. It might be something as simple as saying, "It sounds like you've been working really hard to take care of your family," which helps build rapport and encourages the client to keep going. Reflections are used to repeat what the client has said, showing that you've heard and understood them. Reflections can be simple or complex, but they're a great way to help clients feel seen and heard. Summaries pull together key points from the session, helping clients make sense of their own thoughts and reinforcing the progress they've made.

Another essential MI technique is developing a discrepancy. This involves helping clients see the difference between their current behavior and their goals or values. For example, if a client values being a good parent but is struggling with addiction, you might reflect back their desire to be present for their kids while gently pointing out how their substance use is getting in the way of that goal. By highlighting this discrepancy, you create a space for the client to begin considering change.

Another saying that fits well with Motivational Interviewing is, "Sometimes you get, and sometimes you get got." This is a reminder that life doesn't always go the way we plan. Sometimes, we're in control, and sometimes, things happen that take us by surprise or knock us off course. This applies to the change process as well. Sometimes, clients will feel like they're making progress and other times, they'll feel like they've been set back. As therapists, it's important to remind them that setbacks are part of the journey and that resilience comes from how they respond to those moments.

I once worked with a client named [lviii]Polly, who struggled with alcohol use. Polly was fiercely independent, the kind of person who prided herself on doing everything on her own. She resisted therapy at first, convinced that she didn't need help. But over time, through open-ended questions and reflective listening, I helped Polly explore what mattered most to her, her family, particularly her grandchildren.

Polly often said, "I've been drinking for years, and it hasn't been a problem." Rather than challenging her directly, I used amplified reflections, saying, "So you're saying your drinking doesn't affect your relationship with your grandkids at all?" She paused, then replied, "Well, I guess it does. I can't keep up with them like I used to, and I don't want them to see me drunk." That was the first step in moving Polly from sustain talk to change talk. Once she began to see how her drinking was affecting the things she valued most, she started to consider change.

Through MI, I helped Polly recognize that while sometimes life doesn't go as planned, and "you get got," there's always a way forward if you're willing to stop digging and start looking for the ladder out of the hole. It wasn't about me telling Polly to quit drinking; it was about her realizing, on her own terms, that her values pointed her toward a better path.

Sometimes, circumstances become so overwhelming that offering new knowledge is unhelpful and dismissive of a person's current reality. It's like trying to teach someone to fish when they're too hungry to think about anything other than their next meal. When a person is starving, that's not the time to teach them how to lure in the best catch. The right thing to do is to first give the person a fish, banishing their hunger, and only then teach them to fish.

Far too often, people ignore this common-sense first step. They see someone who is struggling and rush to offer wisdom. But few of us truly understand the anxiety, confusion, and uncertainty that come with overwhelming need. People in the midst of personal disasters, such as those devastated by Hurricane Helene, are reeling. They can't think straight. Their nerves are shot. Their confidence is non-existent. They've been knocked down to the foundational level of Maslow's hierarchy of needs: food, shelter, and water.

Rushing to offer a struggling person long-term advice is not just a waste of time, it can feel like callousness or cruelty. Instead, we must first care for their basic needs and help them regain their equilibrium. Once they are warm, fed, and feel safe, their ears, hearts, and minds begin to open, creating the opportunity to teach new skills that can help them move forward.

In Appalachia, values run deep. Whether it's the importance of family, the belief in hard work, or the pride in making one's own way, these values are the foundation of who we are. As therapists, when we tap into these values, we give our clients a powerful tool for change. Rather than imposing our own ideas of what's best for them, we guide them to use their own values to motivate them toward healthier choices.

For Polly, it wasn't about alcohol being "bad"; it was about how it was interfering with her ability to be the grandmother she wanted to be. Once she saw that for herself, change became not only possible but desirable.

For counselors, the lesson is to be patient and to trust the process. Change doesn't happen overnight, and it rarely happens when we try to force it. Instead, we need to guide our clients toward their own answers, using their values as the foundation for change. We need to be hypervigilant, listening for sustain talk and gently nudging clients toward change talk when the opportunity arises.

For clients, the lesson is simple: the answers are already within you. Therapy isn't about someone telling you how to fix your life. It's about discovering, through guided reflection, what matters most to you and how you can live in line with those values. Whether it's giving up a harmful habit or making a positive change in your life, the key to lasting change is finding the motivation within yourself.

Therapy, much like life in the mountains, is about patience, persistence, and the quiet wisdom of allowing change to unfold in its own time. As counselors, we're here to guide the way, using our clients' own values as the compass, trusting that with the right approach, the change they seek will come.

In the mountains, there's an old saying that reminds me of one of the most important roles of a counselor: "Don't just hand a man a meal; teach him how to plant a seed." This simple phrase captures the essence of what we do as therapists and counselor educators. It's not about offering temporary fixes or solutions that work at the moment but leave the client dependent on us. Instead, our job is to teach, guide, and empower clients to cultivate the tools they need to navigate life's challenges on their own.

The comparison to the more well-known phrase, "Give a man a fish, and you feed him for a day. Teach a man to fish, and you feed him for a lifetime," perfectly aligns with the work we do in therapy. We're not here to simply provide answers or advice that keeps clients coming back to us for every problem. We're here to help them find their own strength, their own solutions, and their own path forward. The ultimate goal of any therapist is to make themselves unnecessary, at least for the particular issue the client is struggling with. This is what creates long-term growth, resilience, and true healing.

I like to think of therapists as guides, much like Daniel Boone was in his day. Boone wasn't just a trailblazer who forged new paths through uncharted wilderness; he was a guide who led others through the Cumberland Pass, teaching them how to survive and thrive in the harsh landscape. He didn't just lead people to safety once, he gave them the tools and knowledge they needed to navigate the wilderness on their own in the future.

As counselors, we take a similar approach. We walk alongside our clients on their journey, helping them navigate the emotional and psychological wilderness of their struggles. We're there to offer guidance, support, and insight, but ultimately, the goal is for them to learn to walk the path on their own. Our clients shouldn't need us to tell them what to do at every turn; they should leave therapy equipped with the skills, confidence, and resilience to face future challenges without needing to come back for the same issue.

It's human nature to seek answers from those we see as experts or leaders, especially when we're feeling lost. Clients come to therapy because they're in pain, confused, or stuck, and it's tempting for both client and therapist to fall into the trap of advice-giving. The client may want quick answers, and the therapist may feel pressure to provide a solution to alleviate the client's discomfort. But if we hand out solutions like quick meals, clients will be fed for a day, but they'll come back hungry the next time life gets hard.

The best counseling doesn't work that way. Instead, it focuses on fostering independence. We encourage clients to find their own answers, to explore their values and motivations, and to build the skills they need to cope with life's ups and downs. Through techniques like Motivational Interviewing, we help them realize that they are the ones with the power to change their lives, not us.

In therapy, it's not just about planting the seed of change; it's about teaching clients how to tend that seed, nurture it, and let it grow into something lasting. Like a gardener, our job is to teach them how to take care of their emotional and psychological garden. We can give them strategies, tools, and insights, but they are the ones who need to water the soil, pull the weeds, and care for what's growing within them.

Let's take Polly, the client I mentioned earlier, as an example. She came into therapy struggling with alcohol use, feeling like her drinking wasn't really a problem, even though it was affecting her relationships. I could have given her all the reasons she needed to quit or laid out a step-by-step plan for how to do it, but that wouldn't have worked. Polly needed to come to that conclusion on her own. Through Motivational Interviewing and other techniques, I helped Polly reflect on what really mattered to her, her family, her health, and her desire to be present for her grandchildren. Once Polly connected the dots herself, change became possible because she was motivated from within.

If I had simply handed her a plan for sobriety, she might have followed it for a while, but the change wouldn't have lasted. Polly needed to learn how to "plant the seed" of change herself so that when challenges arose later on, she wouldn't need to come back to me for the answer. She would have the tools within herself to manage her life without alcohol.

For counselor educators, the lesson here is critical. When we teach new therapists, it's important to help them understand that therapy isn't about having all the answers; it's about teaching clients how to find their own answers. Too often, new counselors feel pressured to "fix" their clients' problems, to give advice, or to provide solutions. But the most effective therapy happens when we guide our clients, not direct them.

As counselor educators, we need to model and teach approaches like Motivational Interviewing, and others, which emphasize collaboration over direction. We should train our students to be patient, to allow clients to sit with discomfort, and to resist the urge to jump in with advice. Our job is to help clients connect with their own values, clarify their own goals, and build their own paths toward change. This requires trust in the process and a deep respect for the client's autonomy.

Life is unpredictable, and clients need to be prepared for those moments when things don't go as planned. Our job as therapists is to help them become resilient so that when life knocks them down, they have the inner resources to get back up.

When we teach clients how to fish, how to plant the seed of change and nurture it, we're teaching them resilience. We're showing them that they have the strength and tools to face life's challenges without needing constant guidance. It's about building independence and helping clients understand that they are fully capable of navigating the hard times. In fact, the best compliment a therapist can receive isn't that a client keeps coming back forever; it's that a client leaves therapy feeling empowered to handle whatever comes next. Our greatest success is when clients can face the world on their own, knowing that they have the skills, confidence, and inner strength to thrive without needing us by their side. In the end, the greatest gift we can offer our clients isn't a solution to their problem, it's the confidence to solve it themselves.

Grandma, Zoni Carroll, after a good day of fishing

Practice What You Preach

There's a saying that you might have heard that gets right to the heart of what it means to live with integrity: "The pot calling the kettle black." We all know what that means it's calling out hypocrisy, and nobody likes a hypocrite. As counselors, we have to be careful that we're not setting ourselves up for the same criticism. We can't guide our clients through their struggles if we're making the same mistakes repeatedly. We've got to live by example. Our clients aren't just looking for advice; they're looking for a role model who practices what they preach.

"Reputation is like fine China; once broken, it's hard to fix."

Counselors, just like anyone else, are flawed. We've made mistakes, faced hardships, and gone through our own battles. In fact, many counselors were drawn to this profession because they faced personal challenges and found healing through therapy. That personal experience can be a powerful tool in helping clients feel understood. But here's the catch: while we've been through tough times, we can't stay stuck in them. We need to grow, learn, and keep walking the path of improvement. Otherwise, we become like that old saying from antiquity, "The blind leading the blind," and that doesn't help anyone.

When I was young, every boy had to take wood shop. The girls, on the other hand, were required to take home economics. Now, I won't get into the inappropriate gender roles that were imposed back then, but let me set the stage for you. In my first shop class, the teacher, [lix]Mr. Johnson, was missing a finger. It had been cut off in an accident years before, and he used that missing finger as a constant reminder of the importance of safety.

When Mr. Johnson talked about keeping your hands away from the saw blades or paying attention to what you were doing, we listened. His experience had weight because it came from personal experience. But here's the thing: if Mr. Johnson had been missing a bunch of fingers, still making careless mistakes, and losing more digits along the way, do you think we would have taken him seriously? Probably not. We would have wondered what he was doing wrong, and eventually, we'd stop paying attention altogether.

That's a lot like the counseling profession. Our clients don't expect us to be perfect, but they do expect us to practice what we preach. They may be willing to seek marriage advice from a therapist who's been divorced because people make mistakes and life is complicated, but they won't want to take that advice from a therapist who's been divorced three or four times and doesn't seem to have learned a thing from it. "Fool me once, shame on you; fool me twice, shame on me." Clients will give you grace for your past, but if they see you making the same mistakes again and again, they'll lose trust in you.

We talk about being guides for our clients. We're there to help them navigate their emotional landscapes, just as Daniel Boone led settlers through the wilderness. But a guide who keeps getting lost is no good to anyone. If Daniel Boone had led his party in circles for days, he would've been run out of town. The same goes for us as counselors, if we keep making the same mistakes without learning from them, we'll lose the respect and trust of our clients.

Clients can see through the nonsense. They're looking for authenticity. "You can't teach an old dog new tricks" might be true for some, but it's not true for us. We have to continue learning, growing, and refining our skills so that we're not just spouting advice but living it. This profession demands it. If we tell our clients to be honest in their relationships, then we better be honest in ours. If we talk about the importance of self-care, then we better be practicing it in our own lives. Otherwise, what are we really offering?

One of the worst responses a counselor can give when a client asks a question about their past or their own struggles is to shut down the conversation with, "This is not about me; this is about you." That may be technically true in the sense that therapy is focused on the client, but let's be honest, clients are coming to us as much for who we are as for what we know. If a client is asking a reasonable and appropriate question about your experiences, it's because they want to know if you're walking the walk, not just talking the talk. In those moments, a little vulnerability can go a long way.

Now, I'm not saying we should unload all our personal baggage on our clients. There's a line between healthy disclosure and inappropriate oversharing. But it's important to remember that when a client is looking for guidance, they're also looking for someone who's been there and come out the other side. "You can't put lipstick on a pig." Clients know when you're dodging or being insincere. They're asking for proof that the strategies and techniques you're teaching them are things you've used in your own life, not just theories you read in a textbook.

If a client asks about your past experiences with marriage, for example, and you've been through a divorce, it's okay to acknowledge that. You might say, "Yes, I've been through a divorce myself, and it taught me a lot about communication and personal growth. I'd be happy to share more about what I learned if you think it would be helpful." This kind of response shows humility and integrity, reinforcing that you're human, too. A human who's been working on these issues for a while.

In our line of work, our reputation is everything. Clients need to trust that we are who we say we are and that the advice we offer is based on lived experience and professional expertise. We can't afford to let that reputation slip by making the same mistakes over and over again. Our clients come to us because they believe we can help them, and it's our job to honor that trust by being the best version of ourselves, not just as professionals but as people.

If you're working with clients on their financial health, but your own finances are a mess, how credible will your advice be? If you're counseling someone on parenting, but you're constantly fighting with your own kids, how can you expect them to follow your guidance? "Do as I say, not as I do" doesn't work in therapy. Clients want to see that you're practicing what you preach.

Being a good counselor doesn't mean being perfect. We're all flawed, we all have our own challenges, and we've all made mistakes. But what sets a good counselor apart is the ability to learn from those mistakes and apply those lessons to our lives and to the lives of our clients. If we keep falling into the same traps, making the same bad choices, and refusing to grow, then we're not helping anyone.

I think back to my old shop teacher, Mr. Johnson. He didn't hide his missing finger or pretend it wasn't there. Instead, he used it as a reminder to all of us of what could happen if we weren't careful. That kind of honesty and humility stuck with me all these years. He wasn't perfect, but he learned from his mistake and made sure others learned from it, too. That's what we need to do as counselors. We need to be open about our imperfections, but we also need to show that we've learned and grown from them.

For counselors, the lesson here is simple: live by example. Don't just give advice, follow it. Don't just talk about healthy relationships, financial responsibility, or self-care; practice those things in your own life. Clients will trust you more, respect you more, and ultimately be more open to change when they see that you're walking the walk.

For clients, the takeaway is this: find a counselor who practices what they preach. You have every right to ask questions about your counselor's background and experience, especially if it's relevant to your struggles. Don't settle for someone who dodges your questions or refuses to be open about their own life. You deserve a guide who's been down the path you're trying to navigate and has come out stronger on the other side. Trust your instincts, and remember: if something feels off, it probably is.

As the old saying goes, "You can't trust a butcher with clean hands." A counselor who hasn't done their own work, who hasn't gotten their hands dirty in the process of learning and growing, isn't someone who can truly guide you. But a counselor who's been through the fire, learned from their mistakes, and come out the other side is someone you can trust to help you do the same.

Lessons for Couples Counseling

In my neck of the woods, family is at the center of life. It's often said, "Blood is thicker than water," and no matter how turbulent things get, there's a sense of obligation to stand by family, to mediate conflict, and to help patch up wounds. My grandfather, ˡˣCortez, embodied this resilience and commitment to family, especially when it came to keeping the peace between his parents. His ability to mediate, to act as a go-between for his mother and father left a lasting impact on the family and on me.

Counseling couples is a delicate task. Often, as therapists, we are called upon to be mediators, just as my grandfather was. We aren't there to take sides but to help couples find common ground, communicate more effectively, and build bridges of understanding. In this chapter, I'll share not only the lessons from my family's story, but also practical advice drawn from the work of experts like John Gottman, the Gottman Institute and the strength of Appalachian resilience.

My grandfather, Cortez, grew up in a home filled with tension. Both of his parents, Tina and George Taylor Wesley, had been married and widowed before they met each other, and they brought their own grief, experiences, and children from previous marriages into their union. While their love may have been genuine, it was often marred by conflict. As the oldest child of their union, my grandfather often found himself in the position of mediator.

When tempers flared and harsh words were exchanged between his parents, my grandfather would step in to ease the tension. He'd stand between them, helping to translate their anger into something they could both understand. He became a bridge of understanding, an essential go-between who helped keep the family together and lessened the stress on his younger siblings, Louis and Effie.

However, when my grandfather got married and left home to build a life of his own, things began to unravel between his parents. Without my grandfather's calming presence and mediation, Tina and George struggled to resolve their differences. Eventually, they divorced, only to remarry later, hoping to rekindle their relationship. But they didn't seek counseling or learn new ways to manage their conflicts, and when the same issues resurfaced, they divorced once again.

In the midst of the second divorce, George made a hasty decision, he gave his house to one of his children from his previous marriage to prevent Tina from receiving it in the settlement. George believed his daughter would return the house to him once the divorce was finalized, but instead, she kept it for herself and her family. This left George destitute, with nothing to his name, and eventually, his health began to decline.

Despite the anger my grandfather felt toward his father for the way he had treated his mother, he couldn't let his father suffer alone. My grandparents, with their three young children, took George in. My dad, James, was just a child at the time, remembered his grandfather living with them until he passed away.

That act of care and compassion, despite the family's painful history, speaks volumes about my grandfather's character. He may have been furious with his father, but he understood the importance of family, even when it was messy and imperfect. In the end, he was the one to care for his father, and in death, he continued his role as mediator. Today, my grandfather is buried alongside his mother, Tina Wesley, and his wife, Doreen, but George Taylor is buried right there beside them, a testament to my grandfather's lifelong role as a go-between, even after everyone else had passed away.

George Taylor and Tina Wesley. The child in the picture was Effie, their youngest.

My grandfather's story holds valuable lessons for counselors working with couples. In many ways, the role of a counselor is similar to that of a mediator, standing between two people who often love each other but have lost the ability to communicate effectively. Just as my grandfather sought to bridge the gap between his parents, we as counselors work to help couples find their own way back to understanding, respect, and connection.

John Gottman, one of the leading experts in couples counseling, emphasizes the importance of emotional bids in relationships, the small gestures or cues partners give each other, seeking connection (Gottman, 2015). Whether it's a smile, a question, or even a complaint, these bids are opportunities for couples to turn toward each other and build emotional intimacy. Couples who consistently miss these bids, or turn away from them, often end up in conflict.

As counselors, part of our job is to help couples recognize and respond to these emotional bids, guiding them toward healthier communication patterns. Much like my grandfather's role as a mediator, we are there to help couples translate their anger or frustration into something their partner can understand instead of letting it escalate into a full-blown conflict.

Appalachian families have long understood the importance of support and resilience in tough times. Families would rally around one another, especially during hardship, offering emotional and practical support. For couples in conflict, it's essential to recognize that they aren't just fighting against each other, they're fighting for their relationship. Couples counseling should emphasize this shared goal of fighting for the relationship, rather than against each other.

In Appalachian culture, there's another saying that comes to mind: "It takes two to hoe a row." Just as two people are needed to keep the farm running smoothly, both partners must be willing to work together to keep their relationship healthy. Couples often fall into the trap of waiting for the other person to change or take responsibility. As counselors, we guide them to understand that change must come from both sides. Each partner has to pick up the hoe and start working, even if they feel like they've been doing all the work already.

One of the most poignant lessons from my grandfather's story is the importance of seeking help before it's too late. After Tina and George's first divorce, they remarried, but they didn't change the way they communicated or dealt with conflict. Without new skills or tools, the same problems resurfaced, and they ended up divorcing again.

For couples in counseling, this is a powerful reminder that reconciliation without change is a recipe for repeated failure. Couples need to not only heal the wounds of the past but also learn new ways to communicate, resolve conflicts, and support each other moving forward. This is why it's essential for counselors to provide practical tools for couples to use in their everyday lives, from conflict resolution techniques to emotional regulation strategies.

In many ways, the repair attempts that Gottman talks about, those small efforts to de-escalate a conflict or bring humor back into a tense situation, are like my grandfather's attempts to mediate between his parents. A well-timed joke, a soft gesture, or even taking a break from the argument can make all the difference in turning a conflict into an opportunity for connection.

It's important for couples to recognize that mediation and support should not fall solely on one partner. In my grandfather's case, he bore the weight of keeping his parents together, and when he left home, the cracks in their relationship became too large to ignore. In counseling, we see this dynamic play out often, where one partner feels like they're carrying the relationship while the other disengages.

As counselors, we must encourage both partners to take responsibility for the health of the relationship. It's not enough for one person to constantly mediate or try to fix things. Both partners must be willing to step up and do the work. This is where Gottman's concept of the "sound relationship house" (Navarra, 2016, pp. 93-107) comes in: the idea that a strong relationship is built on mutual trust, commitment, and effective communication. Both partners must contribute to building and maintaining that house, brick by brick.

For counselors, the lesson is clear: our role is to be a mediator, a guide, and a support system for couples in conflict. We must help them learn new ways of communicating and resolving conflict, drawing from both evidence-based practices like those taught by Gottman and the resilience and strength that comes from Appalachian culture. Just as my grandfather stood between his parents to help them understand each other, we stand between our clients to help them find their way back to connection.

For clients, especially those seeking couples counseling, the message is this: reconciliation without change doesn't work. You can't just hope things will get better without learning new tools to make it so. Just like it takes two to hoe a row, it takes both partners working together to build a strong, lasting relationship. And even in the hardest times, when it feels like giving up is the only option, remember that "a house divided cannot stand." Working through conflict, learning from past mistakes, and seeking support can keep the foundation strong.

In the end, my grandfather's role as mediator lives on, not just in his family, but in the lessons, he passed down. His efforts to keep the peace, even when things were hard, remind us of all that love, understanding, and resilience are the cornerstones of any relationship, and that even in death, the role of a mediator can last forever.

Staking Our Claim

There's a saying in Appalachia that I've heard often: "Life's too short to worry about the mule going blind, just load the wagon." It's a reminder that life is fleeting, and we don't have time to waste on things that don't truly matter. The truth is, every one of us is carrying our own load, walking toward a final destination. And while we don't know when we'll get there, the fact remains we will. That's a hard reality to swallow for most people, and for many of us, it's a truth we try to keep at arm's length. But in the end, we're all staring at our own gravestones, waiting for the date to be etched in beside our names.

"You don't get to pick your last day, but you do get to pick how you live today."

When I was about 18 years old, I went with my mom, [lxi]Norma, and my grandfather, Cortez, to the cemetery at Bethelridge Methodist Church. It wasn't unusual for my grandfather to visit the cemetery; he'd often go to tend to the graves of his parents and ancestors. He took great pride in keeping their resting places clean and cared for, and he'd gather the black walnuts that grew around the cemetery, spending hours cracking them open for my grandmother, Doreen, to use in her baking. But on this particular day, something was different. I think my grandfather knew he was entering the last chapter of his life, and he was thinking about his own final resting place.

We sat there at the cemetery, the afternoon sun casting long shadows over the gravestones, and my grandfather, deep in thought, told us where he wanted to be buried. He pointed to a small space between the graves of his mother, Tina, and his father, George Taylor. My mom and I helped him find some old stakes that had been tossed aside, and together, we staked his claim to that small patch of dirt. I remember how happy he was that we had encouraged him to do it. But I also remember seeing something unusual for a man of his generation: emotion. As we placed those stakes in the ground, I could see how much the thought of being reunited with his mother and father touched his heart.

On the way back to the family farm, I asked him a question I'll never forget: "Gramps, are you ready to die?" His response surprised me. He said, "I don't know." My grandfather was a good man, probably the best I've ever known. He didn't curse, he didn't get angry, and he refused to grow tobacco, even though it was one of the most profitable crops in the area. He lived with integrity. But despite all of that, he still carried a deep sense of shame and guilt from his past. He wasn't sure he was "good enough," and I think part of that came from the belief system he had been raised with.

In Appalachia, faith runs deep, and for many, the teachings of the church are a central part of life. But for my grandfather, and later, for my father, those teachings came with a burden. You see, my grandfather had left the Methodist Church a few years before this visit to the cemetery and had joined a Baptist church. The reason? The Baptists believed in the security of salvation, the idea that once you're saved, you're saved for good. No fear of losing it. But I think, deep down, Gramps still worried that maybe, somehow, he wasn't good enough, that maybe God would still be displeased with him.

That belief system weighed on him, and it also weighed on my father, [lxii]Jim. My dad had grown up in the Methodist Church also, and while he spent many years denouncing their belief that one could lose their salvation, he carried the same guilt from his past. When my father learned he had pancreatic cancer and was facing his own death, he asked us where we thought he should be buried. We told him we preferred Bethelridge, where so many of our relatives were laid to rest. He agreed, but he had one requirement: he would decide what his gravestone would say. When my father passed, his gravestone was engraved with the words, "Eternally Secure." It was his way of raising a middle finger to the methodist belief that he could still end up in hell.

My father's gravestone with the inscription "Eternally Secure" listed on top.

The thing is, both my grandfather and my father were good men, men who carried the weight of their belief system in ways that haunted them throughout their lives. But here's the truth: all we have is today. We spend so much time worrying about what's going to happen in the future, but the future is never guaranteed. "You don't get to pick your last day, but you do get to pick how you live today." That's a lesson we all need to learn, and as counselors, it's one we need to pass on to our clients.

Life is brief. None of us knows when our name will be etched into that gravestone. But instead of living in fear of death, we need to focus on how we're living right now. "Make hay while the sun shines," as they say in the country. We can't wait for tomorrow to make things right, to live authentically, or to find peace with ourselves and our past. Today is all we have.

For my grandfather and my father, their belief system played a significant role in shaping their emotions and behaviors. This is a central concept in cognitive-behavioral therapy (CBT): the idea that our beliefs influence how we think, feel, and act. My grandfather and father both believed that they might not be "good enough" in the eyes of God, and that belief colored their entire lives with guilt and doubt despite the fact that they were both men of great integrity.

There's a biblical saying: "You reap what you sow." It's a reminder that the choices we make today will shape our future. But it's not just about the actions we take; it's about the beliefs we hold. If we plant seeds of guilt, fear, and self-doubt, those are the fruits we'll harvest. But if we plant seeds of self-compassion, forgiveness, and acceptance, we'll find peace.

As counselors, it's our job to help clients see that their belief systems are the foundation of their emotional and mental well-being. Whether they believe they're worthy of love and forgiveness or whether they believe they'll never be good enough, those beliefs shape everything. Our role is to help them examine those beliefs and challenge the ones that are holding them back. It's not enough to live in fear of what might come after death; we need to help our clients live fully in the present.

As I reflect on my grandfather's story, I'm reminded of how important it is to live with intention. My grandfather staked his claim to a small piece of dirt between his parents' graves because he wanted to be reunited with them in death. But what about in life? How are we living each day, and how are we helping our clients live theirs?

There's an idiom that sums it up: "You can't wait for your ship to come in if you never sent one out." We can't sit around waiting for life to happen to us. We need to live with purpose and intention. That means confronting the things that hold us back, whether it's fear, guilt, or shame, and finding a way to move forward.

For counselors, this is an essential part of our work. We're not just helping clients deal with their immediate problems; we're helping them build a life they can be proud of, one that isn't weighed down by old beliefs or unresolved emotions. Whether they're dealing with grief, trauma, or guilt, we need to help them see that today is all they have. The past is gone, and the future is unknown, but in this moment, they have the power to live fully and authentically.

In the end, we're all staking our claim, whether it's to a piece of dirt in a cemetery or to the life we want to live. My grandfather's act of claiming his burial spot was both practical and symbolic. It was his way of saying, "This is where I belong. This is my place." But it was also a reminder that life is fleeting, and one day we'll all face the end.

As counselors, we have the unique privilege of helping people stake their claim, not to their final resting place, but to the life they want to live. We help them confront their fears, challenge their beliefs, and live with intention so that when their time comes, they can look back without regret.

And for all of us, whether we're counselors or clients, the lesson is clear: "The only day you're guaranteed is today." We have to make the most of it. We have to live with purpose, love deeply, forgive ourselves and others, and stake our claim to the life we've been given. In the end, it's not the gravestone that matters; it's the life we lived before we got there.

The Power of Experience

As a kid growing up visiting the family farm, I had plenty of opportunities to explore, learn, and occasionally make painful mistakes. One of the most memorable lessons came from an encounter with my grandfather's electric fence. Grandpa used an electric wire to keep the cows from wandering off, and my brother Tony and I quickly discovered how unpleasant it could feel when we tried to cross it.

But that wasn't the end of our curiosity. We spent the summer learning everything we could about that fence. We found out that not only could we get a jolt by directly touching the wire, but we could also get hit by simply grabbing a wet reed that was in contact with the wire. Over time, we even discovered that when my brother got shocked, and I happened to be touching him, I'd feel the sting too. It was a summer of painful education but one that taught me a lot about electricity, conduction, and, more importantly, cause and effect.

We had been warned by our parents and grandparents to stay away from the fence, but it wasn't until we experienced the shock ourselves that the lesson truly sank in. The consequence of touching that wire became real in a way that no amount of verbal warning could replicate. And after a few painful encounters, we learned to steer clear of it altogether.

That electric fence became more than just a boundary for the cows; it became a boundary for us, too. It was a metaphor for many of life's limits. Sometimes, we can be told over and over again about the dangers of a behavior or situation, but until we experience the consequences ourselves, we don't fully understand. In the mountains, there's a saying that sums this up: "Once bitten, twice shy." When we're young, we need those smaller lessons, the ones that might sting but won't cause lasting damage. Those early lessons teach us to avoid the more dangerous pitfalls later on.

Too often, parents try to shield their children from these early, smaller consequences. They rush in to rescue their kids before they have a chance to learn valuable lessons. But when children are constantly saved from the natural consequences of their actions, they miss out on important life lessons. If kids don't learn to cause and effect early on, they'll struggle to understand them when the stakes are much higher.

What I didn't know back then, during those summers on the farm, was that some sections of the electric fence were shut off. There were parts of the fence where I couldn't have gotten shocked even if I had tried. But by then, I had already developed a conditioned response to the fence. Even now, as an adult, I treat every electric fence the same way, like it's on and will hurt if I touch it. This learned response wasn't all that different from the experiments of Pavlov (Pavlov, 1927) and John B. Watson (Watson, 1920) in classical psychology. Pavlov's dogs learned to salivate at the sound of a bell, and Watson's Little Albert learned to fear a white rat after it was paired with a loud noise. In my case, I had learned to fear the electric fence, whether it was active or not.

This conditioned response served me well. The lessons I learned from that electric fence about cause and effect, respect, and boundaries stayed with me long after the summer ended. It was those early shocks that helped me avoid more serious harm later on. In much the same way, life's early lessons, even the small stings, prepare us for the bigger challenges ahead.

The problem arises when parents, out of love and concern, try to prevent their children from experiencing even these small stings. They shut off the electricity, so to speak, by rearranging life's rules so their children never feel discomfort, failure, or pain. While this may seem like an act of protection, it robs children of the opportunity to learn valuable lessons.

There's a reason the [12]Darwin Awards (Northcutt, 2000) exist: the infamous 'honors' given to people who meet their demise by ignoring basic cause-and-effect principles. While my lessons with the electric fence were painful but harmless, plenty of people in the real world learn their lessons far too late. Whether it's trying to pet a bison in Yellowstone or testing whether a gun is loaded by looking down the barrel, some mistakes carry permanent consequences. The lesson? Some boundaries aren't suggestions—they exist for a reason, and when we ignore them, we may not get a second chance to learn.

In today's world, there's a phrase that perfectly captures what I learned from that electric fence: [13]'fuck around and find out.' It's the modern version of 'once bitten, twice shy,' but with a sharper edge. The idea is simple—if you push boundaries, you'll eventually experience the consequences firsthand. While some

---

[12] The Darwin Awards are a satirical honor recognizing individuals who have "improved the human gene pool by removing themselves from it in a spectacularly foolish manner." Established in the early 1990s by Wendy Northcutt, the awards document real-life cases where people suffer fatal or sterilizing consequences due to extreme lapses in judgment. While humorous, the underlying message aligns with natural selection—those who fail to recognize and respect boundaries often face dire results. The awards serve as cautionary tales, reinforcing the fundamental law of cause and effect in human behavior.

[13] The phrase "fuck around and find out" (FAFO) originated as a colloquial expression meaning that actions have consequences—the more someone pushes boundaries, the more likely they are to face negative repercussions. Though the phrase has existed informally for years, it gained widespread popularity in internet culture and social media in the late 2010s. It was notably popularized by a viral meme graph that visually illustrates the concept: the more someone "fucks around" (engages in risky behavior), the more they "find out" (experience consequences). The phrase has been used in various cultural and political contexts but remains a blunt, modern take on cause and effect, akin to "play stupid games, win stupid prizes."

people learn quickly from small shocks, others keep testing limits until they face a painful reckoning. Whether it's ignoring financial responsibilities, relationships, or even safety, life has a way of enforcing its rules whether we're ready for them or not."

I recently worked with a couple, [lxiii]George and Denise, who had spent years rescuing their son from every mistake. From a young age, they protected him from any consequences that might hurt his feelings or make him uncomfortable. If he broke a toy, they bought him a new one. If he didn't study for a test, they helped him cram at the last minute to avoid a bad grade. They believed they were helping him, but in reality, they were setting him up for failure. Their son never learned how to handle adversity or take responsibility for his actions.

By the time he reached adulthood, the stakes were much higher. He had fallen into drug addiction and had started stealing from his parents to support his habit. They were still rescuing him, letting him live at home, paying his bills, and avoiding the hard conversations that might have set boundaries earlier in life. He had never learned to navigate the boundaries of life, and now he was floundering.

When George and Denise came to me for help, they were at their breaking point. They loved their son, but they knew they had enabled him for too long. Together, we worked on setting firm boundaries. They needed to stop rescuing him and allow him to face the natural consequences of his actions. It wasn't easy for them, they feared what might happen if they let him fall. But they also knew that without learning the hard lessons, their son would never grow.

We helped their son understand that if he wanted to live at home, he needed to get treatment for his addiction and find a job. If he didn't follow through, he would have to move out. It was a tough stance, but over time, their son began to take responsibility for his life. He went to rehab, found work, and started contributing to the household. The process wasn't easy, but it was those boundaries and tough love that finally allowed him to grow into the man he needed to be.

As counselors, we have the responsibility to help both clients and parents understand the value of boundaries and consequences. Setting boundaries and allowing consequences to happen is not cruel; it's essential for growth. When clients come to us, often they're struggling with the effects of avoiding consequences, either because they were shielded from them as children or because they've been avoiding them as adults.

Boundaries teach us about limits. They teach us what's acceptable and what isn't. And when we experience the natural consequences of crossing those boundaries, we learn valuable lessons. As the old saying goes, "You made your bed, now lie in it." The mistakes we make aren't failures; they're opportunities to learn and grow. Whether it's a child touching an electric fence or an adult struggling with addiction, the consequences we face can teach us how to navigate life more wisely.

As counselors, we need to encourage parents not to fear those small shocks that life gives their children. Those early, less dangerous experiences, like touching the fence, are what prepare children for the bigger challenges ahead. Rescuing them from every discomfort only delays the inevitable. Life will eventually deliver its lessons, but the longer they're postponed, the more painful they become.

For our clients, learning to embrace mistakes and face consequences is a vital part of therapy. "You can't learn to swim without getting wet," and in much the same way, we can't grow without learning from our mistakes. In therapy, it's important to help clients see their missteps not as failures, but as opportunities for growth.

The lessons I learned from that electric fence weren't just about electricity, they were about life. My conditioned response to avoid the fence, even when it was shut off, has served me well in other areas. It's those early shocks that teach us to respect boundaries, to think twice before acting, and to understand that every action has a consequence. And it's those conditioned responses that often save us from making more serious mistakes later on.

In therapy, we see how powerful these conditioned responses can be. Whether it's fear, avoidance, or anxiety, many of our clients are reacting to experiences they had long ago. By understanding those responses and where they come from, we can help them unlearn the ones that are no longer serving them and embrace the lessons that will guide them toward healthier decisions.

In the end, the lessons of the electric fence are the lessons of life. Boundaries are there for a reason, and when we cross them, there are consequences. But those consequences are what teach us to respect the limits, to learn from our mistakes, and to grow stronger for having faced them.

Stories That Shape Us and the Metaphors that Heal

In my childhood, and for generations before me, storytelling was a way of life. It wasn't just about entertainment, it was about survival, connection, and meaning making. When my mother, [lxiv]Norma, and her siblings were young, they would gather in the evenings, their chores finished, waiting eagerly for the stories that brought their family together. With no need for television or video games to fill the hours, these tales, woven with moral lessons, humor, and even fear, served as a thread that bound them together, offering guidance on how to live, love, and protect one another.

My mom often spoke about how her family, like many others in the region, didn't have much in the way of material possessions. But they were rich in other ways, particularly in the sense of community and connection that came from sharing stories passed down from older generations. Whether it was a tale of a mischievous child who learned the consequences of his actions or an eerie ghost story meant to keep kids from wandering too far after dark, these stories carried messages that stuck with them for life.

One of the most famous among them was the story of [14]Raw Head and Bloody Bones. This tale, though terrifying, was meant to protect my mom and her siblings from straying into danger. Told in hushed tones around a fire or by lamplight, the story spoke of a ghastly creature that roamed the hollers, looking for children who didn't mind their parents or stayed out too late. As terrifying as the story was, it served a protective function, it kept the children close to home, reinforcing the watchful nature of family. My mom recalled how they would clutch each other's hands when the story reached its climax, not just out of fear but out of shared comfort, knowing they were safe as long as they had each other.

---

[14] The tale of "Raw Head and Bloody Bones" is a traditional story originating from British folklore, later spreading to North America, particularly in Appalachia and the Southern United States. This legend has been used for centuries to caution children against misbehavior, depicting a creature that preys on the disobedient. The character is sometimes described as a water demon haunting deep ponds and old marl pits, dragging children into the depths, much like the grindylow and Jenny Greenteeth. In other versions, Bloody Bones is said to live in dark cupboards, usually under the stairs, waiting to catch children who tell lies or say bad words.

But beyond protection, these stories carried deeper moral lessons. There was often a clear sense of right and wrong, reinforced through characters who faced the consequences of bad decisions or who triumphed through hard work and kindness. Norma's parents used these stories as teaching tools, not through scolding or punishment, but by letting the stories speak for themselves. The children internalized these values as they laughed, listened, and sometimes trembled at the twists and turns in the narrative.

Norma and her siblings loved these moments. They would beg for the next story, eager to see what new lesson would unfold. In a world where entertainment today often pushes people into isolated, independent spaces, where televisions, phones, and video games keep people distracted in separate silos, these stories created a shared experience. Everyone was involved. The children weren't sitting separately, glued to screens or lost in their own worlds. They were together, listening, engaging, and learning from their parents and grandparents. The stories weren't just heard, they were felt.

Looking back, I see that these storytelling sessions were more than just entertainment, they were the foundation of resilience, healing, and identity. What my mother experienced in those childhood evenings around the fire is the same power that narrative therapy and therapeutic storytelling tap into today.

Storytelling allows people to make meaning of their experiences. Just as Norma and her siblings learned resilience from stories about overcoming hardship, clients today use storytelling as a way to process pain, loss, and trauma. When we turn our struggles into stories, they become something we can understand, explore, and eventually reshape.

Therapists have found that telling one's story in a safe environment allows for the release of trapped emotions. This is why talk therapy works, because speaking a painful memory aloud can be the first step to letting go of its hold. Storytelling in therapy allows people to release pain in a way that feels natural and safe, often transforming trauma into narratives of resilience and strength.

In both family traditions and therapy, storytelling is about connection. The act of sharing stories creates a bridge between people, it lets us see our common struggles and joys. In therapy, when a client shares their story and feels heard, they no longer carry their burdens alone. This mirrors how Norma and her siblings felt less afraid when they clutched each other's hands, because in telling and hearing a story together, we feel less alone in our experiences.

One of the most powerful aspects of therapeutic storytelling is the ability to reframe our experiences. Many people see their past through a lens of shame, guilt, or powerlessness. But storytelling in therapy allows them to reclaim their story, focusing not just on what happened to them, but how they survived. Clients can begin to see themselves not as victims of their past, but as authors of their future.

I've seen the power of storytelling play out time and time again in my work as a therapist. I've had clients who, at first, couldn't talk about their trauma, but when

I asked them to tell me their story, they found a way in. Sometimes, it starts with a childhood memory, sometimes a family tradition, and sometimes even a ghost story they once heard. And in the telling, something shifted, they could see their own resilience, their own strength, hidden in the details of their past.

In a way, my mother's storytelling tradition was the first therapy I ever experienced, long before I studied psychology or sat in a counseling office. Those evenings by the fire, where stories of hardship and triumph were told, taught me everything I needed to know about healing, connection, and the power of a well-told story. In therapy, in families, and in communities, storytelling remains one of the most powerful tools we have, not just to entertain, but to heal.

Metaphors are also not just a method of communication, they are the foundation of how we interpret the world, make sense of our experiences, and share wisdom. From tales of resilience and survival to humorous sayings passed down through generations, metaphors are woven into the very fabric of life in the mountains.

As therapists, we often find that metaphors, those simple yet powerful images or sayings, can open doors that logic and reasoning cannot. Metaphors tap into the emotional and unconscious realms, allowing clients to make connections and discoveries about themselves without feeling overwhelmed or defensive. It is a universal language that transcends cultural boundaries, but in Appalachia, it takes on a particularly special meaning. Here, we rely on metaphors not just to communicate but to teach, to warn, and to inspire.

Metaphors are powerful tools for facilitating communication and sparking change. They allow clients to "re-story" their experiences, often reframing deeply rooted emotions or beliefs. For clients from Appalachia, whose lives are often tied to the land and tradition, metaphors resonate in a way that more direct interventions might not.

Let's dive into some of the metaphors we've explored in this book and see how they've played an important role in both my personal life and the therapeutic space.

When working with clients, metaphors help to distill complex emotions and situations into something more manageable. Consider the phrase, "Life is simpler when you plow around the stump." This powerful metaphor has been discussed earlier as a way of helping clients understand that not all trauma needs to be dug up and processed in painful detail. Sometimes, the best course of action is to accept the stump in your path and move around it, rather than exhausting yourself trying to uproot it. It doesn't mean that trauma isn't significant, it's about finding a way to live around it, making peace with what cannot be changed. In therapy, this metaphor helps clients see that avoidance isn't always negative, it's about discernment, about knowing which battles to fight and which to let go of.

Similarly, the phrase "If you find yourself in a hole, the first thing to do is stop digging" offers a profound lesson for those dealing with addiction or self-destructive behavior. It is a reminder that when we are in a downward spiral, sometimes the hardest thing to do is stop. But stopping is the first step to figuring out how to climb out of that hole. This metaphor often resonates with clients who feel stuck in cycles of negative behavior, whether it's addiction, anxiety, or harmful relationships. The image is simple, but the message is powerful: change starts with the choice to stop doing what's hurting you.

Another metaphor that I often use with clients is "When you wallow with the pigs, expect to get dirty." This is a more direct way of helping clients see that they must take responsibility for the people they associate with and the environments they allow themselves to remain in. It's a reminder that if you surround yourself with negativity or destructive influences, you're bound to get caught up in it. This metaphor often comes up in conversations with clients who struggle with toxic relationships or environments, whether that's at work, home, or within their social circles.

In Motivational Interviewing (MI), metaphors can be a gentle yet effective tool for guiding clients toward change. As mentioned in a previous chapter, MI focuses on helping clients explore their own values and use those values to inspire change. Metaphors become particularly useful in moving clients from "sustain talk" (where they defend their current state) to "change talk" (where they express a desire to improve). A metaphor like "Sometimes you get, and sometimes you get got" can shift the conversation toward personal responsibility and accountability. It suggests that life is unpredictable, and while things may not always go your way, you have control over how you respond. It helps clients embrace both their agency and the reality of life's uncertainties.

In a session with one client, let's call her [lxv]Jenni, this metaphor became a turning point. Jenni had been trapped in a toxic relationship and repeatedly found herself drawn back into situations where she felt disempowered and hopeless. When we discussed her feelings of helplessness, I reflected back to her, "Sounds like every time you get caught up in that relationship, you feel like you're losing more and more of yourself." Jenni nodded and admitted that she felt like she was "getting got" each time. It was a subtle shift, but in that moment, she began to see herself as having more control than she initially realized. It wasn't about blaming herself but rather recognizing that while bad things happen, she had a choice in how to navigate those situations moving forward.

One of the most powerful aspects of using metaphors in therapy is their ability to connect with cultural values. In Appalachia, stories and metaphors are rich with meaning, often passed down through generations. These stories are not just a way to communicate, they are a way to teach, to pass on values, and to strengthen bonds.

For instance, the phrase "Give a man a fish, and you feed him for a day; teach a man to fish, and you feed him for a lifetime" could be easily adapted into an Appalachian context: "Don't just hand a man a meal, teach him how to plant a seed." This phrase emphasizes the importance of self-sufficiency, a core value in Appalachian culture. It reminds clients that therapy is not just about solving a problem in the moment, but about empowering them to solve their own problems in the future. This metaphor aligns perfectly with the role of the therapist as a guide, not someone who gives advice, but someone who helps the client discover their own answers.

"If you want change, it's like planting a seed, you have to water it, give it sunlight, and be patient. Growth doesn't happen overnight." This can be used for clients facing long-term challenges, helping them see that change takes time and effort.

Another one of my favorites is the toolbox metaphor. "Think of therapy like building a toolbox. Every skill we work on is another tool you can use when you face challenges." This metaphor empowers clients by framing therapy as equipping them with skills they can use independently.

Another one that is good with Appalachian culture is weather metaphors. For clients in crisis, "You're in the middle of a storm right now, but storms pass. Let's work on getting you the shelter you need to stay safe until it's over." This can help clients in crisis to recognize that pain and hardship are temporary.

The idea of life as a journey is a familiar metaphor for almost every client. It speaks to the uncertainties, milestones, and obstacles we all face. When guiding clients through difficult times, you can use phrases like, "Every journey starts with a single step" or "It's not the destination, but the journey that matters." These metaphors help clients understand that their growth and healing are processes rather than immediate fixes. For instance, in dealing with grief, trauma, or addiction, clients often want to skip the hard parts. But metaphors like "You can't skip to the end of the trail without walking it" remind them that each step is part of the healing process.

In therapy, a counselor might say, "You're at a crossroads right now, and while one path seems easy, the other may lead to better opportunities even if it's harder to climb." This encourages clients to weigh their decisions in the context of personal growth. When combined with Motivational Interviewing, this metaphor can facilitate change talk by helping clients envision the future they want.

Similar to the journey metaphor is the concept of a map. For those who feel lost, a metaphor of needing to find their map can be useful. You could say, "Right now, it feels like you're wandering without a map, but we're going to start plotting your course together." This helps clients feel less overwhelmed, as it implies that they are not wandering aimlessly, and they can regain control over their situation with the right tools.

This metaphor is particularly effective for clients struggling with anxiety or major life transitions. By helping them view therapy as a collaborative process of map-making, you emphasize their role in crafting their path forward.

For clients who enjoy sports or who resonate with competition and teamwork, sports metaphors can be powerful. You might say, "Life is a lot like a game, sometimes you win, and sometimes you lose, but you've got to stay in the game to even have a chance." This encourages clients to keep persevering through challenges, framing setbacks as part of the larger process of growth.

In therapy, you could say, "Right now, you're in halftime, and this is the time to reassess your strategy. It's not about how the game started; it's about how you finish." This metaphor aligns perfectly with helping clients shift from self-doubt or self-defeating talk into taking positive action. It reinforces the idea that each individual can "get back in the game" and achieve a different outcome, regardless of how things have gone so far.

Sports metaphors can also foster a sense of teamwork and collaboration between counselor and client. Phrases like "We're on the same team" or "I'm here as your coach, but you're the one on the field making the plays" emphasize the client's autonomy and the counselor's supportive role.

Metaphors not only facilitate therapeutic change but also honor the deep traditions of storytelling and wisdom within Appalachian culture. They allow clients to see themselves within the stories, to connect their personal struggles to universal truths, and to find hope in the lessons of those who came before them.

Metaphors are more than just tools for communication; they are bridges to understanding. They help clients connect their inner worlds with the external challenges they face, providing a framework for change that feels natural and aligned with their values. In Appalachia, where storytelling is a way of life, metaphors carry a unique power to heal and transform. As therapists, we can use these tools not only to communicate but to honor the culture and history of the people we serve. Through metaphors, we help clients reframe their stories, finding new paths forward and embracing the strength they didn't know they had.

Faith and Reason

In the hills of Appalachia, and the greater South, faith and reason have always danced together, sometimes in harmony, sometimes at odds. My father, [lxvi]Jim, who became a Baptist preacher when I was a young teen, embodied that dance. In his younger years, he had strayed from the faith of his people, seeking something beyond what he had known. Yet, as he grew older, he found his way back, embracing the religious tradition that had shaped his upbringing. His return to faith was a conscious one, a homecoming of sorts, but it wasn't without its own struggles.

My spiritual journey was different. I embraced the faith of my people in my youth, growing up in the religious culture that permeated our community. The church, the stories, the hymns, these were all a part of who I was. Yet, as I grew older, my need for reason, for evidence, began to overshadow the comfort that faith had once brought me. It wasn't that I rejected my people or the values they held dear; in fact, I remained deeply connected to them. But for me, faith and reason often felt like opposing forces. I couldn't stake a claim on what I saw as truth without having evidence to back it up.

In the work we do as counselors, we must acknowledge and respect that every client comes with their own set of beliefs, whether those beliefs lean more toward faith, reason, or somewhere in between. Our job is not to impose our belief systems on them but to work with them where they are. We meet them in their journey, whether they are wrestling with questions of faith, seeking evidence for their doubts, or holding fast to a belief system that provides comfort and structure in their lives.

My Grandma Carroll, known as [lxvii]Zoni, was a woman who accepted what she had been taught about spiritual matters from her youth. Her faith was as much a part of her as her love for her family or her sharp wit. She was a wise woman, and while no one could pull the wool over her eyes, even not with her near blindness, she had no reason to question what had worked for her. Faith had served her well. It provided a foundation upon which she built her life, and she had no reason to dismiss it.

Zoni's faith extended beyond just the religious practices of her community. It also encompassed belief in the supernatural, what she called "buggers" and "haints." I remember trying to get her to explain these terms, and she described a bugger as a kind of apparition, something unexplainable. A "haint", on the other hand, was the spirit of someone who had passed, haunting the living. For Zoni, these weren't just old wives' tales or folklore; they were gospel truth. She believed in them as surely as she believed in the Bible. To her, they were as real as the wind that rustled through the trees outside her door.

For me, these stories were fascinating and entertaining. I loved hearing them, especially coming from someone like her, who had a way of telling stories that captivated you from the first word. But as I grew older, I began to question the reality of these stories. I couldn't help but wonder if there weren't simpler explanations for the apparitions and strange occurrences she described. Maybe the mind plays tricks on us, especially in the dark hollers of the hills. Maybe what Zoni saw could be explained away with reason and logic. After all, as the principle of Occam's Razor suggests, the simplest explanation is often the most likely to be true.

Take, for example, the story of my great-grandmother Celicia Martin, Shelby Martin's first wife. The woman who had 14 children with him, the gift he claimed. Toward the end of her life, as described by her son William Perry Martin in the book *A Unique Family*, Celicia had visions of saints entering heaven. She saw her family among the number, and moments before she passed, she claimed to see angels, asking those around her if they could see them too. For many, this is a comforting story, a sign of an afterlife, a glimpse into the divine. For those who believe in such things, it's evidence of something greater than us, a reassurance that there is more to this life than what we can see or touch.

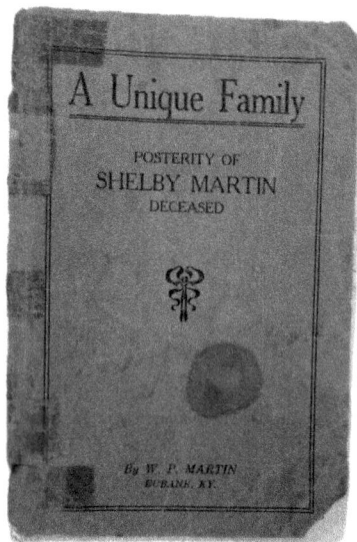

My copy of the book *"A Unique Family"*. I have one of the only remaining copies. It was given to me by my grandmother, Doreen Wesley.

But as a counselor with a background in geriatric mental health, I know that these kinds of visions are not uncommon in those nearing death. They can be explained as part of the brain's response to the dying process, phenomena that are well-documented in medical literature (Claxton-Oldfield, 2024). For me, it's not that I completely dismiss the possibility of an afterlife or spiritual visions, but I approach them with the same rational skepticism I bring to other aspects of life. I'm open to areas of knowledge we don't yet understand, but I need evidence before I can fully accept such claims.

In therapy, we must tread carefully when navigating the intersection of faith and reason. Clients come to us with their own beliefs, and those beliefs can be as varied as the people themselves. Some may find comfort in their faith, while others may be grappling with doubts or a need for evidence, much like I did in my own spiritual journey. Our role is not to challenge their beliefs or to impose our own views on them. Instead, we must create a space where clients feel safe to explore their thoughts and emotions, whatever they may be.

For clients like my grandmother Zoni, who held fast to her beliefs in the supernatural and the divine, therapy might involve using those beliefs as a way to process grief, trauma, or anxiety. Faith can provide a framework for understanding the world, offering comfort in times of distress. Dismissing a client's faith would only alienate them, making them feel unheard and misunderstood.

On the other hand, for clients who, like me, approach the world from a place of reason and skepticism, therapy might focus more on evidence-based practices like cognitive-behavioral therapy (CBT), where logic and rational thought are used to challenge negative thinking patterns. These clients may find comfort in facts and scientific reasoning, and therapy should reflect that.

The key is meeting clients where they are. We must respect their belief systems, whether they lean more toward faith or reason, and work with them in a way that aligns with their values.

For many people, faith and reason are not mutually exclusive. They can coexist, each serving a different purpose in a person's life. Faith can provide meaning and comfort, while reason offers clarity and understanding. In therapy, it's important to recognize that balance and to honor both aspects of a client's experience.

In Appalachia, and the greater South, faith is often passed down through generations, intertwined with family traditions and cultural practices. It's as much a part of the landscape as the mountains themselves. For some clients, faith is non-negotiable. It's a central part of their identity. For others, reason and logic may take precedence, shaping the way they understand the world. As therapists, our job is not to tip the scale in one direction or the other but to help clients find their own balance.

In the end, whether we are working with clients whose lives are shaped by faith, reason, or some combination of the two, our responsibility as counselors is to create a space where they feel heard, respected, and understood. We cannot impose our beliefs on them, nor can we dismiss theirs. Instead, we must guide them through their own journey, helping them find the answers that feel right for them.

Faith and reason will always be part of the human experience, especially in the hills and hollers of Appalachia, where tradition and culture run deep. As therapists, we must walk the line between these two forces, respecting our clients' beliefs while also providing them with the tools they need to heal and grow. In doing so, we honor the complexity of the human experience and the diverse paths that lead to understanding and peace.

If there's one thing you learned growing up in the mountains, it's that life doesn't hand you easy answers. The Appalachian way is full of unknowns, be it the weather, the harvest, or the winding paths you take through the hollers. It's an existence shaped by both doubt and faith, and there's wisdom in that balance. In the same way we don't know if the rains will come or the crops will take, we learn to live with uncertainty. Doubt is part of life here, and while some might see doubt as a sign of weakness or failure, it is, in fact, the opposite. It takes strength to live in uncertainty and still move forward.

This lesson is particularly true when it comes to matters of faith. For many of us born in Appalachia, faith was a constant, a guiding light passed down from generation to generation. Our parents, grandparents, and great-grandparents held on to their beliefs with certainty, and we were expected to follow suit. But the truth is, doubt is just as much a part of faith as certainty is, maybe even more so. Faith without doubt isn't really faith; it's certainty. And certainty leaves no room for growth, change, or discovery. Doubt, on the other hand, is what gives us the space to explore, to hope, and to build our beliefs in a way that feels authentic and real.

Sometimes, they're not rejecting Jesus, but they're rejecting the church because they feel like the church has left Jesus behind.

For many people, especially those who come from deeply religious backgrounds, doubt can feel uncomfortable, like walking barefoot over a rocky trail. But just as you have to pick your way through the stones to reach the green pasture on the other side, doubt is often the path to a deeper understanding of both faith and life.

When I was growing up, doubt wasn't something that was encouraged in church. You were expected to believe fully, without question, and to be certain in that belief. My grandmother Zoni, for example, never questioned what she had been taught. She accepted her faith wholeheartedly, and it served her well. But for others, like me, doubt played a bigger role in the journey. I needed evidence, something tangible to hold on to before I could commit to belief. I wrestled with doubt, but instead of seeing it as a weakness, I've come to understand that doubt is essential even for faith.

As a counselor, I've seen many clients struggle with doubt, especially when it comes to spiritual matters. Some have felt ashamed for questioning what they were taught as children. Others fear that their doubt is a sign that they've failed in some way. But doubt is not a failure; it's an invitation to grow. It's the crack in the door that lets light in. "Doubt ain't nothing but the spade that helps you dig deeper." As the old saying goes, "You can't fix a leak if you never notice the drip." Doubt is that drip; it's the thing that makes us pay attention and go searching for a more meaningful understanding.

One of the hardest things I've seen as a counselor is parents grappling with the fact that their children are moving away from the faith that they themselves hold so dear. For many parents, this feels like a personal failure, as though they've failed to pass down something vital. They often feel guilty, wondering where they went wrong or if they didn't do enough to instill their values in their children.

But here's the thing: certainty doesn't come as easily for younger generations as it did for their parents or grandparents. The world is a lot more complex now, and with that complexity comes doubt. Many of today's young people are wrestling with not just personal faith but with what they perceive as the failures of religious institutions. Sometimes, they're not rejecting Jesus, but they're rejecting the church because they feel like the church has left Jesus behind.

Think about Jesus' message in the Beatitudes: love your neighbor, turn the other cheek, care for the poor, be humble. For many of the younger generation, these are the values they hold close. They've listened closely to the love of Jesus, but they don't always see those values reflected in the church. And so, they question. They doubt. They ask hard questions. But this isn't something to fear or feel guilty about. Doubt doesn't mean that a child has lost their way. In fact, it may mean that they're searching for a more authentic connection to their spirituality.

As the saying goes, "You can lead a horse to water, but you can't make him drink." As parents and counselors, we can guide, teach, and offer love, but we cannot force certainty on someone else. Certainty may have been handed to us in a neat package growing up, but the world today is full of grey areas, and it's okay for our children to navigate those spaces of doubt.

For counselors, it's important to recognize that doubt isn't something to be "fixed." When a client comes to us grappling with spiritual doubt, it's not our job to push them toward certainty. Instead, we create a space where doubt is welcomed, explored, and understood. Just as we encourage our clients to sit with uncomfortable emotions, we should also encourage them to sit with their doubts. Sometimes, doubt is the tool that helps people chip away at the surface and get to something deeper, something truer.

In Appalachia, where faith is often a cornerstone of identity, clients may feel especially conflicted when they experience doubt. The cultural pressure to conform to the faith of one's family can be strong and stepping outside of that can feel like a betrayal. But just like the mountains that surround us, spiritual journeys are full of peaks and valleys. "Ain't no way to climb a mountain without a few slips on the rocks." We must help our clients understand that doubt is a natural part of their journey, not something to fear or avoid.

When working with parents who are struggling with their children's departure from the faith, we need to help them see that doubt is not a reflection of failure. It's easy for parents to blame themselves, thinking they did something wrong. But sometimes, doubt is a sign that their children listened too well to the message of love, kindness, and humility, and they're holding the church accountable for falling short of that message. As counselors, we can help parents let go of their guilt and recognize that their children's spiritual journey may look different from theirs, and that's okay.

For clients, it's important to learn how to live in the tension between doubt and certainty. Faith, after all, isn't about having all the answers. It's about holding on to hope even when you don't have them. Doubt doesn't weaken your faith; it can actually make it stronger because it forces you to wrestle with what you believe and why you believe it.

Think of it like this: "The tallest trees have the deepest roots." When the winds of doubt come, those roots might get shaken, but it's that very shaking that helps the tree grow stronger, digging deeper into the soil to find its foundation. The same is true for faith. When doubt shakes our beliefs, it gives us the chance to dig deeper to find what truly holds us up. Certainty leaves no room for growth, but doubt gives us the space to expand, question, and deepen our understanding.

In the end, doubt is not something to be feared; it's something to be embraced. Whether it's the doubt of a client wrestling with spiritual questions or the doubt of a parent worried about their child's faith journey, we need to recognize doubt as a necessary part of growth.

As therapists, we hold space for this doubt, allowing our clients to explore it without judgment or fear. We understand that certainty can feel comforting, but it's often the cracks of doubt that let the light of understanding in. In Appalachia, where faith runs deep and strong, doubt may feel like a betrayal of tradition. But just as the land changes with the seasons, so too do our beliefs grow and evolve. It's our job to walk with our clients through those changes, guiding them with compassion, empathy, and the understanding that doubt is not a weakness; it's a pathway to deeper faith. "Ain't no river too wide if you know where to cross." And sometimes, it's doubt that helps us find the way.

Building Tolerance

There's an old saying that goes, "You can't make everyone happy, and you're not made of gold anyhow." It's a good reminder that disagreement is part of life, especially here in Kentucky and Appalachia, where strong opinions and even stronger personalities often collide. But here's the thing about disagreement: it doesn't have to tear us apart. In fact, it can be one of the healthiest exercises we engage in, helping us sharpen our thinking, broaden our perspective, and learn from one another. Yet, in today's world, it feels like any form of disagreement is met with accusations of trauma, racism, gaslighting, or abuse. We've lost the ability to have meaningful conversations without turning differences into personal attacks.

As a counselor and someone deeply connected to the values of my people, I've come to see how important it is to build tolerance for disagreement. We need to reclaim the idea that we can argue, debate, and disagree without it turning into something toxic. We need to learn how to tolerate emotional discomfort and how to talk through difficult issues without feeling like we're being attacked.

This is an important lesson not just for my clients but for counselors, too. We must model and guide our clients toward healthy communication. If we can help them see that conflict isn't inherently bad, and that disagreement can be productive, we'll have given them a powerful tool for navigating the complexities of life.

It seems that in today's society, we've developed an increasingly thin skin when it comes to difficult conversations. Disagreement has become synonymous with conflict, and conflict is often labeled as abuse. We've started to treat any unpleasant experience as trauma and any opposing view as an attack. "Taking offense has become the national sport," and instead of trying to understand the other side, people jump to defensive positions.

This is especially true when it comes to discussions of microaggressions. The concept itself was meant to highlight the small, everyday slights that people from marginalized groups experience—things that may not be overtly hostile but still carry weight. And that's important. Words do matter. However, in practice, the discussion around microaggressions has often become a minefield rather than a bridge. Instead of using these moments as opportunities to educate or connect, they have turned into a weaponized list of offenses, leaving people walking on eggshells for fear of saying the wrong thing.

I've seen this firsthand in my work. A well-meaning student, trying to engage in an honest discussion about race, was shut down immediately because she phrased something in a way that was perceived as offensive. Instead of a productive conversation, it became a moment of public shaming. She wasn't trying to be cruel, she was trying to learn. But rather than helping her understand, the moment made her withdraw entirely. I never saw her attempt to engage in that discussion again.

This is what happens when we approach conversation with a gotcha mindset rather than a learning mindset. People stop talking. They stop engaging. And when people stop engaging, nothing changes. Microaggressions are real, but we must find a way to call people in, rather than just calling them out. If our goal is to educate, we need to leave room for people to make mistakes without fearing social exile.

"You can't pick the berries without dealing with a few thorns."

There's a difference between real trauma and the discomfort that comes with having your ideas challenged. Trauma is deeply distressing and often linked to abuse, violence, or severe emotional harm. Disagreement, on the other hand, is simply part of the human condition. Not every argument is a personal affront, and not every difference of opinion is a sign that someone is trying to harm you.

In Appalachia, we understood this. We'd have heated discussions, sure. But we didn't let those disagreements define our relationships. "You can disagree without being disagreeable," my father used to say. And it's true. You can sit on a porch with your neighbor, argue about politics or religion, and still shake hands at the end of the day. You can leave a conversation thinking, "I don't agree with a word they said, but I still respect them as a person."

We need to recover that spirit, where debate is a form of connection, not division. Where ideas are shared in pursuit of truth, not in the pursuit of one-upping or undermining the other person. We must allow for space where disagreement doesn't result in the immediate calling out of words like "gaslighting" or "abuse" unless those things are truly happening. When we overuse these terms, we dilute their meaning, making it harder to identify real harm.

There's a reason why people in Appalachia are known for their toughness. Life here has never been easy, but we've learned to roll with the punches. And that resilience extends to our ability to handle tough conversations. Pain, whether physical or emotional, is part of life, but that doesn't mean we should avoid it at all costs. Pain can teach us, grow us, and help us connect with others.

In counseling, I often work with clients who feel overwhelmed by conflict or who struggle with differing opinions. For many, the emotional discomfort of being disagreed with feels unbearable. But here's the truth: "You can't put out a fire by ignoring the smoke." We need to address the source of our discomfort and learn to sit with it without letting it consume us. In therapy, we often teach mindfulness or grounding techniques to help clients manage emotional discomfort, but these tools aren't about avoiding pain, they're about building tolerance for it.

Painful conversations, whether in therapy, with family, or in public discourse, are necessary. They're what help us grow. Just like the hills of Appalachia force you to climb up steep paths to reach the view on the other side, tough conversations force us to wade through the hard stuff to find clarity and understanding. "You can't pick the berries without dealing with a few thorns."

In the South, we're famous for our sayings, and some of them are a way to soften the blow of disagreement. But we have to be careful not to use these phrases as a way of asserting moral superiority. Take, for example, the phrase "Bless his heart" or "God love em." These sayings, when used in the right context, can be full of warmth and kindness, but too often, they're wielded like a shield. They can be a way of saying, "I'm right, you're wrong, and you're too foolish to see it."

When we use language like this in a disagreement, we're not engaging in honest debate. We're positioning ourselves as superior, as though we're the ones who hold the moral high ground. Phrases like "I'll pray for you" can have the same effect. While prayer can be an incredibly powerful and supportive practice, using it to shut down an argument doesn't give weight to our points; it diminishes the other person's views.

Counselors need to be aware of how these subtleties play out in communication and help clients recognize when their language might be alienating the very people they're trying to connect with. We need to teach our clients, and sometimes ourselves, how to argue in good faith, how to pursue truth together, even when we disagree.

As counselors, one of our greatest responsibilities is to model healthy communication for our clients. We may need to do ongoing roleplays with individuals struggling with difficult conversations with others to build their skills. Here are the main points to keep in mind: First, disagreement is not an attack. Help clients understand that being disagreed with isn't the same as being attacked. Disagreement can signify that someone is invested enough in the relationship to share their honest views. Second, pain is part of growth. Teach clients that discomfort cannot be avoided at all costs. In fact, it's often a necessary part of personal growth. "If you don't stir the pot, the stew won't thicken." Thirdly, mind your language. Be mindful of how certain phrases or tones of voice can be perceived as condescending or dismissive. Encourage clients to debate without resorting to moral superiority or passive-aggressive phrases. Finally, conflict isn't always trauma. Help clients differentiate between actual trauma and the everyday discomfort that comes with navigating relationships. "Don't turn every hill into a mountain."

For clients, especially those who struggle with disagreement, the goal isn't to avoid conflict but to learn how to handle it in a way that strengthens relationships rather than breaking them down. Here's some advice: Stay curious. In a disagreement, instead of immediately defending your point, ask questions. Try to understand where the other person is coming from. "You can't see the whole barn if you only look through one window. Second, Be kind, not right. Sometimes, the goal of a conversation isn't to be right but to be kind. Focus on the relationship over the need to win the argument. And finally, learn to sit with discomfort. When a conversation feels tense or uncomfortable, take a deep breath and remind yourself that discomfort isn't the same as harm. "Tough bark makes a strong tree."

In Appalachia, we know how to disagree without falling apart. We can argue about politics, faith, or family dynamics and still break bread together at the end of the day. This resilience in the face of disagreement is something our society sorely needs to rediscover. In therapy, we can help our clients develop the emotional toughness to have hard conversations without feeling attacked. We can teach them that disagreement doesn't have to lead to division and that sometimes the best growth happens when we're willing to step into the discomfort of opposing views.

At the end of the day, it's not about avoiding disagreement, it's about learning how to navigate it with grace, understanding, and respect. After all, "It's not the storm that breaks you, but how you learn to sail through it."

The Healing Power of Animals

In the hills of Appalachia, animals have always been a part of our way of life. Whether it was the cows in the pasture, the pigs in the pen, or the dogs at our feet, animals were part of the family. But beyond the practical roles they played, plowing fields, providing food, or offering protection, there was something deeper, something harder to put into words. The connection between people and animals went beyond mere utility. Animals could sense things, feel things, and provide a type of comfort and healing that we humans often couldn't express ourselves. And if anyone understood this connection, it was my [lxviii]grandpa Cortez Wesley.

Gramps had a way with animals. He was what you'd call a magician with them. I remember his horse, Pearl, a racking horse that could have been in the movies with how well-trained she was. Grandpa could do anything with Pearl, and the bond they shared was something special. You could see it in the way the horse responded to him, not just with obedience, but with love. It wasn't just Pearl, though. Gramps had that same connection with all the animals on the farm. He could buy wild pigs, and within a week, they'd be lying on their backs, practically begging for belly scratches.

The most vivid memory I have of Grandpa's connection to animals was the way he called his cows. Normally, Grandpa was a quiet man, but when it was time to bring the cows in from the pasture, he would let loose with a loud, booming call: "Sook, Sook... Com-on Cows!". At the sound of his voice, the cows would lift their heads and come running toward him like puppies. They followed him to the barn, one by one, while he talked to them, calling them by name. It was like watching a shepherd with his flock, and you couldn't help but marvel at the trust and respect between Grandpa and those cows.

Grandpa never had the money for a tractor, but I think he preferred his large Belgian plow horses, Amos and Andy, anyway. He trusted them, and they trusted him. With his horses, he could plow the garden with a single plow. He also planted several acres of corn with those horses. My mom and cousins Kaye, Jerry, and Joanie remember helping harvest the crop as the horses pulled the wagon ever so slowly; they would throw the ears of corn in the wagon. In that quiet relationship between man and animal, there was a kind of healing, a bond that gave both purpose and strength. It's something I've carried with me in my own life, especially when I've seen how animals can provide that same healing to others.

Grandpa Cortez Wesley out plowing the field with Amos and Andy.

My father, [lxix]Jim, often talked about his dog, Drum. Drum was more than just a pet; he was my father's best friend growing up. Dad spoke often of the companionship and loyalty Drum offered him during his childhood, but Drum's greatest gift came on the day he gave his life to save my father's.

Dad was outside near a stream when a water moccasin slithered toward him. Before Dad even realized the danger, Drum leaped into action, placing himself between Dad and the snake. Drum was struck by the snake, and despite my father's efforts to save him, Drum never recovered from the venom. My father mourned the loss of his friend, but he always told me that Drum had given him the greatest gift anyone could, the gift of life.

My father, James Wesley, and his dog Drum.

Years later, something similar happened with my youngest child, [lxx]Milo. At the age of 16, Milo was diagnosed with idiopathic thrombocytopenia purpura (ITP), a condition that caused his blood platelets to drop to dangerously low levels. After a stint in the hospital, Milo was finally able to come home, but he had to be extremely careful. Even a small injury could cause uncontrollable bleeding. That's when Wilson, our long-haired dachshund, became Milo's guardian.

One day, after a few days of bed rest, Milo ventured outside near our garden. That's when he noticed a large Rottweiler growling and coming toward him. Milo, still weak and vulnerable, stood frozen in fear. But before the Rottweiler could pounce, little Wilson, no more than a tenth the size of the Rottweiler, launched himself at the larger dog. It was a battle of David and Goliath, and though Wilson was severely outmatched, he didn't back down. The Rottweiler grabbed Wilson, shaking him in his jaws like a rag doll, but something about Wilson's bravery made the Rottweiler retreat.

Milo was saved, but Wilson was close to death. For weeks, our family nursed both Milo and Wilson back to health, side by side. Miraculously, Wilson recovered and lived another 15 years, a testament to the protective, selfless bond that animals can have with their humans.

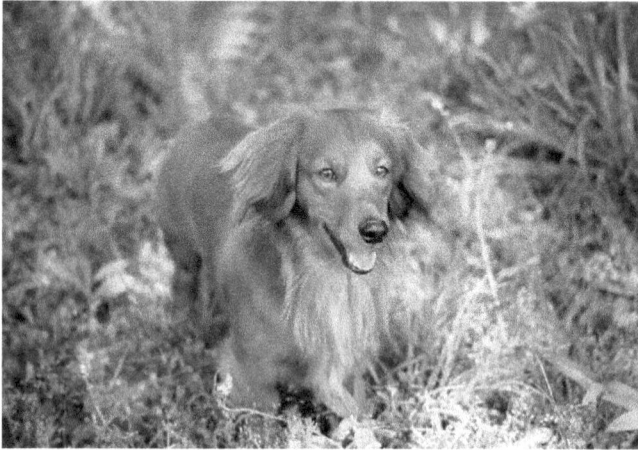

Wilson, our hero dog

My uncle lxxiTruman, a highly decorated Vietnam War veteran, also had a deep bond with his dog, Chief. Uncle Truman had seen more than his fair share of pain and loss during the war, and perhaps that's why Chief became such an important part of his life. Chief, a yellow lab, was more than just a pet; he was family. Even when Chief lost his front right leg in a car accident, his bond with Uncle Truman never wavered. For years, the two were inseparable, with Chief following Uncle Truman around the farm, three legs and all.

Then came the day when Chief's body could no longer keep up. He had an attack while they were working on the farm together, and Chief passed away in my uncle's arms. Uncle Truman, the tough-as-nails soldier who had crawled through tunnels in northern Vietnam, lay down in the field and wept for his beloved friend. That's the power animals have, the ability to break through the hardest of hearts and offer comfort in a way nothing else can.

It's stories like these that inspired me to explore the role of animals in therapy. Twenty years ago, while I was running a substance abuse treatment center in central Kentucky, I noticed how our residents would interact with the wildlife around them, squirrels, rabbits, and the occasional stray cat. The presence of these animals seemed to calm the residents, and it gave me an idea. What if we introduced a therapy dog into group therapy? Could animals help improve the therapeutic alliance between therapists and clients? Could they lower blood pressure and heart rates, leading to better outcomes in treatment?

These questions led to my doctoral dissertation project. I wanted to see if animal-assisted therapy could make a measurable difference in the lives of my clients. For months, I conducted experiments with therapy dogs in group sessions, monitoring clients' physiological responses and the strength of their relationship with the therapist. The results were profound. Not only did the presence of a therapy dog improve the therapeutic alliance, but it also significantly lowered both blood pressure and heart rates in clients. These findings were published in the professional journal Anthrozoos (Wesley M. C., 2009), marking a turning point in my understanding of the healing power of animals.

The bond between humans and animals is ancient and powerful. Whether it's a horse, a dog, or a pig, animals have an innate ability to heal, protect, and comfort us in ways that go beyond words. From my grandpa's magical way with the animals on his farm, to Drum's ultimate sacrifice for my father, to Wilson's bravery in the face of danger, animals have always been there for my family. And as a therapist, I've seen firsthand how they can help my clients heal, too.

Animal-assisted therapy isn't just about science, it's about compassion. It's about understanding that sometimes the best healer doesn't come in the form of a person, but in the form of a loyal, loving animal who sees us for who we are and loves us anyway. In Appalachia, we've always known that. Animals aren't just tools or pets; they're family, and they have the power to bring out the best in us, no matter what we're facing. "Ain't nothing like the love of a good dog to set the world right again."

Today, my wife, [lxxii]Dawn, and I continue to incorporate the healing power of animals into our counseling practice. We have a Bichon Frise named Pierre, who has become an invaluable part of our work with clients. Pierre is not just a pet; he's a therapeutic presence, a joyful little dog who has a way of sensing exactly what our clients need. When someone comes into the office feeling down, Pierre seems to know. He'll nuzzle up beside them or perform one of his funny little dances, instantly lifting their spirits. When clients are struggling with grief or anxiety, Pierre offers silent comfort, lying close and offering his unconditional love.

Pierre brings a lightness to the room that encourages clients to open up, relax, and feel seen. In many ways, he embodies the very essence of what therapy aims to do, bring joy, comfort, and healing. Clients often tell us how Pierre's presence has helped them during difficult sessions, and he reminds me of the many ways animals can support us in ways words simply cannot.

Dawn and Pierre

If there's one lesson, I've learned from years of working with animals in therapy, it's that animals have a unique ability to break down barriers. For therapists, incorporating animals into your practice can create a more welcoming and supportive environment, one where clients feel more comfortable sharing their emotions and experiences. Therapy animals, like Pierre, can serve as a bridge between the client and the therapist, offering a non-judgmental presence that makes it easier to engage in the therapeutic process.

For clients, seeking out a therapist who uses therapy animals might be a game-changer. The calming presence of a dog, cat, or even a horse can lower anxiety, provide comfort, and help clients feel more grounded during their sessions. It's something I would encourage clients to consider, especially those who feel apprehensive about therapy. Animals have a way of making us feel safe, and in a therapeutic setting, that safety can be the key to unlocking deeper healing.

In Appalachia, we've always understood the bond between humans and animals. Whether it's the cows following Grandpa to the barn or Pierre dancing around our counseling office, animals have a way of making life a little bit easier, a little bit more joyful. For counselors and clients alike, embracing that bond could be the missing piece to a truly healing experience. "A good dog and a kind word go a long way toward healing a broken heart."

The Unpredictability of Life

There's a saying in Appalachia: "You can be tough as nails, but even nails rust." Life has a way of surprising us, even those who think they have it all figured out. That's why we must remain vigilant as counselors, friends, and family members, never assuming that resilience alone will carry someone through the darkest moments of their lives. As someone who has trained counselors for over two decades, I've seen the volatility of human emotions and the potential for things to spiral out of control quickly, even with people who seem like they have everything under control.

One of the hardest lessons I've learned came from a mock counseling session in one of my classes. [lxxiii]Amy and Carla were two of my students. As part of their counseling skills course, they needed to present a recorded mock counseling session to the rest of the class. That Sunday, they waited until the last minute to complete their session, with Carla acting as the therapist and Amy as the client. While the goal in these sessions is to deal with real issues but nothing too serious, Amy brought up something deeply personal: her struggle with her marriage and her concerns about her husband's closeness with a colleague.

"You can be tough as nails, but even nails rust."

Carla, using the skills she had been learning, listened empathetically and helped Amy develop a strategy to confront her husband. They ended their session and submitted the recording, preparing to present it to the class on Tuesday. But when Tuesday arrived, Amy wasn't there. We later learned that she had confronted her husband the night before and, in a moment of desperation, took her own life.

Amy was a professional, working in mental health herself, taking courses to become a licensed therapist. She had the knowledge and the skills, and yet, in a moment of being emotionally overwhelmed, she reached for a gun and made a permanent decision to a temporary problem. It's a sobering reminder of how fragile life can be, even for those who seem to have all the tools at their disposal.

As counselors, we have to remember that we are not just dealing with skills and techniques, we are dealing with people, their emotions, vulnerabilities, and potential for harm. Every client we see, no matter how put-together they may seem, could be struggling with something we can't immediately see. That's why it's so important to assess every client for risk, not just at the beginning of treatment but throughout the course of therapy.

When a client is experiencing overwhelming emotions, whether it's anger, hopelessness, or grief, we need to be attuned to the signs of potential risk. These signs can sometimes be subtle: expressions of hopelessness, changes in behavior, withdrawal from loved ones, or even statements like "I just don't see the point anymore." Our job is to create a space where these thoughts can be expressed safely and to take action when necessary.

In Amy's case, there were no obvious red flags during her mock session. She expressed frustration with her marriage, yes, but she was also working through a plan of action. It seemed like she was in control of the situation. But, as counselors, we need to be aware that beneath the surface, there could be deeper layers of emotional turmoil that the client might not yet be fully aware of. This is why ongoing risk assessment, asking directly about thoughts of suicide or harm to self or others, is crucial.

"You can't fix what you don't acknowledge," as the saying goes, and sometimes, just asking the right question can open up a conversation that may save a life.

For clients who may be reading this, I want to emphasize one thing: seek help. Life is fragile, unpredictable, and, at times, overwhelming. But help is available, and you don't have to go through your darkest moments alone. There's no shame in reaching out to a therapist, a friend, or a family member when you feel like you're losing control. In fact, it's one of the bravest things you can do.

One of the challenges I've seen in the Appalachian region, in particular, is the belief that seeking help is a sign of weakness. "Tough it out," they say, "don't air your dirty laundry." There's a cultural pride in being strong and self-reliant. And while that resilience is something to be proud of, it can also be dangerous when it prevents people from asking for help when they truly need it.

Appalachians have always been known for their strength. It's a region shaped by hardship, mining accidents, farming failures, and economic struggles. Families here have learned to weather storms and lean on each other in times of crisis. But no matter how resilient a person or a community may be, there comes a point where even the strongest among us need help.

"You can't mend a fence if you wait for the whole barn to fall down." The key is recognizing when you need support before things spiral out of control. Therapy isn't about fixing what's broken; it's about maintaining your emotional well-being, much like you'd maintain your physical health. It's about having a space to talk about your fears, frustrations, and pain without judgment.

The people of Appalachia are tough, no doubt about it. But we also have to acknowledge that life is fragile. A person can be strong for years, overcoming adversity after adversity, only to break under the weight of one too many burdens. That's why it's important for counselors to recognize that even the most resilient clients are not immune to emotional collapse. And for clients, it's important to know that being vulnerable, asking for help, and admitting when life feels overwhelming doesn't make you weak, it makes you human.

In Appalachia, we understand the unpredictability of life better than most. We've seen loved ones taken by sudden accidents, like my great-grandparents, one who was killed by a horse's kick and the other who fell from a cliff. We live with the dangers of nature, whether it's snakes in the grass or the uncertainty of the next harvest. But even as we understand life's fragility, we also know that "you can't live your life waiting for the sky to fall." We can't avoid the dangers of life, but we can learn to navigate them with support.

Counselors should never assume that a client is safe just because they appear composed. The reality is that many clients, especially those knowledgeable in mental health issues themselves, can mask their struggles. We must build a relationship of trust where our clients feel safe enough to express their deepest fears and darkest thoughts. And we must be willing to ask the tough questions: "Have you thought about hurting yourself?" "Do you feel safe at home?" These are not easy conversations, but they are necessary.

Assess risk consistently, build rapport, and create a safe space where your clients can talk openly. And remember that even the most resilient clients have their breaking points. Just because someone is strong doesn't mean they're invincible.

The story of Amy and Carla is a tragic reminder of how quickly things can go wrong, even for those who seem to have it all together. As counselors, we must always be vigilant, assessing for risk and providing a safe space for our clients to explore their emotions. For clients, it's essential to understand that seeking help is not a sign of weakness; it's a sign of strength.

In Appalachia, we know all too well the fragility and unpredictability of life. But we also know that "even the tallest oak can fall in a storm." It's not about whether or not we'll face difficulties in life, it's about how we handle them when they come. And the first step to handling them is recognizing when we need help.

For those who are struggling, I encourage you to reach out. And for counselors, I encourage you to always be ready to listen and assess. Life is precious, fragile, and unpredictable. But with the right support, we can weather the storms.

Pandemic Lessons

My great-grandfather, [lxxiv]Shelby Martin, was a man who knew the meaning of resilience. He raised 17 children in the rugged hills of Kentucky, and his legacy lives on in the stories of strength and endurance passed down through generations of our family. But one of the hardest chapters of his life, and of our family's history, came in 1918, during the deadly influenza pandemic that swept across America and the world.

Shelby's youngest son, Virgil, had been called to Monticello, Kentucky, to be examined for World War I service. It was there that both he and his father contracted the flu, which had already claimed millions of lives globally. They were isolated in their suffering, with no help in sight. Panic spread through the area, and anyone who showed symptoms of the illness was feared and shunned. People were so terrified of exposure that they couldn't even visit their own family members. Shelby and Virgil were alone in their struggle until Hattie, one of Shelby's daughters, and her husband came to offer assistance. Their bravery stood in stark contrast to the fear that had gripped the community.

The other children, despite their love for their father and brother, had to stay away. Visiting their father would have meant putting their own lives and the lives of their children at risk. The heartbreak of not being able to be by his side weighed heavily on the family, but the pandemic had created a new kind of isolation, one where love and care had to take a back seat to survival. This is a feeling many of us experienced firsthand during the COVID-19 pandemic of our own time.

Shelby did not survive the flu. He was buried without the comfort of his large family in attendance. It was a lonely end for a man who had spent his life surrounded by those he loved. Virgil, on the other hand, recovered and later moved to work for the Stearns Coal and Lumber Company, bringing his widowed mother with him. He went on to marry, have children, and build a life, carrying with him the weight of losing his father during one of the most devastating pandemics in American history.

Many years later, we faced another pandemic. And like Shelby and Virgil, we experienced the fear, isolation, and grief that accompany such an event. But we also had the opportunity to learn lessons from that time, lessons about resilience, compassion, and the fragility of life. As a counselor and counselor educator, I've reflected on these lessons, and they've shaped the way I approach my work today.

The pandemic of 1918 and the COVID-19 pandemic that struck over a century later taught us much about the human condition. One of the most striking parallels between these two events is how they laid bare the interconnectedness of our physical and mental health. The isolation, fear, and grief of losing loved ones were as devastating during Shelby's time as they were during our own. But what sets us apart is the opportunity to learn from those who came before us.

One of the hardest aspects of both pandemics was the forced isolation. During Shelby's illness, his family couldn't be with him in his final moments. This separation, born out of necessity, inflicted deep emotional wounds on those left behind. The same was true during COVID-19. Many of us were unable to say goodbye to loved ones, and the grief of that loss, both physical and emotional, was profound.

As counselors, we've learned that human connection is essential to healing. Even in times of isolation, we must find ways to stay connected with others, whether through technology or other means. I've seen clients struggle with the loneliness that came from quarantine and social distancing, but I've also seen the power of a phone call, a Zoom session, or even a simple message to remind someone that they are not alone.

Both pandemics left a trail of grief in their wake. But what I've learned as a counselor is that grief is unique to each person. Virgil had to move forward after losing his father, and while he built a life for himself, the loss of Shelby was something that stayed with him. Similarly, during the COVID-19 pandemic, people coped with loss in different ways. Some were angry, others numb, and some turned to their faith or community for comfort.

In counseling, we must recognize that grief doesn't follow a prescribed path. Just because someone survived doesn't mean they aren't suffering. Counselors need to offer space for clients to process their grief in their own time and in their own way, without pushing them toward a specific resolution. "There's no right way to grieve," as the saying goes, "only your way."

In Kentucky and Appalachia, we pride ourselves on resilience. Shelby's life, raising 17 children and surviving in a harsh environment, was a testament to that resilience. But even the strongest among us can be brought low by forces beyond our control. The pandemic taught us that while we can endure much, we are also fragile. Life is unpredictable, and no amount of strength can protect us from the randomness of illness and loss.

This is an important lesson for counselors and clients alike. It's okay to admit that you're struggling. Being resilient doesn't mean you're invincible; it means you keep going even when life knocks you down. "The oak tree bends in the wind but doesn't break," they say in the mountains, and that's the balance we need to strike, allowing ourselves to feel the weight of our circumstances without letting them define us.

If there's one thing I've learned from my time as a counselor, it's that empathy is the most powerful tool we have. During the pandemic, the world was filled with fear and panic, much like the days of 1918 when Shelby and Virgil were sick. People avoided each other out of self-preservation, but those who showed up, like Hattie and her husband, were the ones who made a difference. It's the same in counseling.

Clients don't always need us to solve their problems; they need us to sit with them, listen to them, and walk beside them in their pain.

During COVID-19, many of my clients felt isolated and unseen. But by showing up with empathy and unconditional positive regard, whether through virtual sessions or socially distanced walks, we created a space for healing. Counselors don't need to have all the answers; we just need to be present.

Both pandemics reminded us of the fragility of life, but they also highlighted the importance of connection, resilience, and empathy. Shelby Martin didn't make it through the 1918 flu, but his son Virgil carried on, and generations later, we are still learning from their experience.

In counseling, we must remember that no matter how strong our clients appear, they are not immune to the unpredictability of life. But in the face of that uncertainty, we can offer them connection, support, and a space to process their pain. "Life's like a mountain trail, hard and rough, but the company you keep makes the journey worthwhile."

As we move forward, let's carry these lessons with us, knowing that while life can be fragile, it can also be beautiful when we face it together.

Deep Roots, Strong Branches

As this journey through the pages of my family history and the therapeutic lessons learned from my roots in Kentucky draws to a close, I find myself reflecting on the interconnectedness of it all, how deeply our past shapes our present, and how those deep roots strengthen the branches of our lives.

The stories of my ancestors, their resilience, and their unyielding connection to the land have served as a guiding force for me, both as a therapist, professor and as a person. From my great-grandfather Shelby Martin, who raised 17 children amidst the challenges of life and faced the devastation of the 1918 flu pandemic, to my grandfather Cortez Wesley and uncle Truman Carroll, who weathered the storms of family conflicts and the horrors of war, their lives remind me of the strength found in family, community, and faith.

I've woven the lessons from their lives with my own professional journey, using their wisdom to guide my work as a counselor and educator. The values of perseverance, humility, integrity, and empathy, so essential to Appalachian life, are just as crucial in the world of therapy. They shape how we interact with clients, students, and ourselves. My ancestors' stories have taught me that no matter how tough life gets, we are all connected by our shared humanity, and the love and support of family and community are the pillars of our survival.

In these pages, we've explored topics that reach into the heart of the human condition: faith and doubt, strength and vulnerability, resilience and fragility. These opposing forces are a part of all our lives, and the beauty lies in finding the balance between them. We've talked about navigating life's dangers, honoring those we've lost, and the healing power of laughter, animals, and nature. I hope these stories and lessons have resonated with you, just as they have guided me through my life and career.

One of the overarching themes of this book has been the importance of balance between faith and reason, between strength and vulnerability, and between action and reflection. Life in Appalachia, like life everywhere, is filled with contradictions, and part of growing up and growing wiser is learning how to navigate those contradictions without losing ourselves.

My family's history has shown me that while life is often uncertain and unpredictable, we can always draw on the lessons of the past to guide us through the present. Whether it's facing the dangers of the world with courage, as my great-grandparents did, or embracing doubt and curiosity in the pursuit of truth, as I've done in my own spiritual journey, the key is to remain rooted in our values while remaining open to growth and change.

As a therapist, I've also seen firsthand the power of these lessons. Whether I'm working with clients dealing with addiction, trauma, grief, or anxiety, the core message remains the same: we are stronger when we are connected, both to our past and to the people around us. Therapy, much like life, is about tending to the roots while nurturing the growth of new branches. It's about finding strength in vulnerability and learning to live with life's uncertainties without being consumed by them.

The metaphor of a tree has always resonated with me when I think about the work we do as therapists and the lives we lead as individuals. A tree's roots grow deep, anchoring it to the earth and providing nourishment. These roots represent our family, our culture, our traditions, and the lessons passed down to us. They ground us, giving us stability in life's storms.

But a tree's strength is not only in its roots, it's also in its branches. The branches stretch upward, reaching for the sun, growing ever stronger as they weather the elements. Our branches represent our growth, our experiences, our relationships, and our aspirations. They symbolize the ways in which we stretch ourselves to learn, evolve, and connect with others.

In both life and therapy, our job is to tend to the roots while encouraging the branches to grow. Without deep roots, the branches cannot grow strong. But without growth, those deep roots are left stagnant and untapped. It's this balance between tradition and progress, between stability and change, that defines a meaningful life.

As we close this book, I want to leave you with a simple truth: your roots matter. Whether you come from the mountains of Appalachia or the cities of the world, your past is part of you. Embrace it. Learn from it. But don't be afraid to grow beyond it. Just as a tree extends its branches to the sky, so too should we reach for new heights, new experiences, and new understandings.

As a therapist, I have had the honor of walking alongside countless clients and students on their journey toward growth. My hope is that this book has helped illuminate the importance of family, community, and the healing power of connection. We are all branches of a much larger tree, and together, we can create a legacy of strength, resilience, and hope.

"A tree with deep roots laughs at storms." This Appalachian saying captures the essence of what I've learned in life and what I try to impart to my clients and students: life is unpredictable, and hardships will come. But if we stay grounded in our roots, our values, our traditions, and our connections, then we can weather any storm that life throws our way.

May you continue to grow strong, both in your roots and in your branches. May you find peace in the past and hope in the future. And may you never stop seeking the balance between the two, for it is in that balance that we find true strength.

To get in touch with Dr. Martin Cortez Wesley, you can reach him via his personal email at wesleyphd@gmail.com.

Photos and Illustrations

Idioms, Metaphors, and Sayings:

1. "A good dog and a kind word go a long way toward healing a broken heart."
2. "A house divided cannot stand."
3. "Ain't no river too wide if you know where to cross."
4. "Ain't nothing like the love of a good dog to set the world right again."
5. "Ain't no way to climb a mountain without a few slips on the rocks."
6. "Always drink upstream from the herd"
7. "A load shared is a load lightened."
8. "A tree with deep roots laughs at storms."
9. "Ain't no use digging up old bones."
10. "Apple doesn't fall far from the tree."
11. "Bless his heart."
12. "Blood is thicker than water."
13. "Carpe Diem (Seize the day)."
14. "Come and sit for a spell."
15. "Don't air your dirty laundry."
16. "Don't forget your roots,"
17. "Don't get above your raisin'."
18. "Don't get your knickers in a knot."
19. "Don't judge someone by their kin."
20. "Don't just hand a man a meal, teach him how to plant a seed."
21. "Don't put on airs."
22. "Doubt ain't nothing but the spade that helps you dig deeper."
23. "Don't turn every hill into a mountain."
24. "Even the tallest oak can fall in a storm."
25. "Every journey starts with a single step"
26. "Fair to Middlin'."
27. "Fool me once, shame on you; fool me twice, shame on me."
28. "Fuck Around and Find Out" (FAFO)
29. "Give a man a fish, and you feed him for a day. Teach a man to fish, and you feed him for a lifetime,"
30. "God love em"
31. "Grin and Bear it"
32. "Hard times don't last, but tough people do."
33. "if it weren't for bad luck, I'd have no luck at all"
34. "If you don't stir the pot, the stew won't thicken."
35. "If you find yourself in a hole, the first thing to do is stop diggin'."
36. "If you want to go fast, go alone; if you want to go far, go together."
37. "I'll pray for you"

38. "It's a mighty poor man that can't get the better of himself."
39. "It's not the destination but the journey that matters."
40. "It's not the storm that breaks you, but how you learn to sail through it."
41. "It takes a village to raise a child,"
42. "It takes two to hoe a row."
43. "It's the town's job to raise smart kids, and the teacher just happens to get paid for it."
44. "Keep a stiff upper lip"
45. "Keep on the sunny side."
46. "Laughter is the best medicine."
47. "Life's like a mountain trail, hard and rough, but it's the company you keep that makes the journey worthwhile."
48. "Life's too short to worry about the mule going blind, just load the wagon."
49. "Life is simpler when you plow around the stump."
50. "Make hay while the sun shines,"
51. "No man is an island."
52. "No pain, no gain."
53. "Nothing worth having comes easy."
54. "Oook at Me"
55. "Once bitten, twice shy."
56. "Pot calling the kettle black."
57. "Practice what you preach"
58. "Pull themselves up by the bootstraps"
59. "Reputation is like fine China; once broken, it's hard to fix."
60. "Sometimes you get, and sometimes you get got."
61. "Still waters run deep"
62. "The apple doesn't fall far from the tree."
63. "The best sermons are lived, not preached."
64. "The blind leading the blind"
65. "The oak tree bends in the wind but doesn't break."
66. "The tallest trees have the deepest roots."
67. "There's no right way to grieve, only your way."
68. "Tough as Nails"
69. "Tough bark makes a strong tree."
70. "Tough it out"
71. "Trust the Process"
72. "Well, shit fire and save the matches!"
73. "When you wallow with the pigs, expect to get dirty."
74. "When we slaughtered a hog, we used everything but the oink."
75. "You can be tough as nails, but even nails rust."
76. "You can lead a horse to water, but you can't make him drink."

77. "You can't cross the creek without getting your feet wet,"
78. "You can't dance in the rain if you're afraid to get wet."
79. "You can't get blood from a turnip
80. "You can't fix a leak if you never notice the drip."
81. "You can't fix what you don't acknowledge,"
82. "You can't learn to swim without getting wet,"
83. "You can't live your life waiting for the sky to fall."
84. "You can't make a quilt without a few pricks."
85. "You can't make everyone happy, and you're not made of gold anyhow."
86. "You can't mend a fence if you wait for the whole barn to fall down."
87. "You can't pick the berries without dealing with a few thorns."
88. "You can't put lipstick on a pig."
89. "You can't put out a fire by ignoring the smoke."
90. "You can't rush a good thing."
91. "You can't see the whole barn if you only look through one window."
92. "You can't skip to the end of the trail without walking it"
93. "You can't spend your life looking for rattlesnakes under every rock
94. "You can't teach an old dog new tricks"
95. "You can't trust a butcher with clean hands."
96. "You can't wait for your ship to come in if you never sent one out."
97. "You catch more flies with honey than with vinegar."
98. "You don't just belong to your family; you belong to the whole town."
99. "You don't get to pick your last day, but you do get to pick how you live today."
100. "You don't know how strong you are until being strong is the only choice you have."
101. "You made your bed, now lie in it."
102. "You might as well laugh as cry,"
103. "You need a stiff backbone and a soft heart to get through life."
104. "You reap what you sow."

Bibliography

Akbari, R. ,. (2021). The Effectiveness of Music Therapy on Reducing Alexithymia Symptoms and Improvement of Peer Relationships. . *International Journal of Behavioral Sciences,*, 178-184.

Appalachian Regional Commission. (2019). *Health disparities related to opioid misuse in Appalachia.* Appalachian Regional Commission.

Arnold, C. A. (2024). The psychophysiology of music-based interventions and the experience of pain. . *Frontiers in Psychology, 15.* *https://doi.org/10.3389/fpsyg.2024.1361857* .

Baumrind, D. (1967). Child care practices anteceding three patterns of preschool behavior. *Genetic Psychology Monographs, 75,* 43-88.

Beck, A. (1978). *Cognitive therapy and the emotional disorders.* International Universities Press.

Boone, D. &. (1996). *Daniel Boone: His own story.* Applewood Books.

Brillstein, B. P. (1969). *Gloom, despair, and agony on me [Song].* Performed by Buck Owens and Roy Clark on Hee Haw. .

Brown, B. (2012). *Daring greatly: How the courage to be vulnerable transforms the way we live, love, parent, and lead.* . Gotham Books.

Claxton-Oldfield, S. (2024). Deathbed Visions: Visitors and Vistas. Omega (Westport). 2024 Nov;90(1):21-36. doi: 10.1177/00302228221095910. Epub 2022 Apr 29. PMID: 35484996. *Omega (Westport). doi: 10.1177/00302228221095910. Epub 2022 Apr 29. PMID: 35484996.*, 21-36.

Dalezman, A. (2012). Is laughter the best medicine? An evaluation of the physiological effects of laughter. The Science Journal of the Lander College of Arts and Sciences, 6(1), 10–15. *The Science Journal of the Lander College of Arts and Sciences, 6(1),* 10–15.

Dohlman, J. (2024). Urban, Place-Based Ecotherapists: Observations on & Experiences Related to Ecological Justice: A Grounded Theory Approach. *Doctoral Dissertation, National Louis University.*

Dossey, L. (2018). The Helper's High. *Explore doi: 10.1016/j.explore.2018.10.003. Epub 2018 Oct 23. PMID: 30424992.*, 393-399.

Eastman, P. D. (1960). *Are you my mother?* . Random House.

Ellis, A. (1962). *Reason and emotion in psychotherapy.* Lyle Stuart.

Federation of American Societies for Experimental Biology. . ((2010, April 26).). Body's response to repetitive laughter is similar to the effect of repetitive exercise, study finds.. *ScienceDaily,* Retrieved March 15, 2025 from www.sciencedaily.com/releases/2010/04/100426113058.htm.

Ferster, C. B. (1973). A functional analysis of depression. https://doi.org/10.1037/h0035605. *American Psychologist,* 857–870. https://doi.org/10.1037/h0035605.

Gottman, J. S. (2015). *The Seven Principles for Making Marriage Work: A Practical Guide from the Country's Foremost Relationship Expert.* Harmony.

Hunter, M. C. (2019). Urban nature experiences reduce stress in the context of daily life based on salivary biomarkers. *Frontiers in Psychology, 10, 722.*, https://doi.org/10.3389/fpsyg.2019.00722.

Klass, D. S. (1996). *Continuing bonds: New understandings of grief.* . Taylor & Francis.

Kramer CK, L. C. (2023). Laughter as medicine: A systematic review and meta-analysis of interventional studies evaluating the impact of spontaneous laughter on cortisol levels. . *PLoS One. 2023 May 23;18(5):e0286260. doi: 10.1371/journal.pone.0286260. PMID: 37220157; PMCID: PMC10204943.*

Lyubomirsky, S. S. (2005). Pursuing happiness: The architecture of sustainable change. *Review of General Psychology, 9(2)*, 111-131.

McGoldrick, M. G. (2008). *Genograms: Assessment and intervention (3rd ed.).* W.W. Norton.

Miller, W. R. (2023). *Motivational Interviewing: Helping People Change and Grow, 4th Ed.* . The Guilford Press.

Navarra, R. J. (2016). *Sound relationship house theory and relationship and marriage education. In J. J. Ponzetti Jr. (Ed.), Evidence-based approaches to relationship and marriage education.* Routledge.

Neff, K. D. (2011). Self-compassion, self-esteem, and well-being. *Social and Personality Psychology Compass, 5(1)*, 1-12.

Northcutt, W. (2000). *The Darwin Awards: Evolution in Action.* . Dutton.

Pavlov, I. P. (1927). *Conditioned reflexes: An investigation of the physiological activity of the cerebral cortex (G. V. Anrep, Trans.).* . Oxford University Press.

Shermis, S. S. (1978). Social Studies and the Problem of Knowledge: A Re-Examination of Edgar Bruce Wesley's Classic Definition of the Social Studies. *Theory & Research in Social Education*, 31-43.

Stefanelli, K. J. (2025). editation and guided imagery show reduction in chronic stress and increase in mental health-related quality of life for college students. . *Journal of American College Health, https://doi.org/10.1080/07448481.2024.2449426*, 1-11.

Watson, J. B. (1920). Conditioned emotional reactions. *Journal of Experimental Psychology, 3(1),* , 1 - 14.

Wesley, E. B. (1952). *Teaching social studies in elementary schools (Revised ed.).* Boston: Heath.

Wesley, E. B. (1958). *Teaching social studies in high schools (3rd ed.).* Boston: Heath.

Wesley, E. B. (1966). *Too Short the Days.* Cypress Press.

Wesley, M. C. (2009). Animal-Assisted Therapy in the Treatment of Substance Dependence. . *Anthrozoös, 22(2), https://doi.org/10.2752/175303709X434167*, 137–148. .

Yim, J. (2016). Therapeutic Benefits of Laughter in Mental Health: A Theoretical Review. Tohoku J Exp Med. 2016 Jul;239(3):243-9. doi:

10.1620/tjem.239.243. PMID: 27439375. *ohoku J Exp Med. doi: 10.1620/tjem.239.243. PMID: 27439375.*, 243-9.

Stories of Strength and Resilience